WHAT HAPPENS IN BOOK PUBLISHING

WHAT HAPPENS IN BOOK PUBLISHING

SECOND EDITION ❁ EDITED BY

CHANDLER B. GRANNIS

COLUMBIA UNIVERSITY PRESS

NEW YORK & LONDON 1967

Library of Congress Catalog Number 67:19875
Printed in the United States of America

FOREWORD TO THE FIRST EDITION

IT HAS BEEN the cynic's comment on book publishing that publishers are a group of individualists who would not be likely to come together in any common cause or for any joint program. Yet here in this volume is refutation of that criticism, for a score of specialists in the various departments of publishing have accepted an invitation to make contributions which will, in total, provide a well-rounded picture of what book publishing really is or can be.

Such a book has been greatly needed; first, because book publishing is an intricate series of processes which should be respectfully studied while practicing or before beginning, and, second, because it is a business which definitely affects the public interest and consequently is of real importance to the public itself.

One thing is generally true of all American businessmen—that they are quite willing to make available to others those things which each has found out for himself. So, here, some of the experienced people who have earned high place in this business of books have put down for others some of the things that should be common heritage among those who are to practice publishing or are to understand it.

FREDERIC G. MELCHER

PREFACE

❋

THE FIRST edition of this book was aimed at meeting the need for an up-to-date survey of operations in the American book publishing business. Acceptance of the book suggests that it has helped to meet that need. It has been used, as intended, by students in library schools, and in publishing and graphic arts courses. Many publishing houses have used it to provide the new or prospective staff member with a frame of reference for his own work, and to refresh the minds of more experienced publishing workers about operations other than their own. It has helped manufacturers, booksellers, authors, and others to review the publishing aspects of their industry.

This edition, like the first, is an outline of the procedures in book publishing, not a how-to book. It has been brought extensively up to date by the contributors. Most chapters have been largely rewritten, except for those that have been replaced by new ones—for example, in the areas of sales and promotion, children's books, paperbacks (two chapters instead of one), and mail-order publishing. An exception is the chapter on copy editing by the late Dr. William Bridgwater, who had not had the opportunity to rewrite it at the time of his death; only minor revisions have been made. New chapters on order fulfillment and internal services, and on the future prospects of the industry, have been added. And, of course, all the statistics are new. Nearly all of the book reflects the immense changes that have overtaken the book publishing business in the past decade.

The editor acknowledges a deep debt of gratitude to the staff of the Columbia University Press, to his colleagues at *Publishers' Weekly*, to many users of the first edition, to his family, and above all to the authors who have made this contribution to their industry.

CHANDLER B. GRANNIS

June, 1967

CONTENTS

❋

SECTION IV: FURTHER MAJOR CONCERNS

SECTION V: SPECIAL AREAS OF PUBLISHING

SECTION VI: THE FUTURE

APPENDIXES

SECTION I

INTRODUCTION

1

INTRODUCTION: GENERAL VIEW OF A DIVERSE INDUSTRY

By CHANDLER B. GRANNIS

SENIOR ASSOCIATE EDITOR, *Publishers' Weekly*

PUBLISHING, to start with a definition, is to make public—to send forth among the people—the words and pictures that creative minds have produced, that editors have worked over, that printers have reproduced. As applied to books, it is a formidable succession of activities no one of which can, by itself, be called publishing. It is only when a manuscript has been transformed into a book and then distributed to its intended market place, that the process of publishing is complete. To perform an editorial service alone, whether at a risk or for a fee, is not to publish; to purchase printing and binding services alone is not to publish; to promote sales is not, in itself, to publish; to distribute another's printed product is not, in itself, to publish. Book publishing is all of these things together, an integrated process, whether carried out by a single firm or by several. *It is the whole intellectual and business procedure of selecting and arranging to make a book and of promoting its ultimate use.*

THE BOOK INDUSTRY

Around this process are accumulated the other activities which, with book publishing, make up the total complex, the book business or book industry. (The term "book trade" is sometimes used in this broad sense, too, but is somewhat more often meant to refer to the retail part of the industry.) The principal functions of "the book industry" in its broader meaning are performed by these groups (in more or less chronological sequence): 1) the literary agencies through which most manuscripts that attain general bookstore sale are developed; 2) the publishers and their departments, described in this book; 3) the book manufacturers, including the compositors, engravers, printers and binders, and their suppliers of type, ink, paper, binding material, and so on; 4) the book reviewers and critics; 5) the advertising agencies and other services for promoting sales; 6) the warehouse services, and the wholesalers, for redistribution of books to retailers, libraries, schools, colleges, and other purchasers; 7) the retail bookshops and book departments; 8) the buyers of "subsidiary" publication rights for book clubs, reprint houses, magazines, newspaper syndicates, film makers, and broadcasters.

Closely allied are the libraries—public, private, school, college, and special—which, while they are not part of the "business" so far as handling books for profit is concerned, are the greatest of all vehicles for keeping books, once sold, at work.

The Diversity of Book Publishing. Book publishers may be overheard referring to their work, loftily, as a profession; realistically, as a business; ruefully, as a gamble. It is essentially a business—probably more fun than most. It is something of a gamble, too, for it involves considerable risks, even when its effort is directed towards educational or specialized audiences that can pretty well be estimated in advance. But it is a business that has strong professional overtones; it serves all the professions and it has room for a remarkable number of professional skills and non-publishing professional backgrounds. Moreover, it faces a responsibility akin to that faced by educators—but a lot less subject to institutional limitations and frustrations.

As a business, book publishing had in 1965 a $2 billion income, which amounted to less than .03 of the Gross National Product. Yet the book industry turns out somewhere around two billion volumes a year. Its sales have more than tripled in the past ten years. Its promise is for still greater growth. Above all, it is an underlying necessity for the conduct of every trade, industry, profession, useful activity, or recreation. This is what makes it at once the fascinating and the diverse industry that it is.

Its diversity lies partly in the limitless variety of subject matter it must deal with, and therefore in the variety of specialized kinds of publishing and the different ways of reaching specialized markets. It lies, too, in the fact that virtually every book is a product separate from all other books, requiring with few exceptions (for example, standardized series and mass market paperbacks) a separate job of production and promotion.

The diversity of book publishing lies, also, in an economic structure that often seems chaotic. For general trade books, the market potential is inadequately known and even less adequately realized. The basis for business decisions ranges from analysis to intuition. The same book may be sold through different channels in different—or identical—formats, at different prices, at one and the same time. The wholesale–retail distribution system is subject to inefficiencies that persist despite earnest industry-sponsored efforts to lessen them. There is competition not only between publisher and publisher, and between bookseller and bookseller, as should be expected under free enterprise. There is also competition by publishers against the very jobbers and booksellers who serve them. Few individuals out of all the thousands of authors whose works are published can make a living simply by writing books. Yet, despite its problems, the book publishing business survives, grows, and serves the national interest.

It is precisely because of its variety that the world of book publishing holds lifelong fascination for a great many people. There is a place in it for the man or woman who has a lively critical sense combined with a flair for bringing out the talents of other people. There is a place in it for the person who loves language and all that can be done with it. There is a vital function also to be filled by the scientist or the technical person who takes delight in communicating knowledge to others.

At the same time, without the talents of people who truly enjoy solving the mechanical puzzles of wholesale and retail distribution, the book business could hardly have progressed beyond the medieval cloister.

There is a variety of jobs to be done by artists, designers, typographers, and art directors—and their assistants; by librarians; by people addicted to the techniques of research; by bibliographers; by book-minded secretaries and accountants. There is work for people who enjoy contacts with the world of newspapers, radio, and television; for those who can plan advertising and promotion; and for others who can take pride in simply writing routine, straightforward press publicity and catalogue copy and doing it well.

In the wide-ranging book industry, there is an active demand for educators who can write, edit, or organize people and facts. There is an endless need for literate and imaginative salesmen who can deal with the great department stores and food chains, or with the personal bookstores; who can meet effectively with library buyers or heads of university departments or local committees of school teachers. There are roles for the editor who can make deals in Hollywood; for the executive who knows his way around Wall Street, Washington, and the Harvard Yard; and at the same time for the rare supervisor whose pride —and justly so!—is to process all incoming orders within a day of their receipt.

In short, the world of book publishing offers a touch of

glamor, a strong dose of useful routine, and a large amount of rewarding, often creative, labor. Above all, it affords to a great part of the people in it the satisfaction of work that really seems to be abundantly worth doing.

Varieties of Business Organization. The succession of activities which, added up, constitute book publishing, are described in the chapters immediately following, about editorial selection and handling, design and production, selling, publicity, promotion, advertising, subsidiary rights, foreign distribution, business operations, financial management, and legal considerations.

In large firms, these functions may be performed by separate or subdivided departments. In many firms, several of the activities are combined in the busy hands of one individual or department. There is no standard form of organization, and the diverse kinds of publishing would probably preclude any large degree of standardization. There is little concentration of power and ownership, and the industry retains a large degree of individualism.

Forms of business organization are as various as in other industries. Most publishing houses are incorporated. Many of them now are public stock companies, but many are still closely held by small groups of people—families and/or top executives, older employees, perhaps a handful of outside investors. Several firms today represent mergers of several companies, the whole group providing a healthy diversification in its varieties of publishing. Further, some of the giants in communications and electronics have moved into the book business, buying out existing publishers or starting book divisions of their own. It is this trend which constitutes the greatest threat to individualism and creative editorial programs in publishing.

Some publishing houses, on the other hand, are the publishing arms of religious bodies, professional or technical societies, public or private universities, foundations or public service institutions, and are either owned or chartered by them and are responsible to them.

Different Kinds of Publishing. In this book, the main emphasis is on the processes that constitute general or "trade book" publishing, defined broadly as the issuing of books for general retail bookstore sale. These processes, from securing manuscripts through final sale, are in varying degrees common to nearly all kinds of publishing, but special fields require some special procedures. What some of these procedures are is related in the chapters about textbooks, children's books, religious books, technical, scientific, and medical books, university press books, paper-covered books, and publishing for sale by mail. (Of course, some of these specialized activities are also part of trade book publishing, and important in it. Most juveniles, many religious books other than church materials, some technical and scholarly books, and some lines of paperbacks are definitely trade books in their manner of editing, production, and sale, and in their terms to the retailer.)

Each of these major areas of publishing includes some firms that have separate departments in several different fields. Many trade houses have juvenile departments, a few have book clubs, many have paperback departments or affiliates. Some of the biggest money-makers have schoolbook and college text departments. One or two have technical departments far outstripping their general trade departments, and so on. A great number of firms, on the other hand, are strictly specialized.

FIGURES AND PROPORTIONS

A few basic figures will illuminate further the structure of the book industry and the relative positions of its different parts. But first, three parenthetical notes: (1) In this book, and in all the figures we quote, we are talking about publishing under *other than* government auspices; we are not dealing with the extensive publishing that is done by agencies of the federal, state, county, or local governments. (2) More statistical details are given in the appendix to this book. And (3) current data are issued every year by the various book industry organizations and at intervals by government bodies, and are summarized annually in *Publishers' Weekly* early each year and in the *Bowker Annual of Library and Book Trade Information.*

To begin with, how many titles are put out by publishers of all kinds each year? Counting a book as containing more than 48 pages plus covers (UNESCO definition), *Publishers' Weekly* in 1964 and 1965 listed about 29,000 separate titles, of which over 20,000 were brand-new titles and 8,000 or more were new or reprinted editions. Most of the 29,000 were issued by about 520 publishers who brought out at least five titles each in the years covered. About 66 large firms issued 100 or more titles a year and accounted for well over 45 percent of the grand total.

There is no accurate count of how many copies of all these titles are sold, but the available estimates suggest that about as many copies are sold as dollars are received for them—not that this would hold true in any one category of books. At any rate, in 1965, publishers probably got into the hands of customers some two billion books and received about $2 billion for them (at wholesale or direct sale prices). In a few categories the figures are more precise; see, for example, the chapter on textbook publishing.

As for the relative sizes of different parts of the industry, measured by publishers' receipts in 1964–1965, the adult trade books—hardcover and higher-priced paperback—bring in over 7½ percent of the industry total; children's books at all price levels, over 6 percent; mass market paperbacks, about 5½ percent; religious books, Bibles, and so on, almost 5 percent; professional books (law, medical, scientific, technical, vocational, business, and university press books), almost 12 percent; book club editions, over 7 percent; and miscellaneous "other" books, over 5 percent.

This leaves the two largest income-producing sectors of the book industry: the textbook publishing business, with over 28 percent of the publishers' receipts; and the reference book sector, selling mostly by subscription, with almost 23 percent.

Setting these figures against a total of $2 billion would give a fair enough approximation for the mid-1960s. Rates of growth differ in the different branches of the industry. Overall, however, annual increases ranging from 9 to 11 percent have been common for some years. Increased government funds for library and school purchases are bringing immense changes to the book industry, and these will be reflected in the year-to-year totals and proportions.

THE BOOK MARKETS

About 190,000 book titles were being listed in the mid-1960s in Bowker's annual *Books in Print*, the index to the full catalogs of most publishers, bound each year in the *Publishers' Trade List Annual*. The markets for all these titles are many and hard to measure. Probably the markets are, above all, institutional.

For example—leaving aside the school and college textbook market, covered in our textbook chapter—there are more than 17,000 public, college, and special libraries of all kinds in the United States, with budgets changing on such a large scale from year to year that to quote them here would be misleading. (See issues of the *Bowker Annual of Library and Book Trade Information* for the most up-to-date figures.) In addition to these libraries, there is the immensely expanding group

—perhaps 50,000—of libraries in public and private schools. Federal government assistance, first to the public and academic libraries, later—as part of massive general education support—to school libraries, has been soaring in the 1960s. The resulting demands have had profound effects upon book publishers and manufacturers, encouraging their rapid and prosperous expansion, and at the same time taxing their facilities.

Higher-priced children's books are sold primarily to libraries—the percentage of library (including school library) sales being over 90 percent in some firms. Adult trade books have a library sale that is not calculated, but may in some companies account for half the income. Libraries make up major proportions of the markets for university press, technical, scientific, and reference titles.

Direct sales to the individual consumer, by mail, make up another section of the book market, especially for book club and mail-order books, many medical, law, and other professional books.

Compared with these massive markets, the general retail market may seem relatively smaller. Yet it is the retail market that counts in the reputation, prestige, and subsidiary sales of general trade books, and of many a university press book, scientific or religious book, or children's book. It is to the retail market, even more than to the public library or the academic market, that most book advertising and promotion is addressed and for which the important daily book reviews and the weekly and monthly critical reviews are written.

More than 9,300 retail book outlets were listed in the 1965 edition of Bowker's triennial *American Book Trade Directory*, but it is generally conceded that only a fraction of these can be considered full-scale, well-stocked bookstores. An estimate of 1,000 "effective" bookstores would probably be fair—bookstores or department store book sections that have a broad, varied stock of general adult and children's books, good reference, art, religious, and science sections, and a strong representation of paperbacks. At this writing, about 2,000 bookstores belong to the American Booksellers Association. Almost as many belong to the National Association of College Stores—which represents the fastest growing and best capitalized (especially if institutionally owned) segment of bookselling. There are several strong multibranch commercial bookstore groups, notably Doubleday's and Brentano's; scores of astutely managed denominational stores, including those of Methodist, Baptist, Presbyterian, and Catholic bodies; a handful of specialists in technical and scientific books; 300 or so specialists in paperbacks; over 100 antiquarian stores, which handle most of the trade in out-of-print and specialized rare books. In addition, more than 100,000 newsstands each handle small stocks of current, lower-priced paperbacks.

The general and college stores are concentrated mainly in major urban and academic centers; and until both local demand for books and income for booksellers increase markedly, this will continue to be true.

THE MECHANICS OF DISTRIBUTION

Just how a book gets from a publisher to a bookstore or a newsstand, a library or school or college, is outlined in large part in the chapters on sales, order fulfillment, textbooks, and paperbacks. A word should be added here about wholesalers, warehouses, returns, and remainders.

An order for a book, once it is received and processed by the publisher, goes to a warehouse (owned by the publisher, or by a group of publishers, or by an independent company). The warehouse is ordinarily in some location where space is relatively cheap and shipping facilities are handy—and there the order is filled. There is a continuing effort in the industry to make the whole order fulfillment and shipping procedure faster and more efficient, since bottlenecks in this area are notorious in causing delay, loss of business, and increase in cost to retailers.

Wholesaling. A great many books, for purchasers of all kinds, are ordered not directly from the publisher or through his travelers, but from the wholesalers, who buy and store quantities from the publishers. They may obtain the books from the publishers' own warehouses, or, as the publishers do, from the binderies where the manufacture of the books is completed.

In supplying books directly to stores, each publisher offers his own individual schedule of discounts. There are usually other discount schedules for libraries and schools—though the distinction has become blurred in recent years. Wholesalers may be given special discount schedules, but Federal Trade Commission rules under the antitrust, antidiscrimination laws have induced many publishers to set one schedule of discounts for all, and let the jobbers get their needed extra discount by taking advantage of the higher discounts offered for purchase of large quantities.

The Book Warehouse. A book warehouse—there is no standard model—includes an office area (sometimes housing the publisher's entire billing and credit department) and also the main storage area. In this storage area, the books, many copies of each title, are arranged in shelf-bins down long corridors, with reserve stocks behind them. Between these corridors, order-filling carts are rolled by the order-pickers, or baskets or pallets are moved on a sort of assembly line, an endless belt or line of rollers. Other employees pack and address the cartons, affix or enclose an invoice for the purchaser, charge the postage or express cost, and check the whole procedure. Then the parcels go by belt or lift-truck to delivery trucks or a postal substation in the plant. Some small warehouses are less mechanized than this, but on the whole, the larger the operation, the greater the need for automation and, increasingly in the future, for electronic record-keeping and controls.

Usually, there is a space in the warehouse where very large orders are handled separately, direct from the binders' skids (large wooden platforms).

Returns. Usually, too, there is an area in the warehouse for the detailed but necessary business of handling "returns." These are books that retailers have not managed to sell, and which, within specified periods and at 90 or 100 percent of full value, the publisher permits the retailer to send back if "in salable condition." In the warehouse, they are received, examined, rejacketed if necessary, and returned to storage.

Remainders. If a book bounces back to the publisher in too large numbers, or doesn't sell out the entire print order, it becomes something else—not just a book, but a "remainder." Unsold items in an industry that has over 100,000 separate products for sale at any one time constitute a problem that can be dealt with in only two ways: by destroying the surplus product, that is, selling the books to be pulped; or by selling it off intact at a low price. The latter procedure is called "remaindering," and several companies specialize in that operation.

The "remainder houses" buy up all or part of the unsold residue of an edition—from a few dozen to some thousands of copies—and supply it to retailers for low-priced resale. The retailers set their own consumer prices. Many book and department stores regularly use such books for bargain promotion sales at seasons when such sales help keep business stable. Many college stores buy up textbook remainders to use in bargain sales. Secondhand-book dealers cull the remainders with care and an eye to their own specialized interests. Many stores and some mail-order houses run long ads listing in small type the "publishers' overstock" they have bought from the remainder houses. The latter often supply the actual mailing folders and ad mats for these dealers.

Sometimes a retailer will buy from the remainder house the entire stock of a book, and will thereby have its exclusive sale; the quantity will usually be small. Sometimes a publisher will release for remainder sale only part of the unsold stock of a title, and this "partial remaindering" may arouse protests from unprivileged dealers or from authors who suspect a shrinkage in their royalties. Some publishers, notably some university presses, deal with remainder houses scarcely at all, but after a number of years, collect quantities of unsold back-stock and offer it directly to consumers by mail (using specialized-interest lists of names) or to retailers, at low prices.

BOOK TRADE ORGANIZATIONS

National associations within the book industry have come to play a decisive role in its stability and expansion. They watch over the interests of specific branches of publishing or bookselling; they issue informative bulletins and, at times, instructional materials; they hold meetings and seminars—both regional and national—that constitute exciting forums and workshops on industry problems. The retail organizations hold trade exhibits that have an important effect on sales and marketing. People who work in the trade associations are as much a part of the book business as is any employee of a publishing house, and are often in a position to have a broader view of the industry.

Retailers. The principal associations of retailers are these:

American Booksellers Association, 175 Fifth Avenue, New York 10010, founded in 1900, the oldest, largest, and most comprehensive of the retail groups, noted especially for its annual trade fair and convention, its regional meetings, its handbook of publishers' terms, its order-handling services, and its regular gifts of books to the family library of the White House.

National Association of College Stores, 55 East College Street, Oberlin, Ohio 44074, noted for its convention and trade fair, and also for its wholesale services, its training institutes, and its quarterly, *The College Store.*

Christian Booksellers Association, 5611 West Chicago Avenue, Chicago, Illinois 60651, representing conservative evangelical stores, and similar to the above two groups in service to members.

Antiquarian Booksellers Association of America, Shop 2, Concourse, 630 Fifth Avenue, New York 10020, maintaining an exhibition center for members and holding annual consumer fairs.

Publishers' Associations. The outstanding organizations of book publishers are:

American Book Publishers Council, One Park Avenue, New York 10001, representing most active general book publishers; incorporating separate groups of religious, technical, and paperback book publishers; providing extensive statistical, legislative, informational, and credit services; and holding frequent group and general meetings on specific problems of the industry.

American Textbook Publishers Institute, 432 Park Avenue South, New York 10016, representing most publishers of school and college textbooks and encyclopedias, performing functions similar to those of the ABPC (above), but in the area of educational publishing. The ABPC and ATPI are represented by a jointly maintained office in Washington, 1820 Jefferson Place NW, Washington D.C. 20036.

Association of American University Presses, 20 West 43d Street, New York 10036, made up of most university presses in the Americas; devoted to the specialized problems of scholarly publishing. Membership of the ABPC, ATPI, and AAUP overlaps where the interests of the publishers involved overlap.

Children's Book Council, 175 Fifth Avenue, New York 10010, established by the children's trade book publishers; widely known for its year-round children's book promotional materials; sponsor of Children's National Book Week, for nearly fifty years the industry's outstanding program for the promotion of children's reading.

Graphic Arts Groups. Graphic arts organizations specifically concerned with books exist in several cities, and there are many large national groups not focused on book design and production. Two national groups should be named here:

American Institute of Graphic Arts, 1059 Third Avenue, New York 10021, having both corporate and personal memberships; known for its meetings on trade book, textbook, and other printing and design problems, for its exhibitions of graphic arts at its own and other galleries, and for its scholarships and workshops.

Book Manufacturers' Institute, 25 West 43d Street, New York 10036, representing the composers, engravers, printers, and binders of books, with their suppliers of cloth, paper, and other materials; notable for its work on trade customs and specifications, its technical studies, and its meetings on industry concerns.

Other Organizations. Two other extremely important groups should be known to every student of publishing:

American Library Association, 50 East Huron Street, Chicago 60611, the professional association representing the greater part of the nation's librarians; organized in several divisions; meeting, over 8,000 strong, in a different city each year.

National Book Committee, One Park Avenue, New York 10001, a nonprofit association of private citizens, dedicated to "the wider and wiser use of books"; sponsors of National Library Week (held annually in April), the National Book Awards (March), the National Medal for Literature, and other efforts to promote—and when necessary, defend—books.

These are only the basic organizations, the vitally important ones. (*N.B.*: The addresses given above are those of 1966; *they are much subject to change*, and the annual editions of the *Literary Market Place* [Bowker] should be checked for these changes).

In many leading cities there are active groups of booksellers, graphic artists, publishers, or all three. Attendance at activities of these groups can be an aspect both of training and of maintaining trade contacts and keeping in touch with industry happenings. The names and current addresses and officers of these groups can be found in the annual *Literary Market Place;* and events are listed in the calendar columns of trade journals, including *Publishers' Weekly*.

In New York, for example, besides the associations named above, important groups are the Publishers Adclub, Publishers Publicity Association, Booksellers League, Publishers Library Promotion Group, and Women's National Book Association (which has chapters also in Boston, Cleveland, Chicago, and other cities).

In Boston, the Bookbuilders, with its meetings, exhibitions, and workshop courses, is significant, as is the Society of Printers. In other principal publishing cities it is important to keep in touch with the Philadelphia Book Clinic, Philadelphia Booksellers Association, Chicago Book Clinic, Booksellers Association of Greater Chicago, Northern California Booksellers Association (San Francisco), Southern California Booksellers Association (Los Angeles), Western Book Publishers Association (no regular office), Washington (D.C.) Booksellers Association, and so on.

Many other groups are of significance, depending on one's

concerns: to name some examples, the Protestant Church-Owned Publishers' Association, Society of Authors' Representatives, Society of Illustrators, Research and Engineering Council of the Graphic Arts Industry, Inc., and the Bureau of Independent Publishers & Distributors (paperbacks and magazines).

Many more groups, national and local, are active, interesting, and worth looking into; again, the reader is referred to the *Literary Market Place*.

BOOK TRADE AND RELATED COURSES

Courses and lecture series at the undergraduate, graduate, or adult education level, relating directly to the book industry, are at this writing offered by New York University, Radcliffe College, Simmons College, and Pratt Institute.

More numerous are courses in writing and in many aspects of production and the graphic arts. Some of the interesting courses in these areas are offered by New York University, Hunter College, the New School for Social Research, New York City Community College, Printing Industries of Metropolitan New York, Northwestern University, Rochester Institute of Technology, Carnegie Institute of Technology, Syracuse University, and many professional associations. Here again, the reader can consult the *Literary Market Place* for suggestions and addresses.

PROFESSIONAL READING

The necessity to keep up with professional reading is obvious to anyone in the industry, whether student, newcomer, or old hand. As time goes on, and leisure grows less (rather than more, as the sociologists try to tell us), the wise bookman, like the wise engineer or banker, adopts his own criteria for selection.

But he or she will always find it a necessary—and very pleasant—task to read the top magazines in the field. They include:

The principal review media, daily, weekly, and monthly.

Review and critical journals in the bookman's own particular field of work—scientific, recreational, educational, religious, juvenile, management, or whatever.

Publishers' Weekly (Bowker), 1180 Avenue of the Americas, New York 10036; the independently published news journal of the book industry; voluminous information about new books, sales plans, personnel, bookselling, legal and business matters, markets, production and design, industry problems; also previews and full current lists of new books, indexes, statistics, pre-pub reviews.

Library Journal and *School Library Journal* (also Bowker); bimonthly except summer; the major professional journals of the library world, with great numbers of brief reviews by librarian-experts.

Paperbound Books in Print (also Bowker); monthly; descriptive notes on forthcoming paperbacks; subject articles; three cumulative issues a year, currently listing 37,000 to 40,000 books.

Bestsellers, 124 East 40th Street, New York 10016; monthly; listings, notes, calendar, and other data on paperback merchandise; incorporates *School Paperback Review*, with articles on school use of paperbacks.

The Book Buyer's Guide (Baker & Taylor Co.), 1405 N. Broad Street, Hillside, N.J. 10205; monthly; wholesaler's journal addressed to libraries and book dealers; descriptive calendar of forthcoming books.

Book News (A. C. McClurg & Co.), 2121 Landmeier Road, Elk Grove Village, Ill. 60007; monthly; also a major wholesaler's journal; for customers; lists of new books by subject.

Antiquarian Bookman, Box 1100, Newark, N. J. 07101; monthly; news and "want" lists for the antiquarian, second-hand specialist and bibliophilic trade.

Book Production Industry, 201 East 42d Street, New York 10017; monthly; technical and general coverage for book manufacturers, suppliers, production directors, and designers.

American Library Association Bulletin, also *The Book List* and the

Subscription Books Bulletin; (A.L.A.), 50 East Huron Street, Chicago 60611; major news and review journals of the profession.

Wilson Library Bulletin (H. W. Wilson Co.), 950 University Avenue, Bronx, N. Y. 10452; a major independent journal of the profession.

NECESSARY REFERENCE TOOLS

Some of the magazines above, particularly seasonal and statistical numbers of *Publishers' Weekly* (*PW*); reference issues of *Paperbound Books in Print* (*PBIP*); *Library Journal; Booklist;* annual reference issues of *Antiquarian Bookman.* Also Bowker's *Forthcoming Books,* every other month, full author-title listings of books to be issued over a five-month period.

American Book Trade Directory. 17th ed. New York, Bowker, 1965. Geographical list of retail booksellers of the United States and Canada; also wholesalers; other suppliers; leading British publishers and booksellers.

Book Buyers' Handbook. New York, American Booksellers Association. Annual compilation of publishers' trade discounts and terms.

Books in Print: An Index to the Publishers' Trade List Annual. New York, Bowker. Annually updated list of books by title and author.

Cumulative Book Index: A World List of Books in the English Language. New York, H. W. Wilson Co. Current, annual, and six-year cumulations, by title, author, and subject. Definitive.

Literary Market Place. New York, Bowker. Annual directory of publishers, media, manufacturers, suppliers, agents, organizations, services.

Publishers' Trade List Annual. 3 vols. New York, Bowker. Annual compilations of catalogues or lists from publishers; indexed in *Books in Print* and *Subject Guide to Books in Print.*

Subject Guide to Books in Print. New York, Bowker. Titles in *Books in Print* arranged by subject, annually.

Textbooks in Print. New York, Bowker. Annual author-title-subject list.

GENERAL REFERENCES, HISTORY, AND BACKGROUND READING

Bingley, Clive. Book Publishing Practice. Shoe String Press, Hamden, Conn., 1966.

Bookman's Glossary, The. 4th ed.; rev. New York, Bowker, 1961.

Bowker Annual of Library and Book Trade Information, The. Yearly revisions. New York, Bowker.

Bowker Lectures on Book Publishing, The, 1937–1957. New York, Bowker, 1957; subsequent lectures in pamphlets, New York Public Library.

Burlingame, Roger. Of Making Many Books: A Hundred Years of Reading, Writing, and Publishing. New York, Scribner, 1946.

Cheney, O. H. An Economic Survey of the Book Industry, 1930–31. Reprinted with commentary by Robert W. Frase. New York, Bowker, 1960.

Doran, George H. Chronicles of Barabbas, 1884–1934. Rev. ed. New York, Harcourt, Brace & World, 1952.

Economic-Media Study of Book Publishing, An. New York, American Book Publishers Council and American Textbook Publishers Institute, 1966.

Freedom to Read, The. New York, American Book Publishers Council; Chicago, American Library Association, 1954.

Friede, Donald. The Mechanical Angel: His Adventures and Enterprises in the Glittering 1920's. New York, Knopf, 1938.

Glaister, Geoffrey A. Encyclopedia of the Book. Cleveland and New York, World, 1960.

Gross, Gerald R., ed. Publishers on Publishing. Paper (Universal Library). New York, Grosset and Dunlap.

Hackett, Alice Payne. Seventy Years of Best Sellers. New York, Bowker, 1967.

Hart, James D. The Popular Book: A History of America's Literary Taste. Paper, reprint of 1950 ed. Berkeley, University of California Press, 1961.

Hoffman, Hester R., ed. The Reader's Adviser. (Formerly, The Bookman's Manual.) 10th ed.; rev. New York, Bowker, 1964.

Jovanovich, William. Now Barabbas. New York, Harper and Row, 1964.

Lacy, Dan. Freedom and Communications. Urbana, University of Illinois Press, 1961.

Latham, Harold. My Life in Publishing. New York, Dutton, 1965.

Lehmann-Haupt, Hellmut, and others. The Book in America: A History of the Making and Selling of Books in the United States. 2d ed.; rev. New York, Bowker, 1951.

Madison, Charles A. Book Publishing in America. New York, McGraw-Hill, 1966.

Melcher, Daniel, So You Want to Get into Publishing. Pamphlet. Rev. ed. New York, Bowker, 1967.

Mott, Frank Luther. Golden Multitudes: The Story of Best Sellers in the United States. [1947]. Reprinted. New York, Bowker, 1960.

Mumby, Frank Arthur. Publishing and Bookselling: A History from the Earliest Times to the Present Day. 4th ed.; rev. by Max Kenyon. New York, Bowker, 1956.

Portrait of a Publisher: Alfred A. Knopf. New York, The Typophiles, 1965.

Sheehan, Donald. This Was Publishing: A Chronicle of the Book Trade in the Gilded Age. Bloomington, Indiana University Press, 1952.

Smith, Datus C., Jr. A Guide to Book Publishing. New York, Bowker, 1966.

Smith, Roger, and the editors of *Daedalus*. The American Reading Public, a Symposium. New York, Bowker, 1964.

Targ, William, ed. Carrousel for Bibliophiles. Cleveland and New York, World, 1947.

—— Bouillabaisse for Bibliophiles. Cleveland and New York, World, 1955. Anthologies.

Unwin, Sir Stanley. The Truth about Publishing. 7th ed.; rev. New York, Macmillan, 1960.

Winterich, John T. and David A. Randall. A Primer of Book Collecting. 3d ed.; rev. New York, Crown Publishers, 1966.

SECTION II

CREATING THE TRADE BOOK

2

SECURING AND SELECTING THE MANUSCRIPT

By JOHN FARRAR

CHAIRMAN OF THE BOARD, FARRAR, STRAUS AND GIROUX

❋

THE SECURING AND SELECTING of manuscripts in book publishing is an editorial function. The distribution of authority and of particular duties in connection with this delicate and vital performance varies among publishing houses, so much so that perhaps no single pattern emerges. A discussion of the perfect pattern would be highly controversial and I hope, to avoid contentiousness, to present as simple a picture as possible of what this editorial function is in today's publishing—to make clear how things are, not how they ought to be.

WHAT IS AN EDITOR?

In splitting up editorial duties, particularly in large firms, there may be many types of editors with various titles bestowed upon them. There may be special editors such as juvenile editors, religious editors, business editors, garden book editors, and so on.

In some firms the partners themselves enjoy both managerial and editorial duties. Many firms have an executive or managing editor whose duties are usually planning and scheduling the list, coordinating details, and integrating the creative side of the process with the production and business side.

The copy editor's functions of preparation for the printer, house styling, and the handling of proofs are discussed elsewhere in this book. I refer to the copy desk because many people think of all editing as copy editing. The copy editor is usually not the same person as the general editor. In my experience the gift of meticulous care in the correction of punctuation, spelling, and so on does not usually combine with the abilities of an editor who concerns himself with the earlier problems of an author's creative period.

Assume, however, that every publishing house has a principal editor, no matter what his title, with assistants varying in number with the size of the firm. It is obvious that there would be no publishing whatsoever without manuscripts, and that for this precious metal to exist at all there must be authors. It is the author, therefore, his nurture and welfare, that is in a very real sense our chief concern here.

The word "editor" once actually meant "publisher," and *éditeur* is so used on the cover and title pages of books in France today. The word derives from the Latin "*editus*, past participle of *edere*, to give out, put forth, publish." In early days authors wrote their books, delivered them to printers, and the printers were the booksellers. The modern middleman, the publisher and his editors and the various distributors, are the refinement of this simple process.

It is my own pleasure to think of the editor as, primarily, the friend and advocate of the author. I have often quoted Stephen Vincent Benét when he was once called upon to debate with a publisher on the subject of editing. Mr. Benét, it seems, liked editors, the editor liked authors, so the debate became an exchange of compliments. Mr. Benét pointed out that every author *must* have an editor, that writing is a lonely business and that the author must talk over his work with someone, that the someone does not necessarily have to be a publisher, however, but can be teacher, brother, librarian—even a wife or a literate, knowledgeable friend. When this friend turns out to be his publisher, so much the better; it is neat, it is convenient. He did point out, however, that he thought it dangerous for an author to have too many advisers.

During my own lifetime in publishing there have been many fine editors. There are still. Among those who have died in recent years and whose reputations are even so soon somewhat legendary are Eugene Saxton, Maxwell Perkins, T. R. Smith, Rutger Jewett, Guy Holt, John Woodburn, Ray Everitt, Nicholas Wreden, Ben Huebsch, Saxe Commins, Pascal Covici, Donald Friede, and Lynn Carrick. All of them were strongly individualistic in their characters and methods, yet all had certain things in common. Although they had a deep appreciation of the finest things in literature, they were not literary snobs; all of them liked authors as friends and all liked to read and enjoyed a good story; they worked night and day and loved publishing even as it became more and more a business and less a profession. Naturally preferring to work with books they admired, they were willing to undertake more routine jobs.

As we proceed with this description I think it wise to remember that only a small percentage of the books on any list are by any test works of literature. Many titles are, indeed, not produced by seasoned professional writers. Much of the editor's work would be eliminated if all manuscripts aimed at the publisher's desk were perfectly executed. Yet here we are considering all sorts and conditions of manuscripts, from the works of a great artist to a frankly ghost-written opus.

In closing these opening paragraphs I should point out that there is a growing feeling among authors that editors have become too possessively meddlesome with manuscripts, that editors increasingly want to change for the sake of change and override the author's prerogatives. I will not discuss this problem but only point out that the exigencies of today's publishing and the increasing hazards discussed elsewhere in the book have made this natural, if not inevitable. To illustrate the rigorous attitude and to highlight the controversial point without discussing it, I quote here with her permission a letter which that fine writer and wise woman, Marchette Chute, recently wrote me. She says: "I take a rather stern, old-fashioned point of view on the subject of writing. I think the good writers all have a period of struggle and defeat and probably need it, like the fight to get out of a chrysalis, and they end in control of themselves and their material. The other kind, the ones that chase around everywhere looking for help and support and advice, very seldom amount to anything and are mostly not worth the trouble they cause. A first-rate writer is usually stubborn and self-reliant, and the limp ones are seldom of value."

As you meet editors, and I believe this applies to all types of editors, you will find them men of affection, industry, and enthusiasm, and most of them dedicated to their job. That all editors are frustrated writers is a myth; but were it true, I believe it would make them better and more understanding editors. As I attempt to describe this business of editing, I hope you will feel that after lo! these many years, it is a business I cherish.

SECURING MANUSCRIPTS, DEVELOPING IDEAS

How are manuscripts secured? What brings authors to a publisher's door? Do they come neatly to the editor while he waits at his desk or does he go out with a dredge or a butterfly net? He and his various associates do both.

The most important factors in luring a parade of authors to any publisher are the distinction and attractiveness of the books published by a firm and its performance in presenting, advertising, and selling them. One might call this the personality of the house, and part of this is the personality of the members of the firm, the editors and the rest of the staff including the office boy and, of great importance, secretaries, receptionists, and telephone operators. Here we mustn't forget the business department. It must provide the promise of fair dealing and efficiency.

Given such a pleasing frame, the editorial department must work both within and outside it. Its members must be grounded in the history of writing and be aware of current writing in all its aspects. The ideal editor would be a superman, with world events as well as literatures at his fingertips. Many editors, even the most scholarly, read widely and with catholicity of taste. They must if they are to keep their jobs. They are aware of fads and fancies as well as of world events, politics, and philosophies. Editorial departments watch for good writers wherever they appear. They read other publishers' books and catalogues. They read newspapers and magazines—all sorts of magazines. They follow the theater, the radio, and television. They must follow, too, not only creative writing but critical writing, and watch closely the publications of their own trade, the reviews, the book announcements. They often follow writing in the colleges, the work done at writers' conferences. And all this, of course, not only on the domestic scene and in English-speaking countries but over the globe. Interest in translated works has greatly increased in the last twenty years, and is now rapidly extending from Europe to the Far East.

The editor searches for writing talent wherever he can find it, gets in touch with promising new writers, asks to read their work, nurtures them. Prizes are often offered by publishing houses, some of them grants to writers while they are creating their books. As times have become more stringent, this type of fellowship is less usual than it was soon after World War II, but the practice still continues.

The editor must keep an open door to all who come to him

with ideas. Ideas for books may come from the most unexpected places. The editor may be bored by the next door neighbor's suggestion, but it sometimes turns out to be a good one. He may dislike cocktail parties or gatherings of authors and their friends, but they are part of the job. Of course, the tavern-hopping aspects of publishing are overemphasized in fiction and among the columnists. An editor, or someone representing him, must have feelers out in all directions. To be sure, he must know what to do with ideas when they come to him, but that is another part of the chapter. It is usually one of the editors who makes trips to England, the Continent, and, increasingly, all over the globe to interview publishers and authors to seek out books.

Anyone following publishing even casually knows that authors change from one publisher to another. A whole book could be written on the ethics and complications of this fact. Suffice it to say that one source of authors for any publisher is a source for all the rest of the publishers, friend and foe alike.

Ideas for books are often generated within the publishing house itself. It is said of one highly modern firm that a rolling wall-screen is kept with such ideas graphically represented. If an author enters with an idea for a book on, say, "Games My Grandfather Played," the proper scroll is pulled down to display the fact that the editor himself had that inspiration long ago. The practice of developing ideas in editorial departments, then finding writers to do them on assignment, has, I should think, doubled since the 1920s. Some of our most successful books are developed in this manner, and it is doubtful if many successful publishers' lists could exist without them.

A publisher is perhaps interested in biography. He feels that a study of some titan, past or present, would ornament his list. He selects a writer known for his biographical writing, or perhaps a brilliant unknown. Often the writer has no current enthusiasm of his own and is happy to accept the assignment. Or a publisher has an idea for a certain type of book in psychology, medicine, history, what-not. He may want a game book, or a special anthology. He may design a series of books of a certain type. Following the news, some personality may appear whose story, told by himself or ghost-written, may appeal. Current best-seller lists are studded with these. Here the fertile imagination of the editor combines with his knowledge of available writers to produce much profitable merchandise and, indeed, occasionally a piece of real literature. Often the process is reversed and an author, barren for the moment, will come to a publisher seeking an idea. In some houses, editorial meetings are held frequently to dream over such imagined volumes and to produce lists of them for experimentation. Such books are not always ordered; often authors are prevailed upon to produce outlines, a few chapters, as an experiment, usually with some payment for the endeavor. The project may end there.

While an editor does occasionally present a writer with a plot or a theme for a novel, most of his own planning of books is done in nonfiction. Specialized nonfiction lists need much more inside-the-house planning than the general trade list.

Another source of books developed largely since World War II is the so-called package book presented to publishers by various individuals and a few concerns. A package book is usually, although not always, the sort of book that would be developed by the publisher himself as a house-idea book. But in this case, the outside idea man has produced the book entire, dealt with the author, secured illustrations, and so on, and delivers the completed product. There are several clever groups of editors working outside publishing houses who produce such books. They receive special fees or a share in the royalties or both—sometimes from the publishers, sometimes from the authors.

Some printing firms have special individuals or departments that produce package books, requiring the *quid pro quo* that the printing be done by them at their price.

A profitable phase of publishing for many years has been the publishing of books on great industries or industrial figures or on some phase of business of use for commercial distribution—books often heavily financed by the industries themselves. This type of book is very often initiated and brought to completion by the package book firms.

With the development of the paperback book business, book ideas and completed books are now increasingly offered to publishers of hard-cover books by the houses dealing with the paperback books. This is a reversal; in former days the original publisher almost always offered books complete to the reprint houses, although occasionally he discussed an idea with them.

Of all outside aids in the securing of books, the most important are the literary scout and the agent (paid or unpaid), and I shall discuss each of them now.

LITERARY SCOUTS

A literary scout of one sort or another is responsible for bringing to the attention of a publisher almost 100 percent of the manuscripts accepted for publication. He is, of course, an extension of the scouting duties of the editor. The percentage of manuscripts accepted from those that come in "unsolicited," "unattended," or "over the transom" is appallingly slim. One reason for this is that most writers know someone who knows someone in a publisher's office.

Scouts are, first, the good friends who bring the editors advice, assistance, and manuscripts. They are also the publisher's own salesmen on the road. And friendly booksellers. They are legion and they are often unpaid. They become scouts in fact when they are paid, sometimes by outright fees, sometimes by royalties paid by the publisher. Some publishers have elaborate and far-flung scouting systems with representatives all over the world. They are to be found on college campuses, in various cliques, literary and otherwise, in special areas such as business, medicine, the sciences. In any milieu where the background is rich and someone might write something entertaining about it, you may find the literary scout. A few New York publishers have offices in Chicago, in San Francisco, in London, and so on. While these are usually business offices, they also perform scouting duties. Scouts are, perhaps, most useful in securing foreign authors and often specialize in one foreign country or a group of foreign countries.

In a sense, the literary agent is the publisher's most important and active scout. The difference, however, lies in the fact that, in a material and contractual sense, the scout is working for the publisher and is paid by him, the agent is working for and is paid by the author.

Some well-known literary scouts have worked for more than one publisher at a time, but it is usually understood which of several publishers they serve *first*. If this is clearly understood, the seeming division of loyalties has proved manageable.

Scouts have been known to attempt to persuade authors to leave one publisher for another. This may be dangerous procedure and often results in unhappy relations all around, but it is nonetheless a cold fact. The literary scout is not so dramatically active as the talent scout in the entertainment or sports world. Please do not visualize a huge network of well-organized publishers' spies. This would be a misconception. However, the literary scout does exist and is valuable.

LITERARY AGENTS

The literary agent since World War I has risen with increasing rapidity to become one of the two or three most important factors in publishing. An author who does not employ an agent these days is rare, and the publisher who does not advise an author to use an agent is even rarer.

Literary agents in foreign countries are important both in their scouting and business capacities. They often represent specific publishers in placing translation rights. Literary agents in England or in other countries are usually represented by a specific American literary agent if they do not have their own branch office in the United States.

The business functions of the literary agent will be discussed elsewhere in this book. My concern here is with his relation to the editor. When I first came into publishing in the early 1920s there were relatively few agents in the United States. There were more of them in England. They dealt largely with matters of finance then, but there were men and women among them who were advisers in literary matters as well. So closely are the two allied that several good editors have become agents, and vice versa.

Literary agencies vary in size, as do publishers, from the small, highly personalized organization with a handful of people on the staff, to huge corporations dealing in the various ramifications of the literary and entertainment world. The large agencies, as well as the publishers, have their own scouting systems. Some authors use their lawyers as agents, some lawyers specialize these days in literary matters. Some of these lawyers like to fancy themselves as editors—some are good ones, too!

Today a number of the best editors in publishing are among the literary agents. The functions of securing manuscripts, nurturing authors, editing, and the like, are done in varying degree and intensity by these able and hard-working folk. Usually the author's agent and the publisher's editor work together very closely. The extent to which a publisher works directly with an agented author depends entirely on the personalities and desires of all concerned. Some agents carry on practically all contacts with the publisher in the case of certain authors, while with others on their roster exactly the opposite may be true, except in business matters.

The agent is often the author's advocate in questions of disagreement between author and editor. He is, too, adjudicator. If he is good at his job, he does not, of course, always agree with his client. He must sometimes persuade him.

Moreover, the agent's duty to his author is to consider his work from an overall point of view. The agent may think it wise for an author to write exclusively for the magazines, to accept motion picture contracts, and so on. In this proportioning of what time the author is to spend on writing books there is room for much consultation and real disagreement.

The entire career of the author, the long view of his writing and publishing life, is the true duty of both agent and editor. For example, an author's career can be endangered by too frequent publication. He can be unwisely advised to follow too closely the pattern of former success, or to venture into projects beyond his special talents. Myriads of problems arise in this overall picture and, in my experience, it is here that the author most often really needs advice given with wisdom and integrity because his own eyes fail to see too clearly.

Both publisher and agent find that they are often deeply involved in the personal lives of their authors. Much has been written, some of it in rather impish terms, of this fact. In any profession or business is one not involved with one's friends? Are one's friends not temperamental? Aren't bankers temperamental? Aren't bus drivers temperamental? Aren't editors temperamental? So it goes. However, I must say that when arguments arise, as they do now and then between editor and author, it is extraordinarily comforting for the publisher, and the author as well, to have the agent around to pick up the pieces.

RECEIVING AND CONSIDERING MANUSCRIPTS

Receiving and considering manuscripts are of first importance. A loose system of entering and controlling manuscripts while they are in the house can be both time-consuming and hazardous for public relations. Most houses have found that, no matter to whom the manuscript is addressed, immediate carding and acknowledgment of a manuscript at a central point, with notations also as to accompanying illustrations and directions if any for return, is wisest, and that whenever a manuscript is moved, whether to a department or an individual, a notation be made. It is wise to keep relating correspondence with the manuscript, although this is a difficult problem and an expensive one to solve if, as is sometimes the case, folders on all incoming manuscripts are kept. Lists of incoming manuscript are usually circulated among those concerned, so that all responsible people know what manuscripts are in the house, and frequent check-ups must be made to see that manuscripts have not strayed or been under consideration too long. A recurrent editorial nightmare is of a strayed or lost manuscript.

Some publishers reject manuscripts with great speed and, in this case, an acknowledgment of receipt is not always made. While many authors resent speedy rejection, I have always felt that it was professionally fairer to make this process as swift as possible, and not to hold a manuscript for the sole purpose of convincing its writer that it has been read from first page to last, as, indeed, it often is not. I like these two paragraphs from the English publisher Michael Joseph's warm book *The Adventure of Publishing:*

"Publishers will tell you, with their tongue in their cheek, that every manuscript which reaches their office is faithfully read, but they are not to be believed. At least fifteen out of twenty manuscripts can be summarily rejected, usually with safety. There may be a masterpiece among them, but it is a thousand to one against. . . .

"Most authors are born to be failures, and the publisher knows it. He makes his living out of the few successes and if he is indulgent with less successful writers it is not only because there is always the possibility that today's failure may become tomorrow's best seller. Unless he has a genuine sympathy with the author's problems no one can hope to make an enduring success of publishing."

Since authors do not always make clear how they wish manuscripts returned, an involved correspondence is often necessary. Authors occasionally do not even notify publishers of a change of address. It is necessary to hold manuscripts and, unbelievable as it may seem, manuscripts often are held for weeks or even months to be called for. This necessitates a careful recording and filing of manuscripts being held after rejection, and personnel who are aware of all of the details of this complicated process of reception, logging in, distribution within the office, mailing or expressing, the financial details of the operation, and so on.

I have detailed this operation with some care for two reasons: first, to emphasize the necessity of some central and tactful control; and second, to persuade such authors as may read this book that patience is a great help in a process which is so filled with pitfalls and frustrations. After all, manuscripts are brain-children and, no matter what their quality, are precious to their parents; and, in a not so very different sense, precious to the publisher. Because they are so precious, an author must make and keep at least one, preferably more, copies of his manuscript. To send the sole existing copy of a manuscript to a publisher is dangerous and unfair to all concerned.

The question of rejections and their handling is a troublesome one. Printed rejections, post cards, and letters are used by many publishers for many manuscripts. Editors write most carefully to any author who shows promise. It is considered by some unfair to criticize a manuscript in a letter of rejection unless there is a strong possibility that the publisher would seriously consider a revised manuscript. However, when a publisher writes a gracious letter of rejection and says that he would like to see more of an author's work, he usually means it.

Many authors feel that they do not get fair treatment from publishers. I think they are mistaken, but I have never found any way of persuading them of the fact.

HOW MANUSCRIPTS ARE JUDGED

The consideration of book ideas, the reading and judging of manuscripts, leading to the acceptance of a book, are of course the primary concern of a publishing house.

To accomplish this readers are employed, from one to dozens, some working on salary inside the house, some who take manuscripts home to read, some who are specialized experts in various fields. In some houses a so-called "first reader" (there may be more than one) winnows all manuscripts, although usually a manuscript from a known author or one arriving with an impressive endorsement goes directly to an editor.

As I have pointed out, few unsolicited manuscripts are accepted for publishing. Publishing houses, nonetheless, treat them, and at considerable cost, with care, with varying degrees of care, to be sure. How much of a manuscript is read depends partly on the experience of the reader. There are some editors who prefer to weed out these manuscripts themselves, rather than to leave the matter to inexperienced readers. With experience behind him, and a knowledge of the needs of his own house, an editor can perform this operation with speed and with less chance of error.

Whether it is unsolicited or not, a manuscript that shows promise is passed on with a report to a second reader or to an editor. Reports may consist of a sentence or of many pages. A number of houses provide printed forms for their readers which list the various aspects on which an opinion is desired. Spaces are left for a plot outline in the case of a novel or a digest of content for nonfiction, for a discussion of style, and for notation of various types of appeal. When I was first an outside reader for a publishing house in 1919 (Henry Holt & Co.), the form was a several-page masterpiece in which the most careful instructions were given. I have even seen forms which required the reader to give his estimates of percentages of appeal. For example, 5 percent sex, 10 percent adventure. The more informal report, however, or a very simple printed form, is now the general custom.

The easiest thing in publishing, as a rule, is to reject a book. But the hard work and the rewards, in spiritual as well as fiscal satisfaction, are in acceptance. I believe it is not generally understood what we publishers mean by the phrase, "It does not fit the list," but this is the reason why many books can be quickly rejected. A manuscript may conflict in many ways with books already accepted. The list may already be crowded. The subject matter of the book may be one which has proved unsuccessful for that publisher in the past. A book on playing bridge or an inspirational book might be born only to die on one publisher's list and become a national best seller on another's. Some of these facts an editor knows by instinct, some by training, but he must have a sense of the necessities and possibilities of the "complexion" of his own list. This does not stop him, alas, from reading many a manuscript he enjoys although he knows from the first page it is not for him. This only proves he is not so cold a fish as some would suppose. Moreover, there is always the exception. The editor may get so all-fired excited that he breaks all his own house restrictions.

The first delight that happens in the acceptance of a book is when someone, be it first reader or editor, is set afire. He likes the book. It is as simple as that. Not so simple, you say, and ask an editor, what makes *you* like a book?

Ellery Sedgwick, for many years the great editor of *The Atlantic Monthly*, once said that he published many different kinds of articles but never anything that did not please him, and that he had found that if something pleased him it appealed to many people. The late George Horace Lorimer of *The Saturday Evening Post* told me the same thing. They were magazine editors and their publications were very different—but it is a good rule for any kind of editor, provided, naturally, that he doesn't live in an ivory tower.

Not long ago I was talking with a group of my best friends, all of them editors, of varying ages and experience, all of them still excited by their jobs. What was it that made them want to publish a book? I asked. In what frame of mind did they sit down to read a manuscript? All were agreed that their first consideration was the book as a writing performance, as a book, that a consideration of sales possibilities came later.

One of them said that he always had three things in mind when he was reading any kind of manuscript: first, literary quality; second, topical value; and third, the future possibilities of an author. Another claimed that his rule was much simpler. His first judgment came when he got up and left the manuscript, went off for a walk in the woods. If he *had* to go back to the manuscript, he knew that it was worth going on.

Then, he'd put it away for a week. If he still remembered it vividly, he was reasonably sure.

There are no rules except that one must be excited. I do not believe in successful editors who maintain calm. To be very personal but to make my meaning, I hope, clearer, wouldn't you have felt the magic if you had picked up, before they were published, T. E. Lawrence's *The Seven Pillars of Wisdom*, DuBose Heyward's *Porgy*, Stephen Vincent Benét's *John Brown's Body*? If you wouldn't have, then the publishing business is not for you!

After this adventure into magic, we become more practical again. How is the actual decision to publish made after the enthusiasm from one or more readers?

Many successful publishers have made their decisions on the basis of a set of readers' reports, never having read the manuscripts themselves, usually after consultation with the sales department. A good many publishers have editorial meetings at which editors present the books they wish to publish to the management and members of various departments—sales, promotion, publicity, business. In some houses, principal editors have unlimited powers of decision, although they restrict these powers by many methods of checking and must exercise a large amount of personal self-control.

It is very important to consult the sales department. Many books are accepted without their enthusiasm and support, but this is unwise, and the closer an editor works with the salesmen, the sounder his decisions are likely to be.

Last, but in some ways most important, a manuscript's production costs, an estimate of the book, should be made, before its acceptance, in cooperation with the business department. The editor should know, before negotiations are started with author or agent, what the so-called "get out" point for a particular book is. In other words, how many copies a specific book must sell before it pays for itself and starts to make some profit for the firm. With these figures before him, he may decide to take chances, but it is very foolish not to know what chances he is taking.

The firm has now decided that it wishes to publish the book. What are the editor's responsibilities from this point on?

EDITOR AND AUTHOR

After the acceptance of a manuscript for publication, the first duty of the editor is to establish the friendliest and most cooperative relation possible with the author. The more mutual trust there is, the happier their whole publishing life together will be. Often this relation has been established long before acceptance. Together, they will now be sure that the manuscript is as perfect in all ways as it can humanly be before it is presented to the copy editor. A whole book could be written about this mutuality of the editor and author. I have already said as much about it as can readily be told in this book. The relation has been compared to marriage and to that of the psychoanalyst and his patient. At any rate it is delicate and difficult but it can be most rewarding.

The final selection of a title, for example, might seem a simple problem but often becomes a matter of bitter argument among author, editor, salesmen, and promotion and publicity men. A given title must be cleared to be sure that it has not been used too recently or too often. That a book title cannot be copyrighted is true, but there are certain legal problems in relation to repeated titles. It has been my experience that a sales department seldom likes a title when it first hears it, and often not until it has become a best seller. The more original the title, the more discussion is likely to eventuate. I well remember that Carl Carmer's *Stars Fell on Alabama,* Hervey Allen's *Anthony Adverse,* and Carlo Levi's *Christ Stopped at*

Eboli were all considered too odd by most of the salesmen, and that the argument over the Samuel Leibowitz-Quentin Reynolds *Courtroom* went on for weeks. Sometimes the author becomes stubborn about a change. Often both editor and author must call a halt to discussion and say "This is it!" but if a sales department really can be persuaded to like a title it is the healthiest situation. It is they who must first sell the book to the booksellers.

The editor and the copy desk are responsible for the front matter of the book, the list of the author's previous works, the dedication, the introduction or preface, if any, and, in cooperation with the production department, the captions on any illustrations. If the book is to be indexed, this is sometimes done by the author, or by a professional indexer under the supervision of the editor or copy desk, and is usually paid for by the author.

To have more than one manuscript available is wise, one to be the setting manuscript, others for the use of departments other than the design and production department. From this point on in the publishing life of a book, various operations can be carried on simultaneously, and speed is most valuable. How long the process now is from manuscript to publication date—ideally from four to six months for books that are fairly uncomplicated and routine—is not generally realized. Other chapters will emphasize this point but I make it strongly here because an editor is usually primarily responsible for the coordination that is necessary if time is not to be wasted, and the success or failure of a given title often lies exactly here.

The contract for the book is signed at some point before the manuscript starts on its way. It may have been signed long before the book was written, and financing of the author undertaken while the work was in progress. These business arrangements will be discussed elsewhere but I mention them here because many editors are responsible for contract negotiations with author and agent. Some of the best editors of the past have negotiated *all* contracts with authors, interpreting the author's needs and demands, so to speak, to the rest of the publishing house. Other editors have never discussed money matters with authors or, indeed, matters of promotion, advertising, sales, and so on. Which is the better system probably cannot be decided. It depends, in part, on the size of the publishing house and, in part, on the special abilities and characters of the authors and editors involved. Some fine editors cannot add a column of figures. Some editors, and authors too, are surprisingly good businessmen. Some merely fancy themselves as such.

However, the editor knows best the personal problems of the author. He understands the author's intent in regard to a specific work, and his enthusiasm and belief must light up all departments and individuals concerned. I believe that the success of a publishing house lies in the strength of the unity it achieves in its presentation of a single title, as well as in the selection and planning of the whole list. The smaller publisher obviously has less difficulty in achieving this unity, but he also finds it more difficult to stay in business these days.

Since World War II, assigning a particular author to a particular editor has become more and more the practice. "Mr. Jones is *my* editor," the author says with a certain possessive satisfaction. This editor is charged with seeing a book through all its operations or at least with advising and assisting in them. However, in many publishing houses several editors still work closely with one another on various projects and titles.

COOPERATION WITH OTHER DEPARTMENTS

Most of the processes discussed from here on are covered in other chapters, and I shall only indicate what the editor's connection with them is. He may actually do the job, or it may be done by other individuals or departments, but it is done, at best, always with the editor's cooperation, especially when consultation with the author is necessary or wise.

The problem of possible libel may be involved in a manuscript and, if there is such danger, the editor is responsible for consulting with lawyer and author.

One word of caution on libel from the editorial point of view. I have often found that if an author becomes too involved in a consideration of libel danger while he is writing, a dangerous block can result. The safer way is for the author to plunge ahead and let the editor and lawyer worry. However, the author must confess to his editor if his characters come close to living people, or more unpleasant situations can result.

Permission for the use of quoted material and the taking out of copyrights are sometimes handled by the editorial department, but usually not.

In the designing of a book the editor's responsibility is first to interpret an author's ideas or prejudices and then to contribute any of his own ideas as to the jacket or the actual physical make-up of the book.

Without such cooperation the book can be designed right out of its market. For example, an old-fashioned romantic story, if given a modernistic treatment in type selection and arrangement of title page, chapter headings, and so on, may displease potential readers before they ever buy the book. The responsible editor should approve jacket sketches and sample pages before the book actually goes to press. My own feeling is that only for the most special and even experimental types of books should highly modernistic designing be used. From the editor's point of view anything that distracts the reader from his actual reading of the book is an error. The editor, too, should take great care in the numbering methods of sections and chapters, also the selection of titles. Some books demand chapter titles; others should have none. Very often, descriptive material before parts or chapters is an effective method of leading the reader on.

The handling of proofs is the responsibility of the copy desk or production department, but the editor sometimes prefers actually to send the author's proofs to him or, to be entirely safe, also to check galley proofs or pages himself before the book is finally printed.

The writing of copy for the jacket of a book, the preparation of biographical material on the author, securing of photographs, catalogue copy, the preliminary steps toward sales promotion and publicity are sometimes undertaken by the editor. In the case of jacket copy, most publishers believe that the editorial department should be closely involved, if not the actual producers of the copy. Here, again, the author and the editor know best the fundamental idea that lies back of the book. And in the first slanting of copy lies the germ of future plans for exploitation.

Just how much part the editor plays from the time the completely produced book arrives on his desk varies greatly. As the author's representative in the publishing house, he must follow the whole operation closely. He sometimes shares with the publicity department the presentation of the list in advance to reviewers. He often chaperons the author in his progress through the tortuous mazes of personal appearances and literary entertainment. At least, he is a kindly parent when he sees signs of failure leading to despair, or the even more perilous effects of huge success.

The need for meetings, for frequent consultation among different departments of a publishing house, must have become apparent from these discussions. Formal meetings of personnel engaged in the various departments are, therefore, essential, although they can be overdone, and at most of these meetings, whether they concern business, sales promotion, publicity or advertising, or simple publisher's housekeeping, the editor should be present. He can also be useful in advising those concerned with the sale of supplementary rights and reprints. How does he ever get any editing done, you ask? The answer is he usually does it nights and week-ends.

In many ways the most important meeting of all is the full-dress sales meeting held twice, sometimes three times, a year, and discussed elsewhere. However, one of the editor's most important duties is to present the books on which he has been working to the salesmen and others gathered at these meetings. Cleverness in doing this can make or break a book. The editor must not only be prepared to make clear what the book is about, but why and to whom he thinks it will sell. He should be as brief in his talks as possible, but never too casual. By using all the wit and strength he possesses, he must see to it that he *never* bores those who are to sell the books. He must be ready to answer questions and to parry negative reactions. I have never known an editor who looked forward to sales meetings. But unless he is at least vigorous about them, he and the authors he represents are lost. Authors sometimes appear at sales meetings and it is usually the editor who coaches them beforehand.

The editor, then, is the man who is supposed to know what's in the book and what its potentialities are. He, therefore, under the guidance of management, must make the strongest effort to secure the unity in operation that will realize the potential.

PLANNING THE LIST

The planning and scheduling of a list is, of course, the concern of the entire publishing house. The editor, however, is the one who knows from what direction and when the books are coming. The business department tells him what volume of sales is necessary to make a profit. He knows with terrible clarity that maximum sales with a minimum number of titles is the goal. He must bring his knowledge and prophetic powers into play to advise as to the number of copies to be printed in a first edition, and hazard guesses as to probable sales, for a budget is necessary. This is the chief reason why publishing is considered a business only for those with a gambling instinct. In spite of all hazards, a list must be produced every year that will not fall behind calculations. There must be books that are sure of a wide, quick, immediate sale and those which, with a smaller original sale, will become established and, perhaps, sell for many years. No publishing house can really be successful without building such a treasure-house of backlist books.

The human factor, the author's ability to produce on time, is a perilous one. You have counted on a book, you have included it in your budget, and through various unforeseen accidents it must be postponed. Such a hole is sometimes impossible to fill. The inability of a writer to finish his book on schedule is unfortunately too usual. One of the most valuable efforts of an editor is his aid in helping such a writer extricate himself from his writing block. The psychologists have written much about mental blocks of various kinds. They can be very serious indeed. I knew one writer who, after a great success, was so overcome by fear that she was never capable of producing another book. The editor must be the understanding counselor. Sometimes only brief encouragement is needed; sometimes it takes long hours and much study before the work again begins to flow. Sometimes a psychoanalyst is actually consulted. This has always been a fascinating study to me, but one which is haunting, for if one's greatest best-selling author suddenly finds that he cannot write it is easy to see that this violently dislocates one's professional pride as well as the budget.

The great worth of steadily producing authors of quality must be apparent here. The greatest prize for any publisher would be several authors each one of which was sure of producing one book apiece every year that would sell fifty thousand copies or more.

Perhaps because I entered publishing as a magazine editor (a magazine about books, to be sure), I find it useful and comforting to think of a publishing list as two issues of a magazine (spring and autumn). The magazine must have variety. It has special departments. It must have important, known writers and new faces. It must not have conflicts of too similar material within the same issue. All this is true of book publishing. To maintain a reserve of material in magazine production is, of course, easier than in book publishing, and the time between acceptance and publication is not so great.

Editors of the specialized departments of publishing are often tempted to schedule too many titles for one season. Sometimes it is necessary to become stern with authors whose books must be postponed, or even to lose an author, rather than have too many garden books, religious books, and so on, in one season.

The editor, then, must dream his ideal list, work and hope to make his dream a reality and, above all things, coordinate details so that preventable accidents do not stop or delay the production of any book; but the seemingly impossible does happen: the perfectly planned and executed list appears; the authors keep to schedule; production and all the other departments function smoothly. The best sellers arrive. It has been a successful season. The editor may relax, but only briefly, for he must begin to dream of the next season and the next.

AUTHOR AT THE HELM

Should any author or would-be author read these pages, my hope is that he will not find them too cold or matter-of-fact.

Describing the complexities of editing in today's publishing factually and at the same time maintaining a degree of warmth has not been easy. Please keep in mind that I believe firmly in my heart that the author must actually always be at the helm. The publisher, the editor, can be only so great, in spirit and in performance, as the author allows them to be. Great editors do not discover nor produce great authors; great authors create and produce great publishers.

FOR FURTHER READING

Brown, Curtis. Contacts. New York, Harper, 1935.

Burack, A. S., ed. The Writer's Handbook. Rev. ed. Boston, The Writer, 1954.

Burlingame, Roger. Of Making Many Books: A Hundred Years of Reading, Writing and Publishing. New York, Scribners, 1946.

Doran, George H. Chronicles of Barabbas, 1884–1934. Rev. ed. New York, Rinehart, 1952.

Greenslet, Ferris. Under the Bridge: An Autobiography. Boston, Houghton Mifflin, 1943.

Gross, Gerald. Editors on Editing. New York, Grosset, 1962.

Hull, Helen, ed., for the Authors Guild. The Writer's Book. New York, Harper, 1950.

Joseph, Michael. The Adventure of Publishing. London, Allan Wingate Ltd., 1949; New York, Bowker, 1949.

McCormick, Ken. Editors Today. Twelfth of the R. R. Bowker Memorial Lectures. New York, New York Public Library, 1948.

Reynolds, Paul R. The Writing Trade. Boston, The Writer, 1949.

Rodell, Marie F. Mystery Fiction: Theory and Technique. Rev. ed. New York, Hermitage House, 1952.

Prescott, Orville. The Five-Dollar Gold Piece. New York, Random House, 1956.

Strauss, Harold. "The Illiterate American Writer," *Saturday Review*, May 17, 1952.

Weeks, Edward. The Open Heart. Boston, Atlantic-Little, Brown, 1955.

Wheelock, John Hall, ed. Editor to Author: The Letters of Maxwell E. Perkins. New York, Scribners, 1950.

3

COPY EDITING

By WILLIAM BRIDGWATER

LATE EDITOR IN CHIEF, COLUMBIA UNIVERSITY PRESS

❋

TAKE THE MANUSCRIPT of a book. Set it firmly upon a desk or a table so that it cannot slip or slide. Pick up a pencil. Start reading through the manuscript, and as you read correct typographical errors and note passages that may confuse a reader and usages that may cause trouble for a printer. You are doing copy editing.

THE SCOPE OF THE JOB

If the task sounds easy, you do not understand it. There are many complications, not the least of them being that it is a task without thoroughly set limits. What is called copy editing in one publishing house is almost never identical with what is called copy editing in another. Thus it is in book publishing, which exists solely to provide human communication through the printed word, yet violates principles of communication by using terms vague and multiple in meaning, but triumphantly workable. Everyone in publishing knows what copy editing is, so why define it precisely?

It is not editing as such—or general editing as it is called here—for that, as has already been shown in this book, is a supernal occupation concerned with telling an author Yes or No as to whether his book will be published, with admonishing him to alter whole chapters, and with other such high affairs. It is not production work, for that involves familiarity with type, sinkage, the moving of space from one place to another, and other matters shared only with printers. Yet in the spectrum of publishing, copy editing lies between general editing and production. Copy editing is basically the mechanical marking of a manuscript so that it is in literal and literary form ready to go to a printer.

In publishing, the edges within the spectrum are blurred. The general editor may do the copy editing himself. Even the publisher may deign to make all necessary changes on a manuscript (usually in a hand totally illegible to the printer). Sometimes the copy editor is called upon to rise above mere marking and rewrite large portions of a book. Occasionally the bearer of the title "copy editor" has as his only duty the marking of a manuscript with direct instructions to the printer as to matters of typographical style and manufacture, but such workers are more properly called production editors. They are concerned with the manuscript but not with copy.

The fundamental, unavoidable, and not infrequently boring part of copy editing is the discovery in a manuscript of all usages that may hinder the reader or may stop him short and make him leave the book altogether, like a man dragging his feet out of a swamp. And "usages" include not only misspelled words and missing or excessive punctuation, but also more important items, such as meaningless headings and references to nonexistent illustrations. These hindrances the copy editor must find and remove by exercise of his pencil, by suggestion to the author, or by referring the matter back to higher authority (usually the general editor or publisher; in short, the boss).

If, for instance, an author persists in writing *quarternary*, the copy editor simply cuts out the offending *r* wherever it appears. If in a numbered list, Item 3 and Item 5 are present, but Item 4 is absent, he writes a polite note to the author asking for Item 4. If he comes upon a chapter that he knows to be filled with error—in which, for instance, towns and cities of Australia are persistently misnamed and confused and there is a long description of a journey by boat from one place to another whereas in geographical fact neither place is remotely connected with a waterway—he usually takes the manuscript back to his superior. Such actions would at least qualify as normal copy-editing procedure, though other answers might be found. Copy editing will vary with the practice of the house, the nature of the boss, the character of the book, the attitude of the author, the amiability of the copy editor, and sometimes the weather. Yet if no action at all is taken in such circumstances, the worker is no copy editor.

Of these forces that control the scope and variation of copy editing by far the most determinative is the character of the book itself. The more creative the writing, the less the copy editor can or should do.

In books of poetry the author is almost entirely responsible for the whole, including the spelling and the physical appearance of the pages; the responsibility of the publisher is purely to translate the author's intention into terms of type on paper, and this responsibility lies almost exclusively in the hands of the general editor and the typographic designer. The function of the copy editor shrinks to measuring and proofreading, and even the measuring is strictly under orders of the designer and the proofreading under orders of the author (who may, if he pleases, scorn all dictionaries). It is true that in anthologies, texts, or quotations of poetry, the copy editor has somewhat larger duties, but these are still strictly mechanical: determining whether indentions must be kept as in the original publication, whether Elizabethan spelling may or may not be modernized, and deciding like issues, all of them involving meaning and therefore involving the copy editor, but all of them verging upon the prerogatives of the general editor or the designer or both. For the copy editor the requirement for editing poetry is plain: HANDS OFF!

The requirement for editing plays is a bit less stringent: HANDS OFF THE TEXT! The actual words written to be spoken —or, in the case of "literary" plays, written as *if* to be spoken—should normally be regarded as sacred, subject only to proofreading. The acting and stage directions must, however, be tested in detail by the copy editor to be certain that a sane and reasonably intelligent person can follow them. Even this limited function disappears when the author has melded everything into a conglomerate and sometimes deliberately obscure whole. Designer, general editor, and author usually determine what typographical mechanics should be employed, as, for example, whether names of characters speaking are to be in small capitals, in italics, in boldface (rare in these days), or in plain roman. The copy editor gleans the wheatfield after them; he questions inconsistencies, unintelligible abbreviations, and other usages that might trap the reader. Again, as in poetry, he has a greater responsibility in new editions or reproductions of old works. It may fall to his lot, for example, to point out to the author or the general editor that the manuscript contains detailed attempts to "picture" the original in ways that, except in a facsimile edition, are foolish, delusory, or even downright dishonest.

In ordinary prose fiction the scope of the copy editor is less, but not much less, limited. The job of "creative" editing, if it is to be done at all, is within the province of the general editor. Some fiction, such as stream-of-consciousness novels and short stories, even defies the crudest type of proofreading, and here the copy editor's job is almost nil. But the pendulum swings in a wide arc. In most romantic and mystery fiction, the dispassionate eye of a copy editor is of value in checking expression and fact. In one quite distinguished novel, when the author asked that no copy editing be done, none was, and to the disturbance of readers one of the minor characters quite inexplicably changed his name from Bob to Bill in the middle of the book. It is this sort of thing, and not cadence or charm, that is supposed to occupy the time of the copy editor of fiction. Occasionally the copy editor is also asked to cut the copy of a story to a predetermined length. He should have sufficient skill at abstracting to perform such a task without doing violence to what the author has created. No matter what the circumstances, the copy editor never has the slightest excuse for trying to preempt even the smallest section of the author's creative job.

It is in works of nonfiction that the copy editor is called upon to do his broadest and most useful work. The classification "nonfiction" covers all sorts of books, good, bad, and indifferent; cheap in idea and approach or elevated to the point where only the most highly trained can follow what is said; intended to be read to children of two or three years or to be read by graybeards in libraries. Each book varies in its audience and in its demands on the copy editor. Art books, for example, require that copy editors know enough about printing reproduction to be sure that the meaning of the text and captions meshes with the illustrations. Juvenile "fact books" should have copy editors as alert as general editors to the demands of word levels and to the responses of children. Copy editors of textbooks must support the efforts of the publisher to produce books that meet the needs of large groups of students of a particular subject at a stated level; in such books meaning and approach become one with expression and focus. The range in nonfiction and in the resultant demands upon copy editors is infinite. Yet in the copy editing of works of nonfiction of all types there are basic procedures and techniques which must be adapted to the purpose of the publishing house and to the book itself. These principles may be extended to all sorts of copy editing.

FIRST VIEW OF THE MANUSCRIPT

The process usually starts as this chapter does, with a manuscript spread out on a desk. In former days, when printing costs were lower, copy editing was by some publishers permitted to wait until the book was in galley proofs, and in exceptional cases this practice still holds. But the risks of expense for the publisher, exasperation for the author, and frustration for the editor and the printer are great indeed, and copy editing in proofs is inadvisable and rare. Usually the copy editor is handed a manuscript. It is given to him by the publisher, the general editor, the author, or some other agent (even if the author is an Eskimo who has just learned to read and write) and almost always with the admonition that it must be edited immediately and in great haste because of the publication schedule.

A good copy editor listens and heeds these words, even if he has heard them in variant form a thousand times. They are a reminder that in a job largely concerned with discovering faults the temptation is always to find too many and not too few; in a job that must be meticulous if it is to be good, attention to detail can easily absorb too much time and painful effort.

With such sobering considerations in mind, he begins a quick inspection of the manuscript as a whole—or at least the whole of what has been given to him. Not all copy editors make this preliminary run-through, but good ones do. The purpose is two-fold: to get the shape and feel of the book, and to uncover major discrepancies in usage and serious copy-editing problems. Such a full view gives the copy editor a better chance to unify his editing and generally improve the book. Therefore, in Utopia, a copy editor would always receive the full manuscript at once, including the title page, preface, and other front matter, as well as bibliography and notes, if such there be.

Yet in this workaday world schedules frequently make necessary the submission of manuscript in driblets from the editor or the author, and the copy editor must work away on what he has, hoping fervently that there are no large bears behind the bushes in scenery not yet viewed. In some publishing houses the title page, preface, and the like never pass through the hands of the copy editor at all. This practice has the advantage of keeping the copy editor busy at the task in which he is most useful, minute examination of the text. It does, however, have the disadvantage of preventing the copy editor, who necessarily ends by having a more intimate knowledge of the book than anyone else in the publishing house, from detecting in front matter usages and even statements that flatly contradict those in the finished text.

GETTING DOWN TO DETAILS

After the first rapid and informative survey the copy editor buckles down to his real work. He goes through the manuscript chapter by chapter, paragraph by paragraph, sentence by sentence, word by word. He always has in mind how the pages of the manuscript will be in detail translated into pages of type. He is trying at the same time to read the text in terms of the readers expected for that particular book. This judgment is not always arithmetical. Thus, if the book is intended for the wider general public, the copy editor must try to prevent it from containing words, allusions, or tone addressed exclusively to the literati or the cognoscenti.

Such editing does not mean eliminating all difficult words, elegant figures, and serious information. Any reader is by definition literate. Most readers, even when they peruse a book for sheer entertainment, are happy to improve their stock of knowledge, for this is, after all, the essence of reading, and they may even from a hard-boiled detective story or a sex-charged historical novel garner an astonishing harvest of exotic and authentic information. In every instance the copy editor must keep in mind the virtues and possibilities of the manuscript in hand. To each book its own copy-editing problems.

Proofreading and Proper Names. Rudimentary but fundamental is direct proofreading of the manuscript itself. Many authors are proud of their inability to spell and leave such trivial matters as spelling to menials. Copy editors, as those menials, may quietly harbor contrary opinions about the value of spelling, but they must of necessity spend their time in bringing the spelling into line with the pronouncements of the dictionary that the publishing house has chosen as authoritative. To do so is not a simple business of going from manuscript to dictionary and back again, pencil in hand. Always there is the problem of exceptions. The makers of dictionaries must choose among various spellings used and understood by educated English-speaking persons: there is no unanimity in English spelling, and the problem of preference often arises. An author has the right to cling to his idiosyncrasies. If he likes to write *meagre* instead of *meager*, his book should have *meagre*, even though the copy editor must take a note of the exception and watch carefully to change to *meagre* any occurrence of *meager*. Worse, dictionary makers cannot in the nature of things be up to the very last moment in decisions or innovations. New words and phrases are being added almost daily to the English language. They come not only down from science and technology, but also up from popular speech and across from foreign languages. Consider spinors, rock 'n' roll, and caudillismo. An expression or a word that has become current with the author and his audience cannot be despised. Since dictionaries must follow usages and not create them, the copy editor must be familiar with new words before they enter dictionaries.

Among words proper names occupy a special position. Many authors are just as careless with these as with common nouns, and proper names are harder for a copy editor to check. Most editors develop a certain wariness and caution toward names, both personal and place. Authors who spell by ear can easily create orthographic monstrosities; only too often Nietzsche becomes Nietsche and Khrushchev becomes Kruschev. For this sort of error the good copy editor is ready. He is even able to cope with the fact that the name of the sacred city of Xauen may also be spelled Xexauen, Chauen, Shishawen, Sheshawen, or Sheshauen; he merely finds the form most frequently used by the author and asks if that may not be used throughout the book. The author will usually consent, and that particular name problem is solved. If the author wants to follow the practice attributed to T. E. Lawrence of educating the reader by throwing at him all possible English forms of the name, it is legitimate for the editor to point out that the reader is more likely to be confused than educated. He may even go so far as to hint that an eccentricity which the public found enchanting in T. E. Lawrence may prove only annoying in the works of John J. Jones.

The checking of names is a delicate and many-sided operation. Offhand it would seem that an author using foreign names would be in a position to dictate what forms of names should appear. Generally this is true, but the exceptions cause trouble. An American book that has Roma and Firenze and Bruxelles instead of Rome, and Florence and Brussels is pretentious and absurd; an American who tried to say Bruxelles in conversation would be laughed at—and justifiably. A book in English should be in English, proper names and all. A good copy editor tries to steer an author toward name forms that will be usable for American readers.

Even in the editing of an insipid novel names can be an aggravating and complex problem. In considering them the copy editor is always halted by the caution of time. He may look up every American and English personal name in the appropriate *Who's Who,* if the volumes are at his elbow. But he may not devote hours to such checking. A sampling is all that is required. If the samples turn out, on assay, to have small gold content, then the matter must be referred back to the author or the general editor. The copy editor has only a limited number of hours to devote to a particular book.

In the checking of names the copy editor also encounters danger; he may only too easily commit the cardinal sin of copy editing. He may change something that is right into something wrong.

Words, including names, are of prime importance to the copy editor. Facts, as such, are more important to author and general editor and less the concern of the copy editor. One function of the copy editor is, however, to act as watchdog. It is part of his job to be suspicious. The author is responsible for all misstatements, falsehoods, and misapprehensions. He makes the statements, and the copy editor has only a small chance to check them. Yet, so far as a copy editor can review the facts, he must. In every book he edits he brings to bear all his knowledge, derived from experience or from reading. When there is due reason for querying an author's assertion, the copy editor must query all that seems wrong or dubious. He must point out demonstrable errors, giving his reasons for querying. In many cases disagreement with a reference book is not quite sufficient to justify more than a mild query, for usually the author should know as much or more than the author of an article in a reference book. The copy editor is obliged to bring to bear all the knowledge that he has. As a native of Kansas City, he will not tolerate geographical misinformation about that metropolis. If he does, he is being a knave as well as a fool. He must, further, query facts if he has good reason for doubting their authenticity, even if he is not absolutely certain. Usually such queries are addressed to the author, who will take great satisfaction in declaring his statement right and the query useless, if such is the case. When a copy editor finds the queries growing to a bulk too large for comfort, it is usually time for him to ask the editor or the publisher to intervene and request that the author check and rewrite his material or hire someone else to do so; in rare instances only is it the copy editor's business to talk directly with the author on total revision.

The Phrase and the Meaning. Words, facts, and finally usage. The most troublesome part of a copy editor's job is the review of a manuscript in search of grammatical and rhetorical vagaries. It is in making decisions on usage that the copy editor receives most guidance from the house stylebook, if there is one. Such stylebooks vary in an enormous range. They may be glossily written, expensively produced pamphlets intended primarily to impress authors; they may be stodgy collections of decisions about hyphenation (for example: Never hyphenate an adverb ending in *-ly* with a succeeding adjective), word choice (for example: Do not use *implement* as a verb), paragraphing, and chapter division. The prescriptions of stylebooks may be restricted to directions for the author in preparing a physical manuscript: typing in double-space on standard-sized paper, with no short pages or random pieces of manuscript; no use of pins, stapling machines, or Scotch tape to fasten inserts to the pages; and reams of other practical advice. On the other hand, the stylebook may be a compilation of exceptions, additions, and expansions of dictionary rulings. If such rulings are prescribed, the copy editor who is trying to trim up the manuscript must hold to them and try to make the author hold to them.

The true danger for a copy editor who is undertaking revision of expression is a sort of overconfidence, especially marked in young editors. The neophyte is sometimes under the mistaken impression that he has been hired as a literary critic. Without long experience he finds it hard to read a typewritten manuscript with the same respect that he gives to the printed word.

In a course in copy editing I have made the experiment of giving students sentences written by masters of English prose. Always a large percentage of the students with earnest abandon will "correct" the phrasing of Walter Pater and Virginia Woolf. Perhaps their changes are improvements; I am no more in a position to judge their alterations than they are to judge the original. But clearly the alterations are unwarranted interference.

The copy editor should do his rephrasing in material that has palpable errors—incomplete sentences, confusing use of "it" and "this," and other such dreary mistakes. If the author of a manuscript has recently come from some other language area into English, both general editor and copy editor must spend tedious hours testing the prose to be sure that foreignisms have not damaged the reading value of the English. In editing translations the task is even more exacting because translators often have such reverence for the original that they leave bits and pieces of it lying about in the translation, like logs washed upon a beach in a storm. Cleaning up a manuscript is honest work for the copy editor, writing old sentences over again in form more in consonance with the book is invaluable, but useless "improvement" of an author's literary style is futile and wrong. The course that a copy editor should follow is easy to indicate: aid the author, do not judge him.

At the same time certain accepted usages of English writing must be maintained so that a publisher may hold up his head among his fellows and boast of the editing of his books. He employs copy editors to support that pride. Therefore every copy editor should come to his desk for the first time with those usages already firmly in mind. This does not mean that he must know all the rules that schoolteachers in the late nineteenth and early twentieth century attempted to foist upon the language of Shakespeare and Dryden. The most familiar examples of these mistaken ordinances are the prohibitions imposed upon split infinitives and sentences ending in prepositions. The revolt against formulations of this sort was severe, but now it seems to have run its course. Today copy editors may edit on the sure principle that certain usages are accepted as a standard in English without fear of being castigated as reactionaries because they hold to principles at all. Almost no copy editors today attempt to follow the rigid and now discarded rules of yesterday. But almost all of them do think in terms of standard and substandard English, standard English being the body of usages accepted by educated people today (but not necessarily tomorrow) and substandard English comprising all forms frowned upon by those same educated persons. The line between the two wavers, but any good copy editor knows that standard English is the source of dictionary and stylebook formulations, not the product of them. He edits by knowledge of the language, not by rigid rules.

Punctuation. Considering the use of punctuation throughout a manuscript is only a part of the general editing of the text. The mechanical marks for guidance in reading are an intimate and inseparable part of an author's presentation of what he has to say. How intimate a part it can be is shown with blinding clarity in the poetical works of E. E. Cummings. Less astonishing to the ordinary reader than the profuse parentheses and missing periods of Cummings's poems but no less illustrative of the point are the methods of punctuation used by many modern novelists in English, from James Joyce to William Faulkner. Punctuation may be used to set the pace in narrative or the stress in exposition, to push phrases together or to thrust them apart, to slow or to hasten reading, to supply overtones absent from the words themselves. Literary arch-conservatives —among them a few copy editors—who decry such usages as twentieth-century innovations would do well to reread such masterpieces as the eighteenth-century novels of Laurence Sterne and the nineteenth-century works of Lewis Carroll. The employment of punctuation in wry and unusual fashion has a long and honorable tradition. Punctuation is part of the text, not a separate little engine throbbing away at a separate business.

True, for workaday nonfiction intended to inform or entertain the reader, full-blown theories are pretentious and even downright silly. Any copy editor of long experience has come upon authors who punctuate in bland carelessness or ignorance and then defensively claim that the periods, exclamation points, commas, and the rest are intricate parts of a well-laid plan and that it is not mere accident that an appositional phrase has a comma before it and none after it. A favorite explanation is that the punctuation is for the ear or for breathing. To this claim the copy editor is not allowed to answer (a) that if the author takes the book home and reads it aloud there will be in the annals of the book a total of oral readers amounting to one, or (b) that anyone trying to follow the punctuation marks in reading aloud will find himself panting like a dog on a hot day. In extreme cases he may, however, point out the same things in a polite way, saying (a) that since the book is of a type that would be read by most readers with silent attention, perhaps it would be better to punctuate for the eye rather than for the ear, or (b) that readers have the privilege of altering stress to suit their own speaking styles and might find marking according to the author's stress a hindrance rather than a help.

In other words, one may question how an author's system of punctuation may work. One should not question his right to choose a system. If he elects close (or tight) punctuation—that is, inserting a comma, a semicolon, a colon, or some other mark at every conceivable pause—it is the copy editor's business to point out spots that have been neglected. If, instead, the author chooses open (or loose) punctuation—that is, having only the minimum of marks necessary to carry the meaning—then the copy editor may suggest removal of punctuation that exceeds that bare minimum. Every copy editor should know, however, that the present tendency is toward open punctuation and that in cases of doubt the simpler forms have more present-day virtue. Further, if the house stylebook was drawn up long ago or concocted by someone with ideas from long ago, the copy editor must do his best to circumvent the house rules up to the point of actual defiance.

In all editing of punctuation it is well to keep in mind several indisputable facts.

One is that no rules for punctuation were handed down by a stern God from a cloudy heaven. Writing existed before punctuation, and can still serve to communicate ideas with no punctuation as such. Consider ancient Roman inscriptions, or such modern signs as this:

DO NOT LITTER THE STREETS
PUT WASTEPAPER IN THE BASKETS PROVIDED
THIS IS YOUR CITY   KEEP IT CLEAN

Admittedly the dots marking word breaks in Roman inscriptions and the line breaks and spaces in the sign operate like punctuation, but they are hardly punctuation marks. Those marks were invented only to aid more rapid and precise reading, and that is their major function now, though they may be quite legitimately used for other purposes.

A correlative—one might even say a consequent—fact is that punctuation varies from one language to another although they may all use the same alphabet. The Germans put commas before all dependent clauses. The French use *guillemets* to mark off quoted passages. The Spanish warn the reader that a question is coming by putting an upside-down question mark at the start. Though alien to usage in English, these practices have developed according to logic and seem to serve their purposes admirably. They are just as virtue-filled as English usage—but different.

A third fact is that in English punctuation there are fashions, just as there are in women's dress and in popular use of phrases. Certain punctuation practices seem to be fairly stable, for example, the use of capital letters to mark the beginnings of sentences. Some are almost universally accepted by English-speaking readers, for example, identifying a clause as nonrestrictive by introducing it with a comma; these are usually clearer when defined in texts of English composition than when met with in actual manuscripts, where a restrictive clause can approach easily the barrier that keeps it from being nonrestrictive. Some practices are demonstrably obsolete: not too long ago chapter numbers and chapter headings had periods after them; now those periods have the old-fashioned effect of Victorian lamps, beautiful in a proper setting, but ludicrous in a modern décor.

To all these facts a copy editor must be sensitive. The conclusions to be drawn are obvious, but it will do no harm to state them obviously. A copy editor should know that punctuation is inferior to the text in editing, and should avoid becoming a "comma chaser." He should try, within the limitations set by the author, to promote punctuation that will aid the reader today. Period, colon, semicolon, dash, parentheses and brackets, exclamation point, question mark, suspension points, and quotation marks—all are intended to illuminate the text. The copy editor should see that they do illuminate and not obscure.

Copy Editor and Author. Copy editing of a manuscript should fall into several patterns. There are changes that must be made. If an author violates house rules or standard usage—if, for example, he writes *phase* when he means *aspect* or writes *specific* when he means *particular*—the copy editor must make the required alterations in a firm, clear hand. If difficulties arise not from such obvious faults but from ambiguity or possible error, the copy editor should not be so brash; he will note these in the margin of the manuscript or, if there is no room there, on slips of paper attached to the proper page of manuscript. Finally, mere suggestions that the editor thinks may be helpful to the author but in no way essential should certainly not be written on the manuscript itself but only on accompanying slips or sheets of paper, so that they may be removed when the author has settled the question. These distinctions turn out, in practice, to be only rough, but the principle is sound.

In making such changes, queries, and suggestions, the copy editor must keep firmly in mind the truth that he is not a teacher instructing an incompetent student. Any editor who persists in writing notes such as "Awkward" or "Meaning?" or just a contemptuous "?" beside a manuscript passage should be fired. An author, even an incompetent, semiliterate, and pig-headed author, is within his rights in resenting such unhelpful work.

It is in the realm of textual editing that battles between author and copy editor usually occur. Not infrequently copy editors call particular authors "uncooperative," "illiterate," and worse. An author may be plaintive ("My manuscript came back all bleeding") or belligerent ("That editor doesn't know good English when he sees it"). Usually, though not always, such contretemps are the fault of the copy editor. It is his business to see difficulties in advance and to make all adjustments possible, no matter how oversensitive, insensitive, or obtuse an author may be. It is his job, above all, to realize that the book belongs primarily to the author, secondarily to the publisher, and not at all to the copy editor. Even if the author is personally cut off, known only through his manuscript and through letters written to someone else, a copy editor must constantly be aware of him, his abilities and his faults, his crotchets and his genius.

In matters of "apparatus," on the other hand, the copy editor must be to a certain extent the authority above the author. If a copy editor does not know about the form of footnotes, bibliography, and appendixes, it is time for his education. Even if his work at the moment is entirely in juveniles or fiction or how-to-do-it books, in which footnotes are at a minimum, he cannot truly know his craft unless he can place a firm hand upon footnotes and beat them into submission. He may, if necessary, learn by consulting stylebooks, though indoctrination by a skilled copy editor is better.

With their subject matter he cannot be concerned. Either the author has done his research properly and in good order, or he has not. If he has not, the copy editor may discover and sadly report that fact. In rare instances, he may be commissioned to check and reshape the notes. Any copy editor should know how to do it. He should at least know that the entries in the bibliography and the citations in footnotes should be coordinated and have some idea how the coordination should be accomplished. Amateur editors do not realize the unity of all the "apparatus"; professional editors should.

To achieve the simplest and most workable forms of notes, bibliography, appendixes, and subsidiary matter such as tables and charts is specifically the duty of the copy editor. In going through the manuscript he sees whether or not references to notes, tables, and charts match the corresponding notes, tables, and charts. If they do not, he must take measures to restore balance. This can be an onerous business. In one case in my experience the author decided to remove the first three of 159 tables, and all references to the tables had to be altered from beginning to end. The copy editor must in such circumstances plod along, looking at each table whenever a reference occurs. When that job is complete, he turns to editing the tables in series, to insure that the reader is not misled by headings that seem to be similar but are, in fact, different. Notes, tables, charts, bibliography—all these challenge the best efforts of a copy editor, and as sure as there will be some rainy days in a northern autumn there will be some manuscripts with intractable notes, insoluble tables, and unreadable charts.

With illustrations a copy editor may or may not deal, depending upon the practice of the particular publishing house. A usual and wholesome practice makes him responsible for the suitability of the illustrations, responsible for fitting them into the total pattern of the book. Photographs and drawings that neither reflect the text nor supplement what it has to say may be and frequently are used to embellish a book. Yet they gain more value if they are closely related to what is said in words, and this correspondence is the business of the copy editor. In the best of all possible worlds, the copy editor knows enough about reproduction methods to warn the author that material he has submitted for illustrations—a tattered newspaper photograph, for example—will not yield satisfactory results; but his proper business is passing on content rather than form, unless he happens also to be involved in production, which is outside the normal copy-editing scope.

When a book has been thoroughly surveyed, it should be ready to go to the production or manufacturing department and to the printer. In even the least troublesome manuscript, however, there are many problems that must, should, or might be referred to the author for decision. To take full advantage of the services of the copy editor, the publisher should submit the manuscript with all corrections, recommendations, and vagrant suggestions to the author before it is committed to type. To avoid trouble, it is normally wise to send sample editing—say of fifty pages—to the author for his approval before the entire manuscript has been canvassed. Then, further copy editing can be guided by the author's wishes. The author has at least as much proprietary interest as the publisher and will insist upon his rights. If he has at the beginning the opportunity to see some of the copy editing and express his tastes and his distastes, the publisher can gain more benefit from the copy editor's time; it can be an advantage, rather than an annoyance, to the author.

GALLEYS AND PAGE PROOFS

When the manuscript is completed and dispatched, the copy editor is not through with his duties. He must take care of the proofs, and in most houses not only the proofs of the books on which he has done the manuscript editing but also proofs of others. A copy editor must be a proofreader. He may at any moment be called upon to do the actual proofreading and do it professionally. In any case he is compelled to check all corrections made by the author in galley proofs.

Such checking would be easy if all authors knew the limits of proof changes. Unfortunately, despite elaborate instructions in style sheets or letters, many authors do not realize that inserting the word *probably* into the first line of an eighteen-line paragraph is not a matter of a one-line change. It is the business of the copy editor, not the author, to know that type is of metal and therefore not elastic. He must be ready to see that an author's correction is about to create trouble for a compositor and suggest substitute changes that will not cause trouble. He must inspect all alterations that are made and adjust those that would not be clear to a typesetter, since all proof changes are intended as instructions to the typesetter. His function as intermediary between manuscript and type becomes clear at the proof stage.

On the proofs the copy editor must also usually give instructions for the beginning of new pages. He must issue instructions so that the page proofs, when they come, will probably reflect the meaning of the book. If he is charged with the "inventory" of the book, he must make sure by a rapid check of the records that everything the book is to include is accounted for, either at hand or expected at a set date—such things as dedication, preface by some eminent person, acknowledgments, and the like. The table of contents and the list of illustrations cannot be prepared finally until page proofs have arrived, but before galley proofs are returned provision must be made for them.

A few niggling tasks also fall to the lot of the copy editor before galley proofs are returned. Word divisions at line ends must normally be checked and made to agree with the dictionary or the style rule approved by the house. Violently uneven spacing must be noted and in extreme cases changed by transposition or rewriting of the text. All headings should be given special proofreading. And if running heads for the chapters have not been made up and listed previously, they must be written out and submitted with the galleys in usable form.

When page proofs are returned, the copy editor must check all the author's new corrections, repeating the procedure used in the galleys. Pages that for one reason or another have been left long or short by the printer must be examined. If facing pages do not match in length, slight changes must be made. The order of page numbers must be checked for that book, and once again headings must be considered. The running heads must be proofread. The copy editor must see that the tables and charts are placed as advantageously as possible in the text (since printers cannot always follow to the letter instructions issued with the galleys). When a book is "dummied up" to show layout of text, illustrations, and headings, the copy editor is usually, though not always, expected to aid the production department, showing placement of all material. The copy editor must in some way assure himself that he has accounted for all content. If something is missing or wrongly placed, he is guilty, and, despite squirming, he must take the responsibility.

INDEXES

Indexes are a weight upon the spirit of the copy editor, though sometimes he is happily delivered of the responsibility when the general editor chooses to edit indexes himself. The copy editor is, however, best acquainted with the copy and normally best equipped, after the author, to perform a clinical inspection of the index manuscript. Some knowledge of indexes and indexing is of value, but if the copy editor does not have it to begin with he will probably gain it in the most laborious and unrewarding way, by experience.

Indexes, unfortunately, are not finished when they are sent out after editing. They return in proof, with author's corrections, and must be handled like regular page proof. In many houses and under many circumstances all page proof is held until the proofs of the table of contents and of the index are ready to be released. It is a good idea, when possible, for the copy editor to see the whole of the page proofs at once and visualize the book as to entire content. Once this last glimpse is allowed, he has no further chance to change his mind or repent his sins. Even if folded and gathered sheets are sent to him later, he can on them do no more than try to discover catastrophes, for anything milder than catastrophes must be left. There comes a time when a book is finished.

TOOLS, TECHNIQUES, AND QUALITIES

The tools of copy editing are simple: a pencil (in some houses pens are prescribed, but since humans err, a pencil is better), an eraser, some bits of paper, some reference works, and a mind. These must suffice.

Chief among the techniques is the ability to mark clearly on copy. Even the beginner at copy editing should know proofreader's marks and especially know how not to use them. A copy editor who makes the mistake of writing corrections in the margin of the manuscript rather than in the manuscript itself is being not only unprofessional but thoughtless, for he must know enough of printing to realize that a compositor goes through every word of manuscript and therefore is only impeded if he must look back and forth between copy and margin. He should be able to see also that the contrary holds true with galleys and page proofs. In those the compositor is setting only the lines that are to be changed; therefore those lines should be indicated by signals in the margin. The ability to mark manuscript and proof simply, cleanly, and unmistakably is something learned only over the years—and sometimes never.

The capacity to adjust knowledge and habits of copy editing and proofreading to new conditions has been severely tested in some houses in recent years because of new printing techniques. A copy editor must not be surprised today to find himself handling ammonia-scented proofs made from film-set type; checking pages of white type on black background, the reverse of what the printed book will look like; looking at fuzzy blueprints of illustrations instead of glossy engravers' proofs; or reading and decoding printouts from computer-aided composition.

Since many new processes depend upon the camera, the copy editor at some point will be faced with material that is not proof in the old form but a "mechanical" or a "repro" that must be handled with the care given to a photograph intended for reproduction. On this, corrections cannot be marked directly; they are usually made on covering tissues. The restrictions for handling photographic copy prevail; for example, no marks except on the edges; no use of clips, staples, or other metal fasteners; no finger marks; no rough handling. These are, however, but samplings from the present day. There may be new requirements tomorrow. It is the business of the copy editor to be ready to adjust to the requirements of the day after tomorrow.

The duties of a good copy editor are exacting. What are the qualities and interests he should have?

First, I should say, he must love books. Books as such, not just their intellectual content. To say that a copy editor should like reading is supererogatory, since no man in his right mind would undertake the job of copy editing if he had no affection for reading. Only readers need apply. But more than this he should like the touch and the smell and the feel of books—possibly even the taste. He should be interested in how books are made, in general and in detail. It is well for him to know a bit of how they are advertised and sold in bookshops and in drugstores, by peddlers and by mail, if he is to take his proper place in the chain of publishing. It is imperative that he know the rudiments of printing processes.

Second, he must respect authors. Primarily he is the servant of the reader, but secondarily he is the servant of the author, and a servant should learn the methods, aims, and whims of even a secondary master. The worst disease that can attack a copy editor is arrogance toward authors.

Third, he must have an eye for detail and a passion for accuracy in dealing with detail: of this the fabric of his working life is made. Yet minute attention must operate within the frame of good judgment. Too much anxiety for detail will cost the publisher money, the author anguish, and perhaps the copy editor his job.

Fourth, he must be really familiar, even intimate, with the English language and current English usage. Some publishers, many authors, and a majority of English professors would rank this requirement first. It is indeed of prime importance that the copy editor know whereof he speaks on words, grammar, and usage. He should know the old and outmoded usages as well as those that are current, for not all authors have current ideas —some, indeed, seem bent upon perpetuating the most unreasonable regulations that were obsolescent fifty years ago. Yet too great stress upon rules—upon "correctness"—is perilous. If the worst disease in copy editing is arrogance, the second worse is rigidity.

Fifth and finally, a copy editor must be curious, for it is curiosity that spurs him to awareness and to interest in even the dullest manuscript. If he learns a little from each book, he is a little more capable to edit the next. As his curiosity expands, so does his ability.

The ideal copy editor has these qualities and does these things. Could one ask for more: Yes. In special fields, such as science editing, juvenile editing, and reference-book editing, publishers ask for wider qualifications. Such employees are often called copy editors, but here I shall call them special editors and leave them out of account.

The professional copy editor, who sits at his desk with a manuscript planted squarely before him, is not superhuman. He is a humble man in a more or less humble job. Yet upon his shoulders lies the weight of centuries of learning. His calling is honorable, and he stands in line with the Scaligers and the Estiennes. The little marks he puts on paper are for the betterment of mankind.

REFERENCES AND FURTHER READING

Any major standard dictionary.

Bernstein, Theodore M. The Careful Writer: A Modern Guide to English Usage. New York, Atheneum, 1965.

Harper and Row's Author's Manual. New York, Harper and Row, 1966.

Manual of Style, 12th ed.; rev. Chicago, University of Chicago Press, 1967.

New York Times Style Book for Writers and Editors. New York, McGraw-Hill, 1962.

Rules for Composition and Readers at the University Press. Oxford, Oxford University Press, undated.

Style Manual. Washington, D. C., United States Government Printing Office.

4

DESIGNING THE PHYSICAL BOOK

By ERNST REICHL

ERNST REICHL ASSOCIATES, BOOK DESIGNERS

THE PROFESSIONAL book designer—like any other industrial designer—is a child of the first half of the twentieth century. There was no need whatever for his services while the printer and the publisher personally had time and knowledge to attend to the format of their books, as did the great printer-publishers of the first three centuries of bookmaking. But when book production and information processing developed into highly complex industries concerned, like any other industry, with mass production and selling, with merchandising and advertising, with market research and with return on investment, somebody responsible for product design, and for nothing else, became a necessity.

For a long period, however, this necessity was not apparent to publishers and printers. Manuscripts of trade books and textbooks were handed, in a routine way, to large commercial printing houses and binders to be set somewhat like an attached model of a previous publication. The result was a generally low level of book design and production.

This state of affairs was so obvious by 1920 that W. A. Dwiggins could write, in his "Extracts from an Investigation into the Physical Properties of Books As They Are at Present Published" (reprinted in Paul Bennett's *Books and Printing*), "All books of the present day are badly made. . . . It isn't so much that they are badly planned as it is that they are not planned at all. . . . The book-publishing industry has depraved the taste of the public. . . . You can't hope to get anything like a decent book until you do away with the damnable cheap paper and the vile types. And then you will have to start in and teach the printer how to print. Most printing looks like it had been done with apple-butter on a hay-press." He concluded: "The case seems to be hopeless. . . . The whole fabric of Standards of Workmanship will have to be rebuilt from the beginning."

In Europe, where the tradition for fine bookmaking had been entrenched somewhat deeper than in this country, and had received new impetus from the efforts of William Morris around the turn of the century, the accidental and totally unplanned book had met earlier resistance. The same general situation had brought forth a whole generation of excellent graphic artists who had proceeded from title-page lettering, type design, or book illustration, to the design of books as a whole. Eric Gill, Rudolf Koch, Hugo Steiner-Prag, Ernst Schneidler, to mention only a very few, had completely transformed the continental trade book from a machine-made commodity into a source of graphic pleasure.

In the United States, the foundations for a new—though rather classical—awareness of design had been laid a little earlier by a few fine craftsmen in the printing field. Among them were Daniel Berkeley Updike, Bruce Rogers, Will Bradley, Thomas Maitland Cleland. Later, at the time when Dwiggins made his plea, other young men were ready to respond to it. Dwiggins himself was finally retained as "consulting designer" by one of New York's leading young publishing houses (Alfred A. Knopf) less than ten years after he had printed his angry evaluation of the American trade book. The tide had started to turn, and public as well as commercial recognition of the intelligent planning, the attractive appearance, and the meticulous production of books has slowly but perceptibly increased ever since.

Today, few important titles of the major trade book publishers are produced without careful attention to design. Textbooks, which compete directly against each other—something which is only very occasionally true of trade books—generally utilize colorful design as an important device to create visual identity and to make a lasting impression. When the Fifty Books of the Year exhibit of the American Institute of Graphic Arts was started in 1923, and for several years thereafter, it consisted nearly exclusively of limited editions; but forty-odd years later trade books had replaced them to such an extent that a separate exhibition for fine, limited editions was under consideration.

Textbooks got their own show first in 1936, practically boycotted by an industry which at that time was appalled by the prospect of having to compete on the appearance as well as on the contents of their product, but today the acceptance of a title in the yearly Textbook Show of the American Institute of Graphic Arts is a feather in any textbook publisher's cap.

THE AIMS OF DESIGN

Design achieves its purpose when it helps to make a book legible, physically attractive, and suited to its particular purpose. These three terms are, however, altogether rather relative.

Legibility, for one, is a variable of established reading habits. What is easily legible varies considerably among nations, changes from decade to decade, and obviously depends even upon the physical age and condition of the prospective reader. No survey of legibility—and there are many of them—can have more than temporary and local validity. A designer who would be guided, let us say, by nothing but the principles of legibility established in a period when type was set by hand, and printed by methods now rarely used, on paper carefully made in small batches, would be very limited in the kind of work he could successfully attempt. He would, if nothing else, have to forego the use of any twentieth-century typeface.

Again, it is entirely a matter of taste as to what makes a book physically attractive. Whose taste, then: the editor's, the designer's, the author's, or the sales manager's? Their various ideas of beauty must at least be somewhat in harmony if an attractive book is to result.

Finally, the design of a title is most definitely influenced by the particular purpose of the volume. Given two manuscripts of the same length, one an economic thesis of predictably limited circulation, the other a spy story with a large sales potential, the designer surely will want to handle them somewhat differently, aside from all considerations of legibility and attractiveness.

Thus it is the designer in whose hands lies the responsibility for converting the raw materials of manuscript, type, paper, ink, cloth, photography, and drawing into what we call a book, in such a way that the end product carries an idea into as many minds as possible, as impressively as possible, and for as long a time as possible.

AN OUTLINE OF THE PROCESS

The design of a trade book begins generally with the copy-edited manuscript (sometimes, of course, a manuscript is tailored to fit a preconceived design formula). A tentative budget, based on estimated sales, has been worked out between the editorial and the sales staff and the production department. The designer is given all pertinent information, such as the planned trim size of the new book, the desirable number of pages, the number and kind of illustrations, the expected front and back matter. He is told the size of the first edition, which printing process is planned, and who will do the composition, the printing, and the binding. The grade of paper to be used, the grade of cloth, the permitted number of stampings upon the binding case, the area of leaf he may use—all these are vital data at this stage. He may further ask for the publication date, the retail price, and any special promotional or merchandising plans for the new book. If the artwork for the book jacket is available at this time—it often is, since some books are sold before they are made—he will want to see it before he starts. Finally, he is given a deadline by which he must deliver the layouts and specifications.

First, so as to fit the manuscript of a trade book into the required number of pages, a character count must be made—either by the prospective compositor or by the designer himself. There are various kinds of select matter in nearly every manuscript, such as excerpts, quotations, epigraphs, poetry, telegrams, footnotes, subheads, etc. Textbooks, containing all sorts of teaching material, step-by-step demonstrations and technical illustrations, are infinitely more complicated and time-consuming. But all this matter must be properly coordinated to begin with.

By the time the designer has all the various counts in front of him, and has figured out how many characters of each kind he must put on a page to give the volume the desired length, he will be quite familiar with the general atmosphere of the book, whether he has intentionally read it or not. His choice of an appropriate combination of typefaces and sizes depends not as much on his general impression of the manuscript as on the character counts; and he will frequently attempt to persuade the editor to change one or the other of the preliminary instructions.

The designer's final specifications are reviewed, and occasionally altered, by the manufacturing department or by the editors, and sample pages are then set up containing all the different elements of the manuscripts. While this is going on, the manuscript itself is marked up for the compositor in every detail so as to leave no room for doubt and save time lost by equivocal instructions.

Simultaneously a comprehensive sketch of the title page is submitted, and a sketch of the binding is made on the particular fabric which seems suitable or harmonizes with the jacket. All this material together is once more reviewed. The designer is usually given the opportunity to go over galleys, page proofs, foundry proofs, blue prints ("blues") and to solve the new problems which arise from the author's additions and alterations, or from the late addition of an unexpected introduction or index; he will also approve the stamped sample covers for the book.

SOME SPECIAL PROBLEMS

This procedure may be considered normal, but it varies somewhat from title to title and from publisher to publisher. Books of verse, children's books, and illustrated books of all kinds have quite individual case histories because they are laid out page for page. Textbooks, of course, are a chapter by themselves. It is the odd book, however, the book with special problems of one kind or another, for which the designer's specialized talent and experience are most helpful. His professional knowledge of various and sometimes unusual techniques of composition, typefaces, and reproduction processes and of materials makes it sometimes possible to publish a book which could not be produced in the ordinary way.

The binding, which forms an integral part of the book, is usually entrusted to the hands which shape the typography, and a professional book designer's experience therefore generally includes a knowledge of bookbinding equipment, procedure, and materials not required in other graphic arts fields; but the designer's services may extend beyond this point. The selection of an illustrator, the art of an endpaper, and the total color scheme are equally important elements of the "package," and therefore are generally discussed with the designer or left in his hands.

The book jacket, however, is such a vital ingredient of the sales and advertising campaign for the new trade book that it is, more often than not, handled in a different manner, too frequently quite unrelated to the process of designing the book itself. By and large, only jackets consisting of type or photography are considered the province of the book designer, unless he happens to be a graphic artist. In that case, of course, the concept of the book as a whole is likely to benefit from his idea for the jacket.

DOES GOOD DESIGN PAY?

"Does good design help the sale of a book? Does it pay in dollars and cents?"

This question is no longer asked as frequently as it once was. With the growing automation of all graphic arts production processes, it is a matter of frightening day-to-day experience that somebody must have planned the whole before the parts can be ordered. Whether you call it designing or graphic planning, it is disastrous not to do it. The possibility of avoiding costly mistakes and saving money by coordinating one's resources and one's timing is only part of the story. On the positive side one may say that good book design is pretty much like book advertising. A national best seller may not sell much better because of it, and a flop won't sell either with or without it. The books that profit most from good design are in the class between the extremes: all those titles which form a good backlist, and which, in the end, create the lasting reputation of a publishing house.

The cost of book design should be figured more in terms of the time consumed to make a decent book than in terms of money. The design charge, measured against the plant cost (composition and plates), is extremely small; and an intelligently planned book costs so much less to produce than an unplanned one that the professional book designer literally earns his own fee. His most obvious value is that of a safeguard against unpleasant surprises.

While the designer is required to spend the publisher's money where it counts most, he is, today more than ever, in a position to keep down expenses. Obvious ways for reducing printing costs, for instance, consist in planning a book so that the total number of pages will make up into forms of 32 or 64 pages. This can often be achieved by adjusting the sinkage of chapter heads, or by running chapters in (i.e., not beginning each chapter on a new page), in which case the heads must, of course, be set in a fairly prominent type. Economical handling of the front matter to save space, or the avoidance of hand composition for chapter heads and for initials, are other popular ways of stretching a tight budget.

Familiarity with various methods of setting type often enables the professional designer to take advantage of the virtues of a particular process. This range extends today from the most honorably established hand composition to the latest methods such as computer, electronic, and photocomposition on several different kinds of machinery.

Any measure of economy should, of course, be planned at the time a book is designed, because an otherwise decent-looking volume is easily ruined by a last-minute change, throwing the type page out of proportion or destroying the margin scheme.

When it comes to illustration, the proper choice of the appropriate printing process can sometimes effect economies. Offset printing, which reproduces type and halftone illustrations with equal ease, is generally to be recommended when photographs are used. This will not only avoid the necessity of using two different kinds of paper—antique stock for the type matter, coated stock for the illustrations—but will also make it unnecessary to bunch the illustrations in one or two forms, or to jacket them around several forms (a noticeable binding expense), or to tip them on, which costs still more. When a book is to be printed by offset altogether, the designer will consider the choice of type carefully ahead of time, because some faces will print by offset less clearly than others, and the compositor must be equipped at least with good proving facilities or, preferably, with photocomposing equipment.

As for binding a book, there are innumerable ways for a designer to prove his mettle, artistically as well as economically. The cost of binding is one of the largest per-copy expenses—to turn out an attractive and durable book within a sensible budget is a feat well worthwhile. But the lack of attention paid to the binding of a volume ruins many a handsomely printed trade book today.

Printers generally have a fine reputation for imaginative excuses, but they can hardly match the alibis invented by bookbinders for misbound books, clashing colors, or late deliveries.

THE SET-UP OF DESIGN SERVICES

More of the younger book designers, men and women, come today from the field of commercial art than from the field of printing and production; training in typography and book production is essential for all of them. Such specialized courses are available every season at several universities, design schools, and colleges. Good as they are, these courses do not furnish nearly sufficient preparation for a design job; practical experience in a publishing house, a design department, a print shop, a bindery, or preferably in all of them is a necessary adjunct. No wonder that there is such a dearth of all-around practical book designers. It has been said that it takes two years to make a good book production man; if that's true, it would take three times as long to make a professional book designer.

The number of publishing houses that employ a designing staff, or a whole art department of their own, is steadily growing. This is due to the increasing size and importance of textbook departments, and to the success of the sort of trade or mail-order book which originates in an editor's brain, not in an author's heart. These kinds of made rather than written books, growing over an extended period of time in a publisher's office, require an on-and-off process of supervised design more suited to a methodical staff treatment than to the moods of an individual designer. Here design is split up in departments: character counting, type specifying, headline styling, color determination, picture editing, art editing, scaling, caption fitting, and paste-up: it altogether proceeds more like magazine production than conventional book design. The result of the coordinated efforts of so many specialists is generally excellent though somewhat lifeless and computerized. Most of these books, no matter which house they come from, tend to look very much alike.

A few outstanding individual designers are employed or retained by some of the larger trade book publishing houses. These house designers are given an enviable amount of artistic freedom because they are thoroughly familiar with the editorial policy of their firm, and because the quality of their work is admired and relied upon. Other designers are in the employ of some of the larger book manufacturers, and as such must be flexible enough to consider the varying requirements of diverse kinds of publishers. Some publishers like to have a "house style" apparent in all their publications; others prefer to change their style with each book and to have its design indicative of its contents. They employ different free-lance designers who work independently, either as individuals or with a staff of their own.

Many technical developments have reshaped the appearance of the books of our time; there is no choice in this respect. But the question is always present how far one may go of one's own free will, in changing the functional design of a product hallowed as it were by a 500-year-old tradition. Some say, all the way; others, don't move.

Stanley Morison, leading type designer and researcher, feels that "the typography of books requires an obedience to convention which is almost absolute." But Christian Dior, famous in another field of design, has a different attitude. He says: "Changes just come about, and many things contribute when everybody is ready for them."

Take your choice.

FOR FURTHER READING

Bennett, Paul A., ed. Books and Printing: A Treasury for Typophiles. Hardcover and paper. Cleveland and New York, World, 1951.

Dair, Carl. Design with Type. Toronto, University of Toronto Press, 1965.

Lee, Marshall. Bookmaking: The Illustrated Guide to Design and Production. New York, Bowker, 1965.

Lee, Marshall, ed., and others. Books for Our Time. New York, Oxford University Press, 1951.

Mansfield, Edgar. Modern Design in Bookbinding. Boston, Boston Book and Art Shop.

McMurtrie, Douglas C. The Book: The Story of Printing and Bookmaking. 3d ed.; rev. Oxford and New York, Oxford University Press, 1943.

Morison, Stanley. Four Centuries of Fine Printing. 3d ed.; rev. New York, Barnes and Noble, 1960.

Rogers, Bruce. Pi: A Hodge Podge of Letters, Papers and Addresses Written During the Last Sixty Years. Cleveland and New York, World, 1953.

Spencer, Herbert, ed. The Penrose Annual. London, Lund, Humphries; New York, Hastings House.

Steinberg, S. H. Five Hundred Years of Printing. Rev. ed. Paper. Baltimore, Penguin Books, 1962.

Updike, Daniel Berkeley. Printing Types, Their History, Forms and Use: A Study in Survivals. 2 vols. 2d ed. Cambridge, Harvard University Press, 1937.

Warde, Beatrice. The Crystal Goblet: Sixteen Essays on Typography. Cleveland and New York, World, 1956.

Williamson, Hugh. Methods of Book Design. 2d ed.; rev. Oxford and New York, Oxford University Press, 1966.

5

PRODUCTION AND MANUFACTURING

By FRANK B. MYRICK

DIRECTOR, RESEARCH AND DEVELOPMENT,
THE SENDOR BINDERY

❋

IT IS the responsibility of the production or manufacturing division of the publishing organization to insure that the author's text (and illustrations, if any) is transformed into a finished book, ready for distribution and the reviewers weeks before the publication date, at a cost which is within the range of the previously estimated sale price of the book and which will leave a margin of profit for the publisher after all costs are covered and assuming sales meet with expectations.

The average publishers' production department has escalated today into a group of specialists in various phases of the design and manufacturing of the book, though many small publishers combine editorial duties with production, or engage firms which specialize in providing complete production service. The production department may also enlist the services of a variety of specialists such as artist, designer, typographer, etc., and coordinate their combined efforts. Much depends on the financial and marketing capability of the individuals who make up the firm.

A typical production department is likely to utilize the services of up to five or more individuals to supervise the production of the finished book, because of the greatly increased complexity of today's books, especially in the textbook area. Today's production department must also be able to choose wisely among several methods of composition, printing, and binding and a widening variety of materials and sources of supply both domestic and foreign, and to keep *au courant* with a variety of new methods of production, many of which were virtually unknown even a decade ago.

Nevertheless, the physical book in its final format is seemingly little different from the books of centuries ago, except that the route has become more familiar. Editor, designer, production manager—all three together or individually estimate the cost of production in terms of the marketability of the book, and are far better equipped today than in the past to determine these costs.

ESTIMATES AND SPECIFICATIONS

First, a member of the staff, perhaps one of those just mentioned, casts off, or estimates the length of the manuscript in words or, preferably, characters, by taking the number of words or characters on a typical page of manuscript and multiplying it by the total number of pages in the copy. Using printers' copyfitting tables, the designer or production department member ascertains how many characters in a suitable typeface may be fitted into a line and how many lines of type this will produce. After making allowance for margins and other aids to legibility, he arrives at a readable type page that will look well when printed on a trim size that will enable the book to be printed, preferably in multiples of 32 pages, at a cost within the budget. The bulk or thickness of the finished book is another factor. A somewhat risky rule of thumb is that the manufacturing cost may be in the vicinity of 20 to 30 percent of the selling price, but obviously the kind of book and its illustrations have a critical effect on these figures.

Many other points greatly affect the cost of the book: the size and nature of chapter headings, long ones or short, or whether chapter numbers will be sufficient; whether or not there are subheads; the size and number of illustrations, if any; color printing, if any; whether or not each chapter will open on a new page; whether or not there will be running heads; the location of folios (page numbers); whether or not there are part titles; how footnotes, extracts, poetry, tabular matter, or other material interpolated in the text will be handled.

The designer needs to know as much as possible about these and about such questions as double-spread title pages; the false title, if any; copyright notice and its required position; dedication, preface, foreword, or half title (usually preceding the first page of the text); and whether there will be a card announcing other titles by the author. Both he and the production department must secure this information from the editor (or author in some cases) and also must find out if there will be an appendix, glossary, bibliography, and index, or if any such material is to be used in the book at all.

Once all these details are settled, the next phase is to set sample pages, usually a title, chapter, and text page, and examples of one or more of the problems discussed above. After approval, a complete specification is drawn up for the typesetter's guidance, and for the printer and binder, setting forth the method of printing and binding, arrived at preferably by conferences with each, unless the facilities of a plant completely equipped for total manufacture are utilized.

The platemaker is consulted about reproduction of the illustrations, if any, the preparation of copy, and selection of the method of printing. Depending on the practices of the house, estimates may be secured from several sources if the book is in any way difficult, or the order may be awarded either to a complete manufacturer or to several specialists.

By this time the production department has a clear picture

of what supplies and services must be obtained, and when, to produce the full edition or any part thereof. To stay within a budget the designer-editor-production team decides what niceties of design or production may have to be eliminated or modified.

Production dummies are prepared to reflect the number of pages in the book, the trim size, the design of the cover, and selection of the materials. The designer paints in a simulation of the cover design or traces in the outlines of the selected typeface or lettering on a sample of the binding material. The dummy also reflects decisions on the cover decoration, and on the process used to apply it—hot die stamping, ink stamping, printing by offset, or silk screen or some other process. The dummy affords the first preview of the finished book, and once it is approved, the ordering of paper, cloth, dies, screens, printing, etc., may proceed, while the book is being composed—that is, set in type.

Final estimates of production cost are in terms of cost per unit, with figures for additional hundreds or thousands of copies in case advance reviews and sales indicate a successful book. The production department ascertains these costs in advance for reprints and possible reissues in new formats. Most publishers divide their production expenses into two categories, plant costs and production costs. The first covers all costs for producing one copy, i.e., composition, art, plates, cover decorations, dies, etc. The second category covers the cost of paper, binding materials, presswork, and binding for the planned edition.

CHOOSING AND ORDERING PAPER

The choice of paper is usually made by mutual agreement between the publisher and the manufacturer, and depends in great part on the method of printing chosen—letterpress, offset, gravure, or a combination of these. (The three processes are described in a later section of this chapter). The nature of the illustrations play a large part in the selection of the finish, weight (thickness), and size of the stock selected, which can be specially ordered from the paper mill by the publisher, printer, or manufacturer.

Most book paper falls into four basic classifications: antique, English finish, coated, or offset. Each of these major types is available in various finishes depending on the volume of the job, the nature of the text and illustrations to be printed on it, and the method of printing to be utilized.

Most trade books, such as novels, for which only type matter is to be set and printed, will require antique stock—a soft, somewhat rough, and absorbent finish. Type and line print easily on it because the fibers in the paper absorb much of the ink impression. Generally, a wove finish antique is used for such books, because there is no reflection from the paper—a sheet much like the paper used in this book, in finish and color. Some antiques are made with a laid finish which shows faint parallel lines intersecting with other parallel lines at regular intervals. These are created by a network of woven wire over which the wet paper passes as it is formed, the wires causing the paper to be slightly thinner at each of these points. Such paper is usually for books of extra fine quality—it may even be watermarked with perhaps the publishers' emblem.

Antiques are supplied in various degrees of bulk, high bulk referring to a paper so made that the fibers are not pressed as flat as they sometimes are, so that a few hundred pages, may, in the preliminary dummy, make up into a very thick book. The practice of bulking is much less prevalent than it has been in the past.

Some antiques are smoothed by heated rollers which iron the paper into varying degrees of smoothness, such as plate, eggshell, and supercalendered. The latter paper is smooth enough to accept medium-screen halftones. Improvements in papermaking have resulted in the development of a wider line of coated papers, especially those called "pigmented." Here, the base stock is heavily coated with a smooth pigment coating, so that a very level surface is achieved, almost as smooth as full coated. Coated paper is supplied in dull and glossy finish, often termed an enamel.

Midway in this group are the machine and English finishes, frequently used for books of all types. Each is the result of extra calendering in the final stages of the paper machine.

Perhaps the greatest change in paper technology in recent years has been the development of special offset papers for use with that process. Because of the dampening effect caused by the use of water in the offset process, papers were developed that were sized to resist the penetration of the moisture which created certain problems of register in offset color printing. Coated stocks also have been improved so that they, too, may be printed in this manner.

Within the past few years, it was found that offset stock could be developed which could be printed from rolls, in several colors (the web dried after each color), folded into signatures, or slit into sheets. This called for the introduction of many new factors into paper, such as foldability and absorption matched by an increase in ink oxidation under heat, without scorching, cracking, or becoming too limp and lifeless.

Such books as long-run elementary textbooks are predominantly printed by web offset, and a great many others are produced by sheet-fed offset.

Finding the amount of paper required to print the desired edition involves a number of mathematical computations, for although paper is used by the sheet, it is sold by the pound. Each paper is rated at a specific basis weight or substance.

For example, 50-lb. antique means that 500 sheets of a size measuring 25 by 38 inches weighs 50 pounds. The paper may be defined as #50 or 50#. The sheet size chosen will be some multiple in relation to the 25 by 38, and will likely be quoted as #50, 52 by 76 inches. It will weigh approximately 100-plus pounds for each 500 sheets. If the book is to have a finished trim size of 6 by 9 inches, this will be divided into 52 by 76, and will permit 64 pages to be printed on each side of the sheet. Other popular sheet sizes are 38 by 50, 41 by 61, or 56 by 69 inches, and permit a variety of trim sizes to be cut economically out of these sheets. If a book consists of 320 pages, it will require five 52 by 76 sheets per book, and thus if the edition is 3,000, the total paper order will be 15,000 sheets—plus an amount for trim and spoilage (to be explained later).

Paper manufacturers and merchants provide tables showing the number of pounds and price per pound in various packings such as carton, ream, skid, or carload. Paper is produced from pulp from ground-up logs. The pulp is whitened by various bleaching acids. Then, in the papermaking machine, the pulp, still highly fluid, is spread out on a continuously vibrating wire screen. This permits the water to drain off and the paper fibers to mat together, usually in the longitudinal direction of the moving web. As the web of raw paper moves through the machine it is dried and pressed between highly polished steam-heated rollers, and then, in the same machine various coatings are applied. At the end of the machine the paper is slitted and rewound into smaller rolls for web presses, or cut in both directions to form sheets. The edge that runs with the fibers lengthwise or parallel to the long edge is known as "long grain," the other as "short grain." For binding the former is preferable.

Most publishers find it economical to print as large a sheet as is practical on the printer's equipment, and as few sheets in the book as needed, to reduce the number of sheets which must be printed, folded, gathered, and sewn before the final cover is put on. A signature is designated as the finished folded sheet, printed on both sides with the form or plate. It may contain 12, 16, 24, 32, 48, 64, 96, or 128 pages depending on the trim size of the book. Half the number of pages are printed on one side of the sheet, the balance on the other. When folded, the pages will follow in numerical order. A 64-page signature may often be printed so that it may be slit in half on the press or on the folder (occasionally on very large papercutters) and folded as two half-sheets to reduce the swell of the folding.

Arranging the type or plates in the proper order so that a given sequence of folding operations will produce the desired signature is called "imposition." Most large sheets are folded in a succession of right-angle folds on a Dexter or Camco knife folder, which may often take a 64- or even 128-page sheet and fold and slit it so that four signatures are delivered. When a great number of right-angle folds are made in a single sheet, it becomes very difficult to secure good alignment of the pages. A great deal of the margin between them will vanish in the gutter, or center portion, of the signature, making the book difficult to read. The heavier the paper, the more likely this is to happen. Offset paper, which is frequently printed cross-grain and may cause erratic folding, is usually folded parallel (so that all folds are parallel to each other), on a Dexter (Cleveland) or Baum buckle folder, which drives the sheet up against a stop in a plate not unlike a mold, then forces it to buckle and fold at the desired dimension with other folds following. When the paper grain is parallel to the fold, the erratic folding referred to is eliminated, and the 12-, 24- or 48-page signatures may be easily secured without right-angle folds, or perhaps only one.

The size of the sheet purchased is determined by the book's

trim size, the number of pages in the signature, the thickness or basis weight of the paper, the number of folds to be made, the printing process (which affects the paper choice), and the necessity of adding a small fraction on the fore-edge, top and bottom of each page, to permit the book to be trimmed neatly. Thus a 6 by 9-inch trim would have from $\frac{1}{8}$ to $\frac{1}{2}$-inch added to the 9-inch dimension, and a similar amount added twice (top and bottom) of the 6-inch dimension. The most common allowance is $\frac{1}{8}$-inch so that the actual overall page size would be $6\frac{1}{4}$ by $9\frac{1}{8}$ inches. If 16 pages were to be printed on each side of the 38 by 50 sheet, the overall size would be divided into the sheet size, thus: $\frac{38 \times 50}{6\frac{1}{4} \times 9\frac{1}{8}}$ which gives the desired 32 pages.

COMPOSITION, PLATES AND PRESSES

While the paper is being estimated and secured, the first stage of the completed book, the composition or setting into type of the author's manuscript begins. The book manufacturer, or typesetter, who is to set the book carefully examines the copy to see if there are any deviations from the original estimate, such as additional mathematical tables, poetry, or footnotes. The main portion of the copy is distributed among several operators of typesetting machines, so as to hasten its completion.

A great many books are still set on Linotype or Intertype machines, which produce single lines of metal type cast as a unit from assembled lines or matrix letters. Intervening spacing is supplied by spacebands, which fill out any remaining space between words before the line is cast. A keyboard somewhat like a typewriter, but twice as large, is used to release the mats from a magazine, to which they return after casting.

Some books are set on the Monotype, which produces lines of single types, each cast from a matrix case, which is actuated by a punched paper tape, the product of a separate keyboard.

An increasing number of books are set on photocomposing machines, in which a negative of each letter is exposed at high speed by flash exposure on a roll of film, which is then developed and a paper print made therefrom. The negative film may be used for stripping into page position for offset, letterpress, or gravure platemaking. Among these machines are the Fotosetter, Monophoto, Photon, Videocomp, and Linofilm. In addition there is a new (1965–1966) family of machines, such as Photon 900, Fotronic, and Linotron, operated by tape punched on a keyboard, which in turn drives the photographic units—all hyphenation, corrections, and typographic format instructions having been put into the tape before the typesetting is done. Also, many models of slug-casting machines have been converted to tape operation, using the Teletypesetter, a first cousin to the Teletype, which is also driven by a paper tape punched by Fairchild, Friden, Dura, or other tape-punching devices. In turn these tapes activate the keyboard casting-systems on slug machines so adapted at much higher speeds than that achieved by manual operation.

Data-processing computers, including those of IBM, Control Data, RCA, and others, have also been adapted to punch paper or magnetic tapes for controlling typesetting, by film or otherwise. Also, cold-type machines, including the IBM, Friden, Justowriter, and Vari-Typer keyboards, have been utilized to produce acceptable copy for platemaking, usually offset, often used for technical books of short run or difficult copy.

Display typography for chapter heads, title page, etc., may be set by hand or machine, depending on the size and face desired. Foundry type (each letter a single piece of metal) is set by hand in a composing stick and justified by metal spaces of various widths until the line is filled out. Monotype and Ludlow machines produce lines cast from hand-assembled matrices. Also, each of the film machines mentioned has models adapted for display setting.

Letterpress, Offset, and Gravure. Letterpress is the process of printing in which ink is impressed on and partially into the paper by characters or images in relief. Offset lithography or planography causes ink to be transferred first to a blanket surface and then to paper from a plate on which the printing and nonprinting areas are on the same level, but the nonprinting areas are wetted so that they will not print, while the printing area is coated with a greasy ink that resists the water. Gravure, like etching, causes the ink to transfer from a plate on which the image is cut in *intaglio*, or beneath the surface, so that after the plate is scraped clean, the ink remaining in the cells or pits transfers to the paper.

In letterpress, the type itself, or metal or plastic plates molded from it, or original engravings may be used. The type will be locked into chases—steel frames—and mounted on the bed of the press. If plates, they will be mounted on a honey-combed block of steel in which small hooks hold the plates, so that all will be type high. A more recent technique is to mount the plates on a plastic sheeting and employ a vacuum device to hold them in place on the bed of the press.

In flatbed letterpress printing, usually using Miehle or Miller presses, the type or plate bed moves in a reciprocating motion under a revolving cylinder, beneath the inking or form rollers which in turn have been inked by a roller revolving in the press's ink fountain, a trough containing the heavy, oily ink. The paper is fed to grippers which clamp it around the cylinder and carry it around until it has received an impression from the inked form on its return. On the second revolution, the sheet is delivered to tapes which carry it back to the delivery area of the press, after which the cylinder picks up a fresh sheet while the form is being re-inked. Adjustment to the minute variances in printing heights of type or plates is made by makeready—building up low points with bits of tissue or sheets placed under the tympan or impression area of the press packing. It is essential that all type, plates, or engravings be type high, .918 inches. Special makeready sheets of plastic are also used.

Two-, three-, or four-color presses print the black and successive colors one after the other, while perfector presses print both sides of the sheet, sometimes in two colors, the second cylinder taking the sheet printed by the first one and "backing it up." Both offset and letterpress units are available.

Rotary letterpresses such as Miehle's print from curved plates mounted on the plate cylinder. They may be sheet-fed or web-fed, either a sheet at a time or from paper fed from a roll or web or, on some special presses, from sheets cut from a web of paper just before printing. Most web presses today can deliver either folded signatures or cut sheets.

Some rotary web-fed letterpress units (Strachan & Henshaw, ATF, or Goss) print from plates of flexible plastic molded from originals affixed to a mylar carrier sheet, which wrap around the cylinder, as do also some flexible engraved plates. "Wrap around" is a term frequently used interchangeably with "letterset." It refers to a type of press which can print either offset or letterpress, and frequently from either a web or cut sheets. On offset presses (Harris, Miehle, Miller, etc.), the image from the plate is transferred to a rubber blanket, from which the inked image is transferred to the paper by means of an impression cylinder. Offset web presses (Harris, Miehle, Goss, ATF, Cottrell) are most often perfectors printing both sides in up to five colors and delivering folded signatures or cut sheets. Offset is based on the principle that grease and water do not mix, and derives from Senefelder's writing with a greasy crayon on a grainy wet stone, and discovering that the writing transferred to a sheet of paper pressed against it.

Offset plates are made from artwork or mechanicals (pasteups) very much as for photoengraving, except that photostats, proofs of type, or strips of film from photocomposing machines are stripped into place with tape, with similar pasteups made for additional colors. Type matter is usually from repro proofs (sharp, clear proofs) made on special paper or on acetate. Negatives or positives may be so stripped, or even typed manuscript from an electric typewriter, such as IBM or Varityper. Even printed pages from books to be converted into offset may be used. The final combination is exposed to arc light, and the resulting exposed and developed film is photographed onto the sensitized metal plate, which may be of aluminum, zinc, or stainless steel, grained slightly to receive the image. After developing and etching, the plate is clamped around a cylinder, the image portions are charged with ink, and the rest of the plate is moistened by the water solution in the press water fountain. The image from the plate transfers to the blanket and thence to the paper.

Since many books today are being converted to offset by various methods, something is needed to save the cost of resetting or making new electros. The names Brightype, Scotchprint, Cronapress, and Kalvar are becoming familiar. In Brightype, the type form is polished to a high luster, photographed, and the negative used to produce the offset plate. In Scotchprint, the type or plates are proved on a special translucent film, which becomes the negative. Cronapress, another form, requires a print on a special film, which is developed so that the nonprinting areas are opaqued. The Kalvar process calls for heating the type form and making an impression on another special film, which is then processed to make the offset plate.

Other new processes are emerging, notably electrostatics and automatic platemaking machines using aniline processes (Ozalid, Xerography, and paper masters) to generate plates. Many offset plates can now be obtained presensitized and ready for immediate exposure.

Gravure, which, like copper etching, is one of the oldest forms of printing, is based upon the intaglio system. The ink is carried in depressions in the copper cylinder, the excess scraped off by a doctor blade, and the impression made on the paper, with tonal values depending on the depth of the cells. Since type must be screened in the making of the plate, book gravure has largely been limited to halftone illustrative matter, with the type printed by letterpress. However, with improved plates and finer screens, especially in the area of rotogravure, in which thin plates are clamped to copper cores, instead of re-etching the cylinder after every job, gravure has made a notable advance, especially in package printing and bookwork, and particularly overseas.

In making the gravure plate, photographic negatives and positives are carefully printed, first without a screen, and then after all the elements have been mounted into position, through an overall grid which regulates the amount of ink in the cells created by the screen. Light is passed through the positive to a sensitized carbon sheet, which is fastened to the plate, developed, and etched.

The term "letterset" was coined to describe a process formerly known as "dry offset," in which an offset press plate is used, the image transferred to the blanket and thence to the paper, but without a water solution. Letterset presses are usually so designed that they may print either offset or letterpress. The letterset plate is usually a thin plastic, which is etched by a solution very similar to water, and at high speed, so that a relief plate is formed. DuPont and the Miehle Company teamed to popularize this method, and some large web presses operate in this manner.

ILLUSTRATIONS AND ARTWORK

While the manuscript is being set, the illustrations are being produced, after sample illustrations are tested for reproduction by the platemaker, so that all the parts of the book will be ready at the same time—a goal never easy to achieve, and especially difficult if instructions by the publisher are unclear or incomplete.

Most illustrations will consist of photographs, pen-and-ink line drawings, or wash drawings. Toned copy, such as a photo or wash, is reproduced by the halftone process. In photographing the copy, a crossline screen of varying numbers of lines to the inch is introduced between the copy and the engraver's camera, so that the negative in the camera is broken up into a pattern of dots, by the passage of light through the screen. Lighter areas will have smaller dots, widely separated; black or grey areas will be made up of larger dots, close together.

In any photographic reproduction, the copy may be cropped to omit unwanted portions, and to give larger value to wanted portions. Artists preparing a number of illustrations for a book should be instructed to make all art twice or three times final size, the better to render detail and eliminate imperfections. If lettering is included, it must be uniform. Sometimes captions may be set in type, proved on a press, and pasted onto the final art or stripped into the engraver's negative.

If the original work is in color, but is to be reproduced in black and white, it must be rephotographed to obtain an orthocromatic print. If on the other hand, the reproduction is to be in color, the original art, known as reflectance copy, must be separated by camera into the basic primary colors that are used to reproduce most color artwork: magenta, ochre, blue, and black. The artist may make these separations himself, using some of the colored acetate shading sheets or other aids that are available, or the engraver may do it.

In the event that film transparencies are used, separations will be made from these. Today, electronic color separation is frequently used to reduce the amount of handwork necessary to secure faithful reproduction.

Size and cropping of the final art is indicated around the edges of the art (preferably it is mounted on illustration board to keep it flat, with protective tissue mounted over it) and instructions given to the engraver or offset platemaker as to the screen density thereof. Customary screens for bookwork are 120, 133, or 150, meaning that in the engraver's screen, there are that many intersections of crosslines, each forming a small aperture which allows light to pass through and harden the emulsion at that point on the engraver's negative. The negative in turn is exposed on the engraver's zinc or copper plate, and etched with acid which eats away the metal where it has not been protected by the hardened emulsion, so that the nonprinting areas are well below the surface of the plate. In offset, negatives of art and type are exposed page by page on large sheets of grained zinc, aluminum, or stainless steel and in the case of gravure, on copper cylinders or sheets as described earlier.

PROOFS

As the type is set or photocomposed, proofs are taken of the completed type, read and corrected, and then returned to the publisher for the author's and publisher's corrections. If the book has been photoset, the galley may be a roll of photographic paper, an ozalid, or some other form of proof. The galley will contain questions about the copy, perhaps a few minor machine errors. Duplicate sets are usually supplied the author for his reading. In rare instances in which the text has been keyboarded into a computer, the resulting printout may be almost unintelligible to the author, because of the use of special codes to indicate typographic instructions such as italics, caps, etc.

Using generally accepted proofreaders' symbols, the proofreader should mark the galleys carefully with a fine but clearly visible mark by pencil or pen, and preferably with marks aligned with the line in which the correction is to be made. The master set of corrected galleys is generally sent to the printer for his corrections before the type is broken up into pages to conform to the original typographic plan. Copy for title page, heads, subtitles, captions, and running heads should now be in the printer's hands, set, and inserted in the proper location. Page proofs are then supplied to the publisher, and oftimes to the author. Here it is, somehow, that everything that looked correct in copy and galley proof, as to wording or typographical handling, now often seems monstrous. If last-minute changes, thoughts, additions, etc.—author's alterations—are not kept under control, they can add up to staggering charges for extra work and production delay. Generally, most publishers allow a specified amount of AA's and bill the author for excesses.

Final check is made for continuity from page to page, page sequence, pagination, position of heads, footnotes, and final adjustment of pages which may be a line short or long. If the book is to be printed from plates, foundry proofs of the type locked up for molding may be supplied, but errors or changes at this point cost even more.

PLATEMAKING

Many books printed by letterpress are printed from duplicate plates, usually electrotypes or plastic plates. Each is produced from a mold of the original type and illustrations. They are made after type and cuts have been carefully locked up in chases and all surfaces planed down so as to be type high. The mold is made in wax which has been treated with graphite to make it electrically conductive. The mold may also be made in lead, vinyl, or, if quality reproduction of engravings is wanted, tenaplate. The mold or case is placed into an electrolytic bath which deposits pure copper on the mold's surface, after which the copper is stripped from the mold and the copper shell filled with a type-metal alloy to give it a firm backing. The plates are shaved to be type high, and trimmed and beveled so that they may be mounted on the bed of the press. If they are to be run as rotary plates, they will be curved to fit the cylinder.

Stereotypes, which are type-metal molds cast from papier mâché mats, may be plated with copper, nickel, chrome, or other compounds to increase their wear-resistance; so, too, may electrotypes.

Plastic plates, in considerable use today, may be flexible or rigid, curved or flat, and are produced from a vinyl matrix mold of the type, and then molded from a resinous powdered plastic into finished plates.

Rubber plates are made in much the same manner as plastic, and mounted on a copper sheet wrapped around the plate cylinder or flat on the bed of the press. They are not generally used for fine work.

Several new families of plastic plates have emerged, including Chemotype, a three-layer plate composed of a hard outer plastic coating, a resilient core, and a hard plastic backing.

Others are the Collage, Daxene, Wilsolite, Flexotype, and the Thomas plate. All are multilayer plates of various compounds.

Other photomechanical plates earning increased attention are the photopolymers, Dycril, Magplate, Kodak relief plate, and Techniplate. In most of these, photosensitive plastic is rapidly etched at a much higher speed than in conventional methods.

BINDING

Imposition and Folding. The pages for any given form in the book are imposed (arranged) in such a manner by the pressman that, when the sheet is printed front and back and folded, the pages will fall into proper sequence. It is essential that the publisher, the printer, and the binder (or book manufacturer) are fully in accord on what imposition will be used, and whether it is practical. If the sheet is printed without first securing an imposition from the binder, it may prove impossible to fold it, or once folded, to bind it properly.

As the number of folds in a sheet of paper increases, more and more paper is accumulated at the back of the folded sheet or signature and more and more air is trapped in the folds, forcing the signature to pop open and resist handling. The binder can specify how many folds may be safely made in a given weight, size, and finish of paper. In general, antiques may be handled up to #60 in 32's, and some lighter stocks in 64's. Often they can be folded as 64's but slit into 32's or 16's as they come off the folder. Most folders perforate the signature at the head and sides to allow the air to escape and prevent gussets from forming. A favorite book imposition is a Dexter Quad or Duplex Quad imposition, in which a large knife drives the sheet between a series of folding rollers. Smaller forms may be folded on buckle folders, in which the sheet is driven into a folding "plate," where a stop-and-deflector blade causes it to buckle and fold at the selected point.

The imposition is the key to the location of color pages in the book, especially if color has been limited to one side of the sheet. The printer or the platemaker will make up his forms from an imposition given him by the binder, which will guide him as to the location of color pages. As a rule of thumb, alternate spreads can be printed in color, if color is to be limited to one side of the sheet. In web printing, however, color often can be printed on both sides at once, or in the same pass of the web, which is being angled and turned so that color can be applied on both sides.

Individual pages of illustrations are tipped to the outside of the signature by machine, as are the end sheets which connect the body of the book and the cover. Frequently illustrations are printed in signatures so that they may be wrapped around other signatures, or may be included as smaller signatures within the book. Because many books today are printed by offset with the illustrations included with the text, there is less need than there once was for tip-ins. Tipped-in illustrations, usually on a different kind of paper, and usually coated, are pasted within the signature and necessitate handwork to open, paste in the tip, and reclose.

After all the signatures are folded, they are jogged together, the air is squeezed out in a hydraulic press, and then they are bundled or stacked for further processing.

Gathering. Assembling the printed signatures is for the most part performed on large automatic gathering machines, in which the pockets, sometimes as many as forty, are loaded with bundles of signatures. Mechanical arms draw a signature from each pocket and deposit it on a moving chain-and-belt. Correct sequence of signatures is essential, and to simplify checking, many printers print a small black mark on each sheet, staggering from the head downward, so that when the sheets are folded and gathered correctly, the marks will show a step-like diagonal line.

Sewing. The majority of trade books are thread-sewn on a machine (usually Smyth) which sews through the saddle (inside fold) of the signature with three to six stitches of cotton, linen, or nylon thread. The operator opens each signature at the fold, and hangs it on a saddle or arm which carries it into the machine. Needles drive through the paper, pick up the thread and loop it through to complete the stitch, then hook it to the next section, and so on through all the signatures of the book. In addition, many machines are now available with automatic feeders, which need only to be kept loaded. Some books, when the runs are large enough to warrant it, are printed, gathered, sewn two-up, and cut apart only before insertion in the covers.

It is possible, and particularly economical on long-run paper-backs of small trimsize, for example, to print two books at a time from one set of plates, by what is known as the "come and go" imposition.

Reference books and a great number of textbooks are sewn on a special stitcher, the McCain, which sews through the signature very close to the back. Previously, a strong tape is applied over the back, thus making a very strong book but one which does not open as easily as a saddlesewn book. Juveniles and thin books not used in schoolrooms—containing often only one, two, or three signatures—may be Singer saddle-stitched at high speed.

The more signatures to a book, the more thread in the back, which requires the binder to nip the edge to flatten the thread. But the book must not be sewn so tight as to burst when subjected to the strain of further processing.

Smashing, Gluing-off, Trimming. Most books will usually be "smashed" to remove all air, to press the folds, and to bring the bulk of the book to the chosen dimension before forwarding. The books are fed to a giant compressor after which they are glued-off in bunches or singly. They are carried by a conveyor over a glue roller and brush combination that drives glue a slight distance up between the signatures and coats the back of the book with a thin, flexible adhesive. The books may be instantaneously dried by heat before being trimmed in bunches or singly. A tumbler trimmer clamps a stack of several books to a revolving block which allows three knives to trim the front, top, and tail (the bottom edge). Other types of trimmers (Lawson and Sheridan) clamp the books, but do not revolve, while the knives perform their work and discharge the book to a conveyor belt. Books bound two-up may be split and trimmed or sawed apart.

Rounding, Backing, Lining. The trimmed book will be rounded and backed, i.e., the book is held stationary, while rollers on either a Smyth, Sheridan, or Dexter unit form the rounded back and shape the joints by irons that impart the slightly flared edge which fits into the hinge of the cover and on which the book swings when it is opened.

Another machine, a liner—one of the three makes mentioned—will apply the back lining, usually a strip or two of gauze applied after the book has again been glued. The gauze is about an inch or so wider than the book bulk, and slightly less in length than the spine. Another coat of glue and a strip of lining paper or perhaps another gauze and a final paper lining are attached. If required, headbands, the bits of cloth at the head and foot of a well-made book, will be applied at another station.

Endsheets. These are the connecting link between book and cover, and generally use paper stronger than the text paper, unless the book is a self-end—printed on a paper generally equivalent in weight to a good endleaf, usually around 80. If endsheets printed separately from the book are to be used, one should be certain of their strength, while the ink should be sufficiently dry so that it will not mark the facing leaf when the book is pressed. The endsheets are usually tipped by paste to the first and last signatures, and may be reinforced by tape around them or whipstitching if extra strength is needed for a heavy book.

Binding Materials. Coincident with all these stages in production, the selection, specification, and ordering of binding materials should be well along. The cover has been designed, the artwork prepared, the type set, the plates made, or the dies engraved. Depending to a great extent on the budget for the book and the designer's plans, the book may be bound in a great variety of combinations, all to some extent concerned with the life expectancy of the book. It may be bound in cloth over board, paper over board, or a combination of the two, or various forms of plastic coated materials, or completely in plastic.

The soaring market for paperback books has led to a tremendous increase in the amount of perfect-bound (adhesive-bound) books, in which the production cycle is much the same as for a hardbound book up until the sewing stage. By a variety of both large and small binders—Sheridan, Dexter, Martini, Sulby, Mueller, and others, usually of great size and speed—the assembled signatures are tightly held in a clamp while the backs are trimmed or sawed off, the edges roughened to some degree and coated with a plastic glue, and a heavy-weight paper cover wrapped around the book, which is then trimmed flush on all three sides. Because of their smaller size and large quantities, considerable economy can be realized in their production by using web presses, special impositions, and in-line binding systems, often producing books at speeds of over 200 per minute.

Book cloth is essentially a lightweight cotton cloth which

has been dyed and filled with a colored starch filler; for textbooks and more expensive books, a heavier cloth base impregnated with a wear-resistant, waterproof pyroxylin or vinyl finish is used.

Recently several types of nonwoven (man-made fibers) materials have been tentatively approved for textbook covers, and in those areas in which there are no specifications for manufacture, such as college books, nonwovens and other plasticized materials and papers are being used.

Starch-finish cloth is available in natural finish, in which the cloth contains an imperceptible amount of filling, and smooth and linen finishes, secured by ironing out the starch or by imparting a linen pattern.

Book cloth is graded by weight of the base material in a progression from A to F (based on U.S. Commercial Standards), and subdivided into price brackets and grades. Grades A to C over the light, medium, and heavy cloths. Extra heavy buckram is used for library bindings and for books, such as dictionaries, that will get hard wear.

Cloth and nonwovens are priced somewhat alike by the running yard and are sold in rolls from 36 to 42 inches wide. Papers may be sold in similar manner to book papers, but cover papers are likely to be sold by the yard.

All materials must generally be able to accept glue or paste without its oozing through, and must be able to be stamped, silk screened, or printed by any process without undue difficulty.

Frequently books will feature a cloth spine with some other type of material on the sides, almost up to the joint. These are known as three-piece covers. Two-piece covers are also available.

The amount of cover material needed is usually computed by the binder, but a general working average is from eight to nine books per yard, to which spoilage must be added, with an additional amount for multiple-piece cases, since the pieces overlap.

Making the Cover. Covers may be made from binder's board, a solid paperboard made in one thickness in one operation; chestnut board, a board made in plies; and pasted board, built up of several layers of thin board. The binder will be glad to advise or discuss the proper board.

The designer's plans for the cover decoration meanwhile have been put into effect. If it is to be stamped, relief dies in brass, copper alloy, or magnesium have been ordered, the technique much the same as ordering engravings for the text, except that stamping dies will be deeply etched, so as to withstand the pressure of the heavy embossing presses used to incise the design deeply into the cover material and the board. If economy is essential even heavy gauge linecuts, if the run is in the vicinity of 1,000 copies, may be used.

Usually covers are stamped from rolls of metallic leaf, either imitation gold or silver, and occasionally genuine gold, or from rolls of pigmented color foil. The dies are mounted in the press and heated. Heavy duty Chandler & Price or Kluge platen presses, or special Sheridan flat die presses, or even small rotaries may be used. Light colors on dark cloth may need more than one impression. Some plants use a Dexter press which can stamp or emboss several impressions or colors at a time at high speed.

Covers may also be offset-printed, or silk screened, and the unfinished cloth may be preprinted by textile coating methods, and the cloth then covered with a protective coating. Paper covers may even be laminated. Silk screen is particularly economical on short runs for which large dies would be required. The heavy paints are applied through a screen, usually cut photographically.

The covers, or cases, are usually made several days in advance of use, so that they will have dried sufficiently. Covers for small editions are sometimes made by hand, but generally by a casemaking machine from sheets of cloth or other material, strips of board, and paste. The binding material is coated with glue, the boards and backlining strip for the back of the covers are deposited on the material, and the edges of the cloth turned in over the board, the finished case pressed to insure a tight fit. The cases may be produced on one of several makes of equipment: Smyth and Kolbus, which operate with individual pieces of cloth and board; Sheridan and Dexter, the former from rolls of the binding material, the latter usually from sheets, though a rollfeed design has been introduced. Various combinations of sides, backbone, etc., are possible.

Putting the book into its covers, or casing-in, is the next to final stage of bookmaking. Automatic machines, also made by Smyth, Kolbus, and Dexter, position the book above the cover, spread paste smoothly over the flyleaves, with extra amounts in the joint of the book, press the book and cover together, and eject it into the next phase. The operator checks the position of the book to see if it is centered precisely in the cover, leaving suitable squares protruding.

For many years it was an industry practice to stack the cased-in books between metal-edged pressboards and store them under pressure of screw-operated standing presses for twenty-four hours or more to allow the glue to dry and the book to set. Today most books are fed automatically to in-line building-in presses, such as those supplied by Smyth, Crawley, and Dexter, which apply heat and pressure over the parts of the book that are still moist from the adhesive, and which enable the books promptly to be jacketed, cartoned, and shipped.

PRINTING THE JACKET AND JACKETING

Jackets are usually printed by letterpress or offset, in from one to four colors from plates usually made from complete full-color art. Favorite stocks are antique, offset, and sheets coated on one side. Enough extras are run to provide for losses in shipping, storage, and library and bookstore handling. Most jacket printers will provide layouts which enable the production department to determine the correct size for art work to cover the front, the flaps which tuck under the cover, the spine, and the back cover. Most jackets are varnished but glossy inks may be sometimes used. Often, too, jackets are run with colored varnish in split fountains on the press. By carefully preventing the merging of the inks, several colors may be printed at one impression; or the inks may be merged for special effects.

Although numerous jacketing machines have been introduced to the industry, in which the covers are opened and the jacket folded around them and the whole pressed flat, jacketing still remains largely a hand operation, in part because the workers who wrap the books can also make a cursory examination in the process. Other inspection of the product is made all along the manufacturing line.

IMPORTANCE OF BEING SPECIFIC

Because so many talents, so many materials, so many processes are used in the production of the simplest book, it is essential that control be exerted from start to finish. Beginning with the production jacket, no detail should be left to guesswork, and the source and responsibility for each component must be spelled out. Colors must be cited. Complete details must be given on: the composition, paper, number of pages in each form, imposition, trim size, bulk, source and printer of illustrations, endsheets, cover, type of plates, total edition, number of copies to be completed, final trim size as well as untrimmed size (if untrimmed, what edges are to be left rough); if to be stained or gilt used, on what edges; type of sewing, location and method of binding tips, wraps, etc.; kinds of board; reinforcements; tight, hollow, round, or square back; whether the book is to be perfect-bound, sewn, or wired; linings for the backbone; headbands or not. Each step is related to its predecessor, and all have a sharp bearing on cost—fractions of a cent per copy multiply quickly!

Production staffs should be constantly searching for new and better methods, and reevaluating the older ones. In particular, they should make it a habit to study and visit suppliers so as to familiarize themselves with their operations. To do so pays dividends in lowered costs, improved quality, and more salable products.

REFERENCES AND FURTHER READING

All books listed at the end of the previous chapter, especially Lee, Bookmaking, and Williamson, Methods of Book Design—handbooks of both production and design.

Allen, Edward M. Harper's Dictionary of the Graphic Arts. New York, Harper and Row, 1963.

Groneman, Chris. General Bookbinding. Bloomington, Ill., McKnight and McKnight, 1958.

Melcher, Daniel, and Nancy Larrick. Printing and Promotion Handbook. 3d ed.; rev. New York, McGraw-Hill, 1966.

Technical publications, Graphic Arts Technical Foundation, 4615 Forbes Avenue, Pittsburgh 15213.

Technical publications, Printing Industries of America, Inc., 20 Chevy Chase Circle NW, Washington D.C. 20015.

SECTION III

DISTRIBUTING THE TRADE BOOK

6

THE SALES DEPARTMENT, INSTITUTIONAL SALES, AND SALES PROMOTION

By FON W. BOARDMAN JR.

VICE-PRESIDENT, SECRETARY, AND ADVERTISING AND PUBLICITY MANAGER,
OXFORD UNIVERSITY PRESS

❈

THE SALES DEPARTMENT

A SALES DEPARTMENT exists to sell books. However, in discussing this obvious function of such a department in a publishing house, one must begin by defining the kinds of books one is talking about, since the publishing industry issues several distinct categories and uses several different selling methods. Here we are concerned with selling in the area of "general trade publishing," thus taking in adult trade books (both fiction and nonfiction), children's books, "quality," or trade, paperbacks, and, in most cases, religious books. We are not concerned here with school or college textbooks, medical, scientific, technical, and scholarly books, mass market paperbacks, or Bibles, although for the relatively small number of Bible publishers, the selling process has many points in common with general trade books.

The Sales Picture. The new books of each season and each year receive the most attention from the sales department, but older, backlist books are often fully as important in total sales.

There is a never ending flood of the new books. In 1966 there were 1,619 new fiction titles, 2,375 juveniles, and 1,477 religious books, without mentioning the many nonfiction titles in categories such as biography (819 titles), poetry and drama (728), and sports and recreation (441) which were also general trade books. On top of this, there were 7,340 new titles and new editions in the field of trade paperbacks.

In 1965 the total sale of these books amounted to about $366 million. All categories showed an increase over the previous year and, overall, a gain of about 93 percent compared with 1958. Geographically, the six states of New York, Illinois, Massachusetts, California, New Jersey, and Pennsylvania account for almost two-thirds of all domestic sales. To some extent, though, this is misleading because the large wholesalers are concentrated in New York, New Jersey, and Illinois. The books they purchase are resold all over the country to retail stores and libraries. In fact, many of those sold by New York publishers to the Baker and Taylor Company in New Jersey come back to New York for sale to the ultimate consumer. Not surprisingly, book sales are highest where there is the greatest population and the major concentrations of government, business, and education. The District of Columbia and the eleven states to the north of it account for nearly half of all trade book sales in the whole country, although again allowance must be made for wholesalers. Nearly 12 percent of total sales are made in the three Pacific Coast states, nearly 25 percent in nine Midwestern states.

Seasonal variations in sales are an important part of the picture also. Although there does not seem to be as much of a summer slump as there once was, sales do ascend during the spring, fall off in the vacation months, and rise sharply in the fall. The great peak is the Christmas season when books are widely bought as gifts. The retail bookstores of the nation do over a third of their year's business in the two months of November and December.

Wholesalers and Retailers. Trade publishers sell mostly to wholesalers, retail bookstores, and libraries, rather than directly to individual book buyers. Wholesalers, as in other industries, buy from the manufacturer for resale to the retail dealer. In the book trade, wholesalers also do a large business in selling to schools and libraries. There is no one definition of a wholesaler that everyone accepts and therefore no way of saying just how many of them there are. The *ABA Book Buyer's Handbook* lists thirty-seven, but some of these specialize in certain areas, such as paperbacks or medical books. Some sell only to schools and libraries and provide an important service, especially for smaller libraries, by acting as one central source through which the library can order the books of all publishers. In the field of general trade books, the American News Company, Baker and Taylor Company, Bookazine Company, Inc., Campbell and Hall, Inc., Cosmo Distributing Company, Dimondstein Book Company, Inc., and A. C. McClurg and Company are among the leading wholesalers.

It is possible to compile a list of nearly 10,000 retail bookstores of one kind and another, but the number drops rapidly when pared down to those of practical importance to the trade publisher. Sometimes these stores, at least in publishers' minds, are placed in three categories: general bookstores, book departments of department stores, and college stores. The American Booksellers Association, with 2,000 members at this writing, is the trade organization of the retail book dealers. The ABA member stores, representing most of the bookstores in the country selling general trade books, on the average do about 75 percent of their business in books, the rest in sidelines such as greeting cards and records. The ABA also calculates that the average discount these dealers receive from publishers is in the range of 38 to 40 percent, and that the lower figure is the minimum a retailer must have to stay in business.

About half of the ABA stores sell less than $20,000 worth of books a year; at the other extreme are a handful that do more than $1 million a year in books. Retail bookselling, by American standards, is not big business, but it is growing. ABA membership ranges from more than 250 stores each in New York and California, to 1 in South Dakota and 3 in North Dakota. A little more than half the stores are located in the New England, the Middle Atlantic, and the Midwestern states east of the Mississippi. The ABA provides its members with a variety of publications and services, including "basic book lists" of both hardbound and paperbound titles, a staff manual for bookstores, and a monthly newsletter. It also acts as liaison with the publishers through their trade organization, the American Book Publishers Council.

Of the 2,000 college stores in the country, more than 1,500 are members of the National Association of College Stores. (Of this 1,500, about 500 also belong to the ABA.) From the publisher's point of view, they differ somewhat from the average ABA store. For many years most college stores did more business in sweatshirts than in Shakespeare, and in the book end itself textbook sales were heavily dominant compared with sales of general trade books. This picture has been changing rapidly since World War II and today some of the largest and most important outlets for trade books, especially paperbacks, are college stores. This has come about through a number of factors: the GI Bill; the increase in college enrollments; the increase in the number of colleges and in the number of teachers; the partial abandonment of the old-style textbook in favor of a number of books per course (reading Plato instead of reading *about* him); the coming of the inexpensive paperback; and last, but not least, the growing affluence of the country, with more money flowing along the pipeline from parent to son and daughter at college. The increase in total volume (trade and textbooks) is astounding: one West Coast college store that in 1937 sold only $18,000 of books of all kinds did business totaling over a million dollars in 1965. In some college stores, sales of trade books are beginning to surpass the dollar volume of textbook sales. A survey of 150 stores showed that in a year the average sales per student of *nonrequired* books was $56.

The NACS, through its subsidiary NACSCORP, is an important wholesaler of trade paperbacks. In 1965 it was supplying to its members more than 8,000 titles of sixty publishers.

The sales manager and his salesmen have a great variety of retail outlets to deal with. In the large city, stores may be within walking distance of each other, their stocks of books large and varied, with emphasis on the latest best sellers. In the Far West, a salesman may drive all day to call on one or two stores whose stock and needs are comparatively small. In the college community, tastes will be more intellectual—and more faddish. In some stores, the traveler will deal with the owner himself, in others with a salaried buyer who may have to abide by the same rules and system as the buyer of office machines or women's coats. Retail bookselling is a challenging business, and even though it is a growing one, cooperation and understanding between publisher and bookseller are absolutely vital.

Prices, Discounts, and Returns. Publishers set a list price for each book. Usually this is printed on the jacket and is the price the consumer is expected to pay. The publisher then grants to wholesalers, retailers, schools, and libraries, various discounts from these list prices. In some houses there are separate and different discount schedules for wholesalers and retailers; in others the schedule is the same but the wholesaler, or jobber, is expected to have an advantage because he buys in larger quantities. In either case, the amount of discount to stores and jobbers increases as the quantity purchased goes up. Publishers try to discourage orders for one copy of one title, but fill them at a discount of anywhere from 20 to 40 percent. Discount rates then go up gradually to 45 to 48 percent for hardbound books, the highest rate applying to quantities of anywhere from 1,000 to 5,000 copies, depending on the publisher. The discounts on trade paperbacks tend to run a little higher and go to as much as 50 percent. Discounts to libraries are lower, ranging mostly from 15 to 30 percent and usually not increasing with quantity. In addition, many publishers give stores an extra 2 percent cash discount if a bill is paid within a stated time. Under United States law, and unlike Great Britain for example, publishers and booksellers cannot get together and agree on discounts and other terms. Consequently, there are almost as many different schedules as there are publishers. This leads to greater overhead costs for everyone, but presumably it encourages competition.

A generation ago, when a jobber or retailer bought a book from a publisher, that was the end of it so far as the publisher was concerned. Now, however, most trade books are sold on a returnable basis, so that a dealer takes little risk in ordering his stock. For practical purposes almost any store can return almost any trade book. Publishers normally require that books not be returned until some time after their publication date—usually at least 90 days, in some cases a longer period. Also, books will not be accepted if a store wants to return them more than a year after publication. The purpose is to insure that, for a time at least, each book has its chance to be seen and purchased, although there are a few well-authenticated cases of books being returned by a store before publication date. There is, of necessity, a good deal of red tape involved in returning books and issuing credits for them. The store must pay the return shipping costs. Both publishers and dealers try regularly to cut down on the number of returns and to devise simple procedures for handling them. It is clearly to the advantage of both to estimate as correctly as possible how many copies of a particular book a store will need to have on hand to satisfy the demands of its customers.

Book costs and prices are of mutual concern to publishers and dealers. All costs have gone up in recent years, and book prices have risen, too, but are not out of line with increases in other fields—bread, or theater tickets, for example. There have been increases in the discounts offered to stores. As seems to happen every so often, there has in the past few years been a new wave of price-cutting, with discount stores and some department stores selling books to the consumer at prices as much as 40 percent below the publisher's list price. Current best sellers are, for the most part, the books offered at such prices. There has also been concern in some circles about the competition from other media, especially television. There is, however, no evidence that this has harmed book sales and, in fact, in some ways television has stimulated book reading. More important, though, has been the population increase, the general rise in the standard of living, and, most of all, the increase in the number of students in schools of all levels. Publishers of juvenile books and of trade paperbacks have benefited particularly from the educational boom and should continue to do so.

The Sales Manager and His Department. The sales department is the part of any publishing house that is on the firing line, dealing directly with the booksellers and with all the constantly changing factors that affect the number of books sold. Sales department personnel have far more contacts with customers than any other part of a publishing house. Within a house, the sales department stands between the editorial and the business sides. It receives from the editorial department the merchandise (books) it must dispose of, and it has to sell enough of the books, without incurring more than normal costs, so that the business and financial management of the house will be satisfied with the net result in dollars and cents. A 1964 survey by the American Book Publishers Council found that, for the publishers taking part, the average selling expense in the case of adult trade books was 6.3 percent of sales, and for juveniles, 6.9 percent. Most of this consists of salaries and traveling expenses.

A sales department is made up of the sales manager, his office staff, and a number of salesmen, or travelers, who call on jobbers and retailers. Because the financial success or failure of a publishing house depends so directly on the sales manager's effectiveness, it is not surprising that his job is recognized as one of the key ones in any publishing house. Usually he is the second- or third-ranking executive in the firm, and his compensation is in accord with this position. His administrative ability, his salesmanship, and his planning will largely determine how many dollars worth of his firm's books are sold in a season, but some of his most important functions are less tangible. Except for the salesmen out on the road, he has far more personal contact with dealers than anyone else in the house. He must be a diplomat, explaining his house's policy on such things as the return of unsold books; he must soothe the dealer who received a shipment of books two weeks late and who expects the sales manager to do something about it. He attends conventions and other meetings and must be able to speak and negotiate concisely and effectively. To some, his image is the public image of a whole publishing house.

At the same time he must inspire and manage a group of salesmen who spend most of their time traveling around the country and who often feel forgotten and neglected by the home office. This part of his job should come naturally to a sales manager, for almost every manager reaches that position by having been a traveling salesman himself for a number of years. In fact, most sales managers continue to do some traveling and selling, and one feels that every so often a bit of the old wanderlust strikes them.

One of the sales manager's most important tasks is to set, or to recommend to the other top officers, the house's policy on such matters as discounts and returns. He usually has something to say in editorial policy, at least to the extent of rendering judgment on the potential sale—or lack thereof—of a manuscript under consideration.

Once a book is accepted and is ready to be published, the sales manager must prepare his plans for selling that particular title. For one thing, he will estimate how many copies should be sold to wholesalers and retailers in advance of publication so that they will have the right amount of stock on hand for their customers. He will then split this total up among the travelers, giving each a quota. He will need to consult with the advertising and sales promotion managers (in a number of houses they are directly under the sales manager) to plan advertising in both trade and consumer media and to prepare circulars or posters for the dealers' use when these are appropriate. As time goes on, he must follow through on all these plans to see that the right things are being done at the right time, and to change plans when circumstances change. From time to time he will need to communicate by direct mail with all the stores.

A small number of publishers currently have automatic distribution plans for new titles and the operation of this is also a responsibility of the sales manager. Under such a plan, a bookstore agrees to let the publishing house decide how many copies of a book it will need to start with, the house having to take back unsold copies, of course. Such plans speed up the process of getting new books to the stores where they can be seen and purchased. On the whole, the plans are used by large publishing houses such as Doubleday and Company, Harper and Row, and Random House. In its simplest form, such a plan consists of a salesman, on the basis of his experience with a particular store, deciding how many copies of each of the new books that store will need. The store has a chance to disapprove the quantities suggested, but otherwise the books are shipped when ready. This system appeals to smaller and middle-sized stores because it saves them time, it assures them of a supply of new books by publication date even if a salesman does not call on the store several times a season, and the conscientious salesman will make up an order that includes backlist books and results in the best possible discount for the store.

The "Doubleday Merchandise Plan" is the most comprehensive and mathematical of these schemes and is used by more than 500 stores and dealers, including large department store chains and jobbers. An adaptation of the basic plan is available to smaller stores. The salesman plays a part since he must take an inventory in each of the stores assigned to him every month or every other month. In essence, the plan, using mathematical formulas, bases the estimate of a store's future needs on its past sales, and the chief merit claimed for it is its ability to increase the store's turnover.

In the process of managing his department, the sales manager must pay attention to its internal workings as well as its personal contacts with customers. He will have a secretary, probably an office assistant or two, and such other clerical help as is needed. Sometimes the sales department is responsible for every inquiry that comes in about a book, its availability, its price, and anything else to do with it as a piece of merchandise that potential buyers may be interested in. In other houses, this part of the work is handled by personnel in the business office rather than in sales. In any event, the sales manager will want to keep an eye on everything to do with customer relations, whether it is directly his responsibility or not. The sales department will have many contacts by mail and telephone with dealers who have some special problem; it must communicate with the travelers regularly, sending them material and information; it must keep records, help determine when more copies of a book should be printed and bound, and often answer inquiries from authors (the most usual one being: "I couldn't find a copy of my book in Jones's Bookstore today").

The Salesmen. The trade travelers, or salesmen, may number from only one or two to more than fifty, depending on the size of the publishing house. They divide into two classes so far as compensation is concerned. Most sizable houses have their own travelers, who receive a salary and their traveling expenses and who sell the books of the one house only. In some cases they also receive an incentive bonus on sales over some predetermined figure. Other salesmen are "commission men," who receive no salary but rather a percentage (usually 10 or 12.5 percent) of their sales to retailers as their compensation. They pay their own expenses out of this commission and, in many instances, they sell the books of more than one publisher. There are several selling organizations in which a number of men, working under the direction of one independent manager, offer to publishers selling services over a large geographical area.

The larger the volume of its business, the more salesmen a firm will employ. A 1964 study carried out by the American Book Publishers Council shows that trade publishers with sales up to $1.5 million averaged 7.3 salesmen, while those with sales over $6 million averaged 21.7. The average total compensation of these salesmen (not including university press salesmen) ranges from $7,400 for the smaller houses to $14,300 for the larger. Overall, compensation may be as low as $4,000, or, for a small number of men, more than $20,000. The average starting salary for inexperienced salesmen was shown to be $6,000.

Each salesman, this same study indicated, calls on around 200 different accounts—that is, customers. The average travel and entertainment expense per salesman runs from $2,200 if he works for a smaller trade house to $4,300 if he is with one of the larger firms. Most trade travelers do not start in as such, but come to the job from some other position in publishing, or from outside sources, such as bookstores, the paper industry, and various entirely unrelated businesses. That most publishers when hiring a salesman want someone already experienced is indicated by the fact that more than half the salesmen hired in 1964 were engaged by persuading them away from another publisher's sales force. On the whole, no great amount of experience is needed if a person seems to have the other general qualifications, and all publishers, of necessity, have their own training programs, some quite formal, some completely informal.

The trade traveler enjoys—or suffers under—a unique two-way relationship in his job. On the one hand he is the roving ambassador, the reconnaissance scout for his firm, traveling about the country persuading the bookseller to buy its products. He may be the only physical embodiment of a particular publishing house the small dealer ever sees. On the other hand, he is also the best channel of communication a bookseller has for getting his viewpoint, his complaints, his suggestions, back to the publishing house, especially to the sales manager and the business office. A traveler must not sell out his own employer by failing to defend him, but he often feels that the home office doesn't understand either him or his customers. Every once in a while, a sales manager wonders if his man in the upper Midwest is working for him or the booksellers. Probably this is a healthy readjustment of a balance that tends to tip to the publisher's viewpoint—a viewpoint that by the nature of the business tends also to be the landscape as seen from New York City only.

The term "traveling salesman" is seldom used any more—not to mention "drummer," which has disappeared entirely. It is also true that salesmen do less traveling than they used to. Half a century ago, a salesman set out by train with heavy trunks full of books. In city after city he set up his display in a hotel room, to which the local booksellers came and ordered their stock for the coming year. Then the salesman repacked his trunks and went on to the next city. It was a long time before he saw the home office again.

With a larger population and greater book sales, it is now economically feasible to have more salesmen and so each man does not have to cover as big a part of the country. Also, where the old-timer usually worked out of the home office, today's salesman probably lives in the territory to which he is assigned. This has been a growing trend for some years and means that a salesman can understand his territory better and can also enjoy more weekends at home than in the past. Nevertheless, a salesman spends a good deal of his life flying or driving around some assigned section of the country, sleeping in different hotels and motels, and eating in all kinds of restaurants. He still needs a strong back and a strong stomach, despite jet planes, air conditioning, and lighter sample loads.

What, then, does the salesman do when he is out on the road? Before he goes, he must prepare an itinerary that gets him around his territory one or more times before another season is upon him. He must send some notice ahead else he may miss half his customers. The number of times any one account is called on will depend on its importance in terms of dollar volume of sales, and its location. Small accounts, off the beaten track, will be visited once a season, or perhaps only once a year. The largest accounts in such cities as New York and Chicago can be called on every week, or checked every day by phone if necessary.

While he no longer totes whole trunks full of books, the salesman must have adequate materials to help him make as many sales as possible. Catalogues, jackets, sample pages, proofs of circulars and advertisements, advance opinions from influential critics, checklists, and order forms are the usual ammunition of a salesman. He sits down with the store owner or buyer and goes through his house's list of books to be published in the coming season. On the one hand, since most trade books are returnable these days, it doesn't matter as much as it used to if he oversells. On the other hand, a bookseller doesn't like to have more copies of a book than he needs—the accounts show he owes the publisher for them, and if he returns them he has to pay the costs. But then he doesn't want to be out of stock when a book is in demand for he will probably lose sales. Thus the conscientious salesman and the experienced bookseller attempt to decide on a rational basis how many copies of a given book should be ordered months before anyone knows what the reviewers are going to say about it or how the public will feel about it.

For a book of poetry or a biography whose subject and author are neither very well known, the order may be for only one or two copies. First novels are even more of a gamble for they may—and usually do—sell very few copies. Or, they may be enormous best sellers—the trade still remembers such books as *Gone With the Wind* and *From Here to Eternity*. The total advance sale to stores all over the country may be only a few hundred copies, or it may be many thousands. Samuel Eliot Morison's *Oxford History of the American People,* although priced at $12.50 and telling an oft-told story, had an advance sale to retailers and wholesalers in 1965 of about 30,000 copies. Finally, the good salesman checks the backlist stock in the store to see if steady selling items, both hardbound and paperbound, should be reordered.

At the end of the day the salesman must write up his orders and mail them back to the office, including any notes about dealers' complaints. He will also, his employers hope, have time to make suggestions of his own. More than one salesman on his travels has come upon a lead to a publishable manuscript. After a few years a salesman will have good friends spread over several states, and he will know as well as his customers how many of certain kinds of books they can sell. Like all callings, traveling as a salesman has its advantages and disadvantages. Many book salesmen apparently prefer it to an inside job in the home office.

The Sales Conference. One of the traditional rites of the publishing business is the seasonal sales conference. Most houses hold two such conferences a year, although some of the larger houses now have three, and a few hold regional conferences. The conferences are held in December or January, and in May or June. At the former—the spring sales conference—the books to be published in the first half of the calendar year are presented to the salesmen; at the latter—the fall sales conference—the books to be published in the second half of the year. In practice, few trade books are published in the summer period of June, July, and August.

The sales conference is attended by the sales manager, the salesmen, the editors, the advertising and publicity staff, one or more representatives of the house's advertising agency, and anyone else who may be concerned with launching the next batch of new books. Usually the sales manager stage-manages the conference and presides. The salesmen are the primary audience. While they sit with an ever-growing pile of catalogues, galley proofs, and other material accumulating around them, the editors describe with great enthusiasm the books that are about to appear. They attempt to tell the salesmen what a book is about and, more important for this occasion, why it will sell and what kind of readers will buy it. The advertising and publicity managers announce what will be done in their areas of promotion to help sell the books. The salesmen get a chance to ask questions and to express opinions, which don't always agree with those of the editors.

In a house that publishes only a few books a season, one day will suffice to present all the books. In a large house, especially one that has a variety of kinds of books, the conference will take the better part of a week. Then, too, since normally all the travelers are gathered together only twice a year, it is a good occasion for the sales manager to go over with them any matters of general interest and policy, such as dealers' complaints about the house's shipping service, or the credit standing of certain stores.

SELLING TO SCHOOLS AND LIBRARIES

The institutional market has for many years been the foundation on which book publishing is built, to the extent that it provides a steady, year-in-and-year-out market for a substantial number of the books produced. In the case of children's books, most publishers estimate that up to 90 percent of their sales is to schools and libraries. The percentage may be as great for some very scholarly and specialized books, much less for lighter and more ephemeral titles whose sale is chiefly to individuals for entertainment. Schools and libraries are a prime market for reference books of all kinds.

This market is also a steadily growing one. There are more than 23,000 public, college, and special libraries in the United States (not counting the small public libraries with book budgets of less than $500). In 1965 they were able to spend about $125 million a year for books, although all of this does not, of course, go for general trade books. In addition, the libraries in elementary and secondary schools, pressured by mounting enrollments and aided by more funds (local, state, and federal) have been growing rapidly, both in numbers and in size of book collections. Not long ago the librarian of a newly consolidated regional high school in New Jersey had $60,000 to spend on books just to get the library started. There are approximately 50,000 elementary and secondary public schools with centralized libraries in school systems having 150 pupils or more. It is estimated that in the 1966-67 school year they have spent well over $100 million on books (not including textbooks), and the amount grows every year. In addition, there are about 34,000 more schools without centralized libraries, but many of them buy trade books for classroom collections.

On top of this, a number of federal laws enacted in very recent years have made available to schools and libraries more money than they ever dreamed of. The National Defense Education Act, the Elementary and Secondary Education Act of 1965, and the Higher Education Act are the best known and the most directly applicable to book purchases, but there are a number of others, among them the Older Americans Act, the Economic Opportunity Act, and the Vocational Education Act. It was estimated that in the year ending June 30, 1967, there would be more than $4 billion of federal assistance available to all types of education. While much of this goes for items other than books, there never before has been so much money of this kind spent on books.

It is no wonder, then, that publishers are making new and

greater efforts to sell books to schools and libraries. In fact, there is no aspect of book promotion within the broad area of trade book publishing that is expanding so rapidly. Of course, publishers have always made strong efforts to sell to institutions, especially libraries. As librarians are well aware, they are on many lists for all kinds of catalogues and circulars, and their professional magazines, such as *Library Journal*, *ALA Booklist*, *ALA Bulletin*, and *Choice*, carry book advertising.

Until recently, in many houses most promotion aimed specifically at schools and libraries was oriented to the juvenile department, perhaps because it has long been apparent to such departments just how important the library market is. Now there is a trend toward a broader approach, encompassing all of a house's books, and directed by the sales manager. More firms are establishing separate library promotion departments, or enlarging within the sales department the amount of such promotion. Although many publishers have for years had "standing order" plans for libraries which wished to buy automatically all the new books, or those in certain fields, these are being expanded to offer more services to the library and hence more incentive to the library to sign up. The McGraw-Hill Book Company, for example, has a "College Library Service Plan," which not only provides automatic shipment of books in any desired category, but will also supply with each book its proper Library of Congress catalogue cards. School and library service companies supply packets of catalogue cards and catalogue materials. The most comprehensive organization for servicing libraries may well be that of Crowell-Collier and Macmillan's "Collier Macmillan Library Service." *Business Week* said of this company that it "distributes its own books through a subscription plan, which has served as a model for other publishers."

Library Selling Methods. Many publishers have a few salesmen calling on libraries, but fewer than a dozen have large, separate sales forces of school and library men. Of course, the kind of books a firm publishes, as well as its overall size, will influence the extent of its efforts in this field. A house with high-priced sets of reference works, or with many titles particularly suited to supplementing the curricula will find it more worthwhile than some others to go after the institutional business intensively. Crowell-Collier and Macmillan, for example, has more than fifty men calling on both schools and public libraries. While such men present books and write up orders, their emphasis is on service: on explaining discounts and standing order plans, and on setting up the machinery that will best serve a particular library system in securing and evaluating information about new books as they are issued.

A position of growing importance is that of school and library consultant. About seventy-five houses now have them, and more are being employed all the time—except that there is a shortage of persons with this kind of experience. The SLC's position may be directly under an institutional sales manager, if there is one; otherwise, he or she probably works for the sales manager. A SLC spends part of the year visiting school systems and public libraries in an effort to secure information, build good will, and open up the correct channels of communication. His job is to find out who selects what kind of books, and when, and what the size of the budget is. He will make sure the right supervisors and specialists are on the list to receive examination copies of new books. In large school systems and public libraries, one person's appraisal of a book may result in the purchase of 100 copies or more. In other cases, departments of education and library agencies make up approved and recommended lists of books on the basis of these examination copies. The SLC, and all others concerned, must keep in mind that school and college libraries are a growing market for general trade books, not just for books intended for educational uses.

In the office, the SLC will normally be in charge of the direct mail, such as graded and subject catalogues and newsletters, aimed at schools and libraries, and in a small house may do the writing and compilation himself. While basic direct mail techniques apply to selling to libraries, there are special and somewhat technical considerations that differentiate it from direct mail selling to individual consumers. Teachers and librarians are less influenced by large pictures and color printing. They need all the facts about a book, especially what has been said about it by the professional reviewers. In catalogues for schools, the books usually are arranged by grade level or subject. Backlist books are as important as new ones because new schools and new libraries need to purchase basic collections. In direct mail, as in other aspects of library promotion, paperbacks are more and more entering the picture, with school libraries ahead of public libraries in making use of them. While some paperbacks are prebound in hard covers, or reinforced in some other way, more of them are being used as purchased in the soft cover. This adds a new dimension to library promotion.

The SLC will also have a good deal to say about the firm's advertising in school and library media and for listings in jobbers' catalogues. Here again, the approach in an advertisement aimed at school librarians will be considerably different from that used in book ads in daily newspapers. The SLC, or someone else in each house, will work with the various book industry and community groups concerned with promoting the use of books, especially among young people, and will handle arrangements for a number of education and library conferences each year (see below). One of the newest book industry organizations is the Publishers Library Promotion Group, which in just a few years has moved from its initial orientation around juvenile publishing to a much broader approach. The American Book Publishers Council has recently activated a School and Library Committee, while National Library Week is long established as an annual program for increasing reading, and, especially, the use and support of libraries.

Population, education, affluence: these are three key words in considering the future of the institutional market for books. The rapidly growing population insures an increased demand for books at all levels and from all kinds of schools and libraries. Education, too, reflects in its school enrollments a continued high level of book needs. This is important in terms of books used in schools but even more important in the long run is the fact that the more education a person has, the more likely he is to go on reading books in later life. Finally, the United States, barring enormous war costs, is now affluent enough both in terms of personal income and national economic resources to be able to spend a larger proportion of individual and tax income in social and cultural areas. The outlook for the continued growth of the institutional market for books is excellent, and publishers will certainly expend more time and thought on selling to it in the next few years.

SALES PROMOTION

Sales promotion consists of certain materials and techniques, other than advertising and publicity, which are used to help sell a product. For the most part, sales promotion materials are not aimed directly at the consumer by the manufacturer but are prepared for the use of the retail dealer. In book publishing, sales promotion consists chiefly of point-of-purchase display material, direct mail material to be mailed by the dealer, booksellers' catalogues, exhibits, and miscellaneous schemes such as contests. Direct mail by the publisher comes under the heading of sales promotion when it is used by him to sell to bookstores. For the most part, sales promotion work attempts to sell *to* the consumer *through* the dealer.

In recent years sales promotion has been emerging as a separate function, but few publishing houses have separate departments on the same level as sales, advertising, or publicity. Sometimes sales promotion is part of the sales department, sometimes part of advertising. Logically, it would seem to be a sales function if it is not to be a separate department. Yet in many cases the advertising manager may be better equipped to handle the production of sales promotion material. At least, this points up the position of sales promotion as part of what should be the coordinated work of sales, advertising, publicity, and sales promotion.

Point-of-Purchase Displays. In highly competitive industries, such as soap, soup, and cigarettes, millions of dollars are spent each year to produce bigger and brighter point-of-purchase display materials to attract attention and sales, within stores, to one brand rather than another. Whether fortunately or not, the competition within the book industry is not so great. In general, books do not compete with each other the way cigarette brands do. On the other hand, retail bookstores are small, on the average; they have only so much room for posters and counter cards; and they will not knowingly waste space on a poster for a book they think they can't sell when so many others are available.

Nevertheless, publishers are now turning out more display material than ever before. This is in keeping with the general trend in the business, and is perhaps influenced somewhat by new or improved processes and techniques which make it possible to produce more colorful materials at fairly reasonable cost. There are various names for the different kinds of display materials, which come in all shapes and sizes from small window stickers costing a few cents each to electrically operated displays costing around $25 each.

Window stickers, or streamers, became more popular when adhesives that do not require wetting were developed. Stickers and streamers can be produced quickly and at relatively little cost, but obviously no dealer is going to put up so many of them at one time that a customer can't see in the window. Posters and counter cards come in various sizes. For window use, a usual size is 14 by 22 inches; for counter use, 11 by 14 inches. At one extreme in size are the four- or five-piece panel affairs requiring six or seven feet of linear space, and the life-size cut-out figures. At the other extreme are the "slit cards" which fit on to the top of a copy of the book. Also popular are "giant books," reproducing the jacket, much enlarged, on a light wood three-dimensional frame.

Most posters show the jacket of the book. This is an identification device and can save money on artwork costs also. Copy, of course, must be brief to be grasped by a person walking past a store window. Posters and other display materials can be produced to feature a prepublication offer in such a way that this part can be removed so that the poster is still usable after publication.

Display racks made to hold copies of a book, or series of books, also vary in size and cost. Relatively simple and inexpensive ones to hold a small quantity of one book can be made of cardboard, with part of the display acting as a poster also. With the growth of paperback publishing, bookstores were offered larger and more elaborate display racks than ever before. Some of these are quite expensive, of wood or metal construction. The purpose, of course, has been to get more attention for one line of paperbacks as compared with another. So many racks have been produced and so many paperbacks published that most stores are now dispensing with publishers' racks and are displaying all publishers' lines on their own shelves and racks. More books can be accommodated that way, and they can be arranged for the greater convenience of the customer.

In some cases ideas can take the place of materials. A publisher may suggest appropriate items to display with a book, and may even set up a sample window, photograph it, and show the results to booksellers. However, even though the idea may be good, the dealer must decide whether he can afford the time necessary to assemble the material.

Materials for Mailing. To help booksellers get old and new customers to come into the store or to order by mail, publishers provide them with a great variety of printed material. This ranges from the simple "statement stuffer" to the elaborate, ready-to-mail promotion package.

A statement stuffer, as its name implies, is meant to be mailed out with other similar material to a customer list, or with the end-of-the-month bills and statements of the store. In its simplest form, it is one leaf, about 3½ by 6 inches. This type of circular is usually offered without charge to bookstores, and the offer normally includes imprinting with the dealer's name and address. Sometimes, as with large circulars, the number a dealer may request is related to the number of copies of the book he orders in advance of publication. While such circulars can be printed at small cost per copy, the quantity is usually more than 100,000, sometimes many more, and imprinting a hundred or more relatively small quantities and mailing that many packages adds to the cost.

Such circulars, and those somewhat larger, are usually produced for books with a wide, general market, and a store may mail to its entire customer list and to other names acquired in one way or another. As circulars get more elaborate, they tend to fall into two groups: 1) those for expensive books (art, for example), aimed at the general market; and 2) those for books of more specialized interest where the total market is smaller but where a dealer, if he has a selective mailing list, can hope for a higher rate of return from the mailing. Circulars of four or more pages, especially for the more elaborate books, often reproduce a type page and one or more of the book's illustrations. The more expensive the circular, the more careful the publisher is in allocating quantities to those stores with appropriate mailing lists, or stores that specialize in the subject matter of the book. At the summit as a promotion production are the complete mailing packages: circular, order form, possibly a sales letter also, and a mailing envelope. The dealer addresses the envelope and pays the postage.

The latter kind of mailing package is sometimes tested in advance. A publisher gets a few stores to try a mailing to part of their lists even before the book is published. Two different types of circulars may be used to test different selling approaches. In fact, in a few cases this is done to test the appeal of the book itself even before the decision is made as to whether to publish it or not.

Circulars are offered to stores either by a mailing (with a sample enclosed) from the publisher, or by the salesmen on their rounds, or in both ways.

Booksellers' Catalogues. There are two catalogues issued throughout the year and distributed by booksellers in which a publisher can purchase space. One of these is the bimonthly *Book Chat*, published by Booksellers Catalog Service, Inc., Chicago (part of the Kroch's and Brentano's Bookstore operation). In October, 1965, for example, 102 stores purchased about 250,000 copies of *Book Chat* for mailing or over-the-counter distribution to their customers. A publisher pays (1966) a minimum of $125 for space in this catalogue. *The Latest Books* is issued monthly by the Baker and Taylor Company in a less elaborate format, and about 50,000 copies of each issue are purchased and distributed by about 300 booksellers. Here a publisher, in 1966, might take space for a book at a cost of $13 to $30.

At Christmas time, catalogues and equivalent promotion are as numerous as department store Santa Clauses. Booksellers Catalog Service issues a Christmas number of *Book Chat* in a larger format. In 1965, 166 stores used half a million copies and publishers paid $250 and up to include their titles. The R. R. Bowker Company has produced for many years an annual Christmas catalogue of which 350 stores used approximately 400,000 copies in 1965 and for space in which publishers paid a minimum of $200. In addition, the Doubleday Book Shops chain has a promotion plan which includes both advertising in the *New Yorker* and a reprint of the ads as a catalogue sent to its entire mailing list. Brentano's gets out a sixteen-page supplement distributed with the New York *Times*, advertises in other cities also, and uses the supplement as a mailing piece to its customer list. Catalogues devoted only to books for children are produced and many department stores issue supplements distributed with local papers in which one or more pages are devoted to books as Christmas gifts.

"*Gimmicks.*" "Gimmick" is a convenient term to use to describe various promotion ideas and materials. It can be extended to everything from an ordinary paper bookmark plugging a particular book to more exotic stunts such as giving away an orchid to the first hundred purchasers of a book on home orchid-growing. Contests of one kind and another can be included, although they are not widespread because of the complicated, detailed work involved. The gimmick depends more on the idea than the material, and should be appropriate to its subject. An author of a book on big-game hunting might wrestle a lion in a bookstore window; but a clergyman-author cannot be expected to exhibit himself in the same way wrestling with sin. At least up to now none has.

Exhibits. Exhibits—displays of books and accompanying material, usually in connection with the conference or convention of some organization—can be divided into three kinds, two of which concern us here. Those with which trade publishing is not primarily concerned are the annual conventions of scholarly and professional organizations such as the American Historical Association and the Modern Language Association. These are textbook-oriented, although serious trade books should be exhibited and many trade paperbacks are of much interest to scholars and teachers for class use. Sales and sales promotion departments, on the other hand, are the ones most concerned with the other two kinds of exhibits: 1) those for booksellers and teachers and librarians, and 2) those which are attended by individuals with some special personal interest.

In the first group are the annual conventions of the National Association of College Stores (in April), the American Booksellers Association (in June), and the Christian Booksellers Association (usually in August). The NACS is becoming increasingly important as more college stores devote more space and attention to general trade books, especially paperbacks. The ABA is the most important trade exhibit of the year for book publishers who make a special effort to present advance information and to build advance enthusiasm among the booksellers for what they hope will be the big sellers of the fall and the most wanted Christmas gift items. The ABA convention is now attended each year by more than 2,000 people, and there are about 300 exhibits. The CBA meeting is of great value and importance to publishers of Bibles and of inspirational and conservative Protestant religious books.

The two most important library exhibits are those of the annual meetings of the Special Libraries Association (in June) and the American Library Association (usually in July). Thousands of librarians from all parts of the country attend these and their fields of interest are as broad as all the subjects that can be found in books. Publishers also exhibit at the meetings of the Catholic Library Association and some of the state education and library associations. Important in the educational field are such meetings as those of the National Council of Teachers of English, the International Reading Association, and the Association for Supervision and Curriculum Development.

Most other exhibits are those sponsored by groups with some special interest. Most colorful, perhaps, are book fairs for the general public, organized to show juvenile books to parents and children during Children's National Book Week late in the fall. Others may be as specialized as those of surgeons or atomic physicists. There are many, however, at which general books have a place. If a publisher in such a case does not think it worth his while to have his own exhibit, he can show his books through such an organization as the Combined Book Exhibit, which arranges for and mans displays of the books of a number of publishers.

Exhibits pose problems of display material that will attract attention, giveaway material for visitors to the exhibit, and a considerable amount of organization and arranging to ship material to the site of the meeting, get it set up, and staff it. In a sense, any exhibit is a temporary bookstore, or a branch office of the publisher. Its cost in time and money is not inconsiderable. When one adds up of the cost of the exhibit space, the materials, and the travel expenses of one or more persons, the cost to the publisher can easily be $1,000 and up. Such displays seldom pay off in direct sales, nor are they expected to, but may pay off indirectly in dollars and cents and in their public relations aspects.

Production and Budgeting. Who produces the sales promotion materials? There may be a separate department, either independent, or most likely, under the sales manager. Or the work may be dispersed functionally. An advertising or publicity copywriter may also produce circulars for stores. Display material may be designed entirely within the house, or one of the firms specializing in such things may take over, much as an advertising agency does in its field. In the same way, the more elaborate mailing pieces for stores may be handled by firms specializing in direct mail work. There is no one, clear, pattern in publishing, and sales promotion work seems generally to be set up within each house in whatever way best fits its volume of such work and the talents and abilities of the promotion people on its staff.

What are the basic problems of sales promotion within a publishing house? First, as always, is the matter of cost. Whatever is spent on sales promotion is part of the total promotion budget for an individual book or series of books. Should some of the money be spent on a circular for stores, or on a poster? Should the advertising manager take a large part for his end of things, or should a large proportion be put into various sales promotion projects? Here one has to face that constant book promotion problem: every book is a different product and consequently has a relatively small budget in contrast with the company that is spending all its promotion money all year round on one brand of soap.

Equally important is the matter of coordination among sales, advertising, publicity, direct mail, and sales promotion. The finest poster a sales promotion man ever produced will be a complete waste if the sales department has not put a sufficient number of copies of the book in the stores that will build a display around the poster. The money spent will not sell the books it should if the sales promotion manager is late with his posters so that they don't reach the stores in good time.

Then there are the problems that exist in the relationships between the retail store and the publisher's sales promotion. Will enough stores use a poster to justify the cost of producing and distributing it? Will stores use your circular for a mailing or that of some other publisher for some other book? This is a twofold problem. In the first place, judgment is required as to which books are sufficiently salable in the eyes of the booksellers to make them want to use posters and circulars. Second, material that will sell the book to the booksellers' customers is what is wanted, not material that pleases the sales promotion man or the sales manager. And one should keep in mind that other publishers are competing for the booksellers' time, money, and window space.

IN SUMMARY

Like most any other merchandise, books don't sell themselves. Someone has to get out and do something to call them to the attention of those who might be interested if they knew of their availability. In actual practice, book publishing, because it is not a very big industry by American standards and because it is broken up into many comparatively small units, is not in a position to splash about gaudily in the mass communication media. No book publisher has ever sponsored a Western on network TV. Sales managers, and all who work with or for them in the selling end of the business, must therefore be all the more businesslike in making plans. They must be sure promotion money is well spent, that the target is pinpointed, and no detail left unattended. To this extent, carrying out the functions described in this chapter is not a carefree way of life. However, when these selling functions are performed efficiently they can give one the satisfaction of having successfully sold a product. And beyond that they give the men and women in book sales and book promotion the satisfaction of having sold a product that in most cases really benefits the consumer whom they have persuaded into parting with his money.

ADDITIONAL REFERENCES

American Book-Trade Directory. 17th ed.; rev. Biennial, with bi-weekly updating. New York, Bowker, 1965.

American Library Directory. 2d ed. rev. Biennial. New York, Bowker, 1966.

Book Buyers Handbook. Publishers' discounts, terms, requirements. Annual, with looseleaf supplements. For ABA members and associates. New York, American Booksellers Association.

Manual on Bookselling. Pamphlet series. New York, American Booksellers Association.

7

BOOK ADVERTISING

By FRANKLIN SPIER

ADVERTISING CONSULTANT; FOUNDER AND FORMER PRESIDENT, FRANKLIN SPIER, INC.

A BOOK is a book only when it is read; without a reader it is merely so much paper, glue, and cloth. The job of advertising is to find the maximum number of readers at a cost which will permit the publisher to make a profit. There is always an optimum advertising figure for any book, below which you are not getting all the readers you should, and above which you can get additional readers—if at all—only by spending so much as to turn the profit on each book sold into a loss.

The purpose of this chapter is to describe the process by which a book gets itself advertised; the specific functions of the various people who are concerned in this process; and something of the basic principles which govern their thinking and planning.

THE PURPOSE OF BOOK ADVERTISING

At first glance, it would seem that publishers advertise books in order to sell them to book buyers. Yet that is an over-simplification. In the broadest sense, publishers advertise books in order to create readers.

Accurate statistics in the publishing business are hard to come by, yet it seems certain that the number of book readers far exceeds the number of book purchasers, for many people borrow the books they read, either from friends or from public or rental libraries. Less than half the sales of trade books to individual consumers take place through bookstores or book departments of department stores; probably as many, or more, get to the public through the medium of book clubs, newsstands, drugstores, mail-order houses, and miscellaneous outlets. In addition, many books are read by people who buy books only rarely, and at long intervals; this is apt to be true especially of the big best sellers—like *Anthony Adverse*, *Gone With the Wind*, or *The Spy Who Came In from the Cold*. Books like these attract even non-bookminded people simply because "everybody is talking about them." The same is true of books with a strong religious theme (*The Robe*) as well as those which have achieved a reputation, deservedly or not, for realism in dealing with sex (*Peyton Place*, *Lolita*).

Nevertheless there is a hard core of regular book readers whose support the publisher must depend on, and whom he must influence first, if he hopes ultimately to reach the much larger circle of occasional readers among the public at large. These are apt to be regular bookstore patrons and readers of those magazines and newspapers which consistently carry book reviews. It is this hard core—the regular bookstore customers and readers of reviews—which is the number one target of publishers' advertising.

Publishers' advertising has several subsidiary functions to perform besides that of selling books, or even making readers. Among them are:

1. Influencing the "trade"—that is impressing book jobbers and retail booksellers with the fact that the publisher is actively backing a certain title and that it would be good business for them to stock and push it.

2. Influencing authors and their agents. Many an author has

left one publisher for another because he felt that the first publisher was not giving his book enough advertising support.

3. Influencing reviewers. The implication here is not that any reputable reviewer can be "bought" by the use of his paper's advertising columns, but reviewers are apt to watch publishers' announcements (particularly those that appear in the trade papers) for information which will aid them in selecting books for review, and in deciding which ones to feature or to review at length.

4. Influencing the sale of book club, reprint, and other subsidiary rights. Publishers sometimes advertise solely to keep a book on the best-seller list while a projected movie sale is in prospect. Occasionally this works the other way round: movie producers have been known to contribute generously to the ad budget of the initial hardcover edition so as to reap the benefit of best-seller publicity for their film, when it finally appears. The same reasoning may be followed by the firm that has bought the reprint rights; usually the two editions (original and reprint) are advertised separately unless they happen to be published simultaneously, in which case the advertisement may be shared by both. But once in a while a reprint publisher may contribute liberally to the expense of advertising the original edition, without the reprint (which will come later) even being mentioned in the ads! The purpose, of course (as in the movie instance mentioned above) is to build up the public's awareness of the original issue; the reprint publisher hopes to capitalize on the success of the original publication when he brings out his own reprint edition later.

THE OVERWORKED AD DOLLAR

Since ad budgets are usually computed solely on the basis of sales to retail bookstores and book jobbers it is obvious that the publishers' advertising dollar has to work extra hard to accomplish all the things which are expected of it. Some, but not all, publishers throw in a definite proportion of the moneys received from subsidiary rights into the advertising of the book which has earned this "extra" income. Such subsidiary rights income may be known even while the original edition is being planned, since in more and more cases, the movie, TV, reprint, and book club rights are sold as part of a "package" deal. (Several times all these "rights" have been sold even before the author has written a word of his book!) But with many or most trade book houses, the subsidiary incomes are looked on as windfalls, spelling the difference between profit and loss at the end of the fiscal year; so those in charge of drawing up the original, hardcover ad budgets are usually required to base their figures on the expected (or hoped-for) sales of the books through normal trade channels.

Once the percentage formula for advertising has been established—whether it be the usual figure of 10 percent of projected net sales, or a greater or smaller percentage—a total dollar figure is first established for all advertising outlays for a particular season, and then this figure is allocated roughly to the individual titles to be promoted, in accordance with their needs, and with a portion held back to meet unforeseen contingencies and to have money available for a book which suddenly begins to develop a runaway sale. But whatever the budget figure, the money must be made available to cover: 1) trade advertising; 2) consumer advertising; 3) sales promotion, including posters, circulars, and other dealer helps; 4) publicity, including the distribution of review copies; 5) the publisher's own catalogues; and 6) in some cases, all or part of the advertising department overhead.

The 10 percent figure mentioned above is not a rigid limitation on each title. Actually, the percent of income allowed for advertising (as for sales, sales promotion, and publicity) simply means that an outside figure has been set for all such functions during a given fiscal period, beyond which the house cannot go without risking loss. But an individual title will often have as much as 15 percent (or even more) of the expected sales income earmarked for space advertising alone, depending on its special needs and on the publisher's estimate of its potential market. The author's contract, too, may call for a definite sum to be spent which may be at complete variance with the normal advertising percentage.

New Books vs. the Backlist. In addition, the publisher must allocate his available money each season between his new books and such of his older titles as merit continued support. However, since many backlist titles do very well, year after year, with only a minimum of advertising, this increases the amount available, proportionately, for the promotion of the new titles.

Trade Advertising. One question frequently asked is: What proportion of the advertising budget should be devoted to trade-paper advertising (directed primarily at the booksellers and librarians) as distinguished from the (consumer) ads which are addressed to the reading public? It is hard to give a categorical answer to this question. An "ideal" figure for most publishers' trade-paper advertising would probably run from 5 to 10 percent of the total expenditures for all advertising space; nevertheless, at certain times of the year the proportion of trade space may run as high as 20 or 25 percent of the monthly total.

Trade advertising has a particular job to do; therefore the copy and approach are apt to be quite different from that of consumer advertising. The first knowledge most bookstores receive about new books and the publisher's plans for them is through trade ads. The essentials of a trade ad therefore include:

1. Editorial slant of the book ("Why we are publishing it"), and the handle or angle to use when selling it to the customer. This should not be consumer copy, but a very short summary of the contents, sales record of the author's previous books, information about book club selections, size of first printings, serial publication, etc.
2. The book's physical make-up—very important for nonfiction, art books, biographies, picture books, and juveniles.
3. Advertising budgets and plans.
4. Promotion plans and publicity tie-ins.
5. Promotion materials available to bookseller—circulars, posters, special displays, cooperative advertising, etc.
6. Publication date and price.

Trade advertising is also used to announce new printings before publication, new editions of older books, free offers, and special discounts.

The Library and School Markets. Closely akin to the trade advertising aimed primarily at booksellers is that addressed more directly to the libraries and to "institutional" buyers (mainly schools and colleges), who may place their orders either direct, or through booksellers or jobbers, but who themselves make the decision what titles to buy. The phenomenal growth of the library market—which has mushroomed in recent years in tune with the educational explosion and the adoption of federal programs of financial aid to schools and libraries —has shifted much of the emphasis of publishers' advertising. In part, this field is covered by the same trade papers that go to the booksellers. But there are more than 73,000 libraries of all types in the country (including over 49,000 school libraries); new ones are being established each year and existing ones expanded under the impetus of federal spending.

To make sure of reaching all of these, therefore, the publisher may use a wide variety of media edited with the professional needs of the libraries in mind, among them *Library Journal*, the *ALA Booklist* published by the American Library Association, *Choice* (Association of College and Research Libraries), the *Wilson Library Bulletin*, and others. In the important children's book field (and in the category of "books for young adults"), he may use *Top of the News* (ALA Children's Services Division), *School Libraries* (American Association of School Librarians), *Horn Book, Scholastic Teacher, The Instructor, Grade Teacher*, etc.

Some publishers, especially those with large juvenile or educational lists, may go into those media on a regular schedule; others will run ads only in special issues, such as the spring and fall announcements or Children's Book Week issues. In any case, these are additional advertising tasks for which money must be provided in advance.

Another section of this book gives further details of other forms of promotion to the school and library markets, such as exhibits, graded catalogues, and other devices. The costs of such operations—as well as the amounts spent exclusively on advertising to the school and library market—are normally covered by a separate "library promotion" budget which is calculated on the expected sales to libraries, in the same manner as the budget for advertising regular trade books is based on anticipated sales to bookstores and jobbers. The "ad budget" must cover *all* forms of advertising—trade, consumer and library—but the trend today is to operate library promotion as a separate department, with its own budget.

Consumer Advertising and Finding the Consumer Market. Every book presents its special problems. Even if the same amount of money were available for advertising, your approach would be vastly different if you were handling a book of poems or essays, a technical work of interest to industry, or that amorphous animal, the so-called book of "general interest"—

either fiction or nonfiction—for which there *may* conceivably be millions of eagerly expectant readers. (The authors are apt to think in such terms, anyway!) But each book (however large or small its ultimate readership may turn out to be) deserves to be presented at least adequately—and especially to be brought to the attention of those readers who are known to be interested in the particular author or the particular subject.

There are about 1,750 daily newspapers, 560 Sunday papers, and 8,190 weekly newspapers published in the United States; in addition there are 8,600 weekly, monthly, and quarterly magazines. When your problem is a book of general appeal—particularly fiction—you have obviously a wide choice of media in which to advertise. Now, since you cannot possibly hope to blanket the nation's press with an appropriation of, say $1,500 to $2,500 (an average amount for a new novel), your problem boils down to this: you must present your book first to the group of steady readers of the better-known newspapers and magazines which over the years have fostered and developed a known audience of book readers; second—and then only if available money permits, and if the response to your initial advertising justifies expanding your effort—you can add to your list a limited number of other good newspapers and general magazines.

However, your choice of media can be narrowed down considerably if you are dealing with a scientific, technical, or scholarly work (such as a university press publication)—or even a "general" book intended for people with special interests or hobbies. Books on hunting, fishing, home economics, dressmaking, chess, and other vocations and hobbies are obviously "naturals" for the specialized magazines in those fields.

However, it does not follow that these are necessarily the best, or the only, media which could be used to advertise such books. A great many men who golf or fish undoubtedly read the *New York Times Book Review;* only your own experience will show whether you can more easily and economically interest readers of the *Times Book Review* who are also golfers or fishermen, than you can find people who are "bookminded" among the readers of *Golf* or *Field and Stream.* (Note: Some of the larger magazines appealing to special interests—for example, women's interests—have regional editions which give you a chance to test out the appeal of a book, or of a copy angle, on a coupon basis on a portion of their total audience, naturally at lower cost than if you bought the full circulation).

National vs. Local Advertising. The complaint is frequently made (particularly by book dealers in the smaller towns) that publishers tend to concentrate their advertising too much in the big cities, particularly the New York papers. Of course the truth is that the publishers can reach more *known* book buyers per dollar spent through the columns of the nationally distributed newspaper book supplements and through national magazines, than through any combination of small-town or medium-town local papers. Furthermore, the circulation of the big city newspapers is definitely *not* limited to the city limits; for example, more than a third of the Sunday New York *Times* circulation goes outside the metropolitan trading area; the Chicago *Tribune* gives thorough coverage of five states of the Midwest, and has a sizable circulation in many other states. *Book Week,* originally issued as the Sunday edition of the New York *Herald Tribune,* later became the book review section of papers in Chicago and Washington also.

And it is even more true of the "quality" magazines like *Atlantic, Harper's, The New Yorker,* and *Saturday Review* whose distribution patterns parallel closely that of bookstore sales throughout the country.

Other magazines, with smaller circulations, but whose editorial content is apt to appeal to the habitual readers of books

—like *The New Republic*, *The Nation*, *New York Review of Books*, *Commonweal*, *Commentary*, and *The Reporter*—also receive coast-to-coast distribution, and are particularly strong on the college campuses, which are of strategic importance in the launching of the more serious and "literary" titles.

"Local" advertising usually means ads placed in a local newspaper, or TV or radio station. Local advertising is obviously called for when a book has a strong regional interest (like books about national parks, or the tourist attractions of a city, San Francisco for example), or when the author has a big local following. Regional advertising in some of the big general magazines that offer "geographic splits" (*Better Homes and Gardens*, *Holiday*, *Look*, *Life*, etc.) is another way to hit a particular section of the country, though this is obviously more expensive than using local newspapers. But local advertising is used to *supplement* a national campaign as a rule, not as a substitute for it.

It is apparently true that an enthusiastic review by a trusted local reviewer will do more to stimulate sales in bookstores in *that* locality (and to start a "run" in the local library) than will an equally favorable review in one of the big, nationally syndicated book review supplements. But it does not follow that an *advertisement* in the local paper would necessarily be more effective than the same ad in the national media. For one thing, the paper may not have a decent book page, or a regular one of any kind. If so, the publisher's ad is apt to get lost among the miscellaneous ads for products and services of all kinds, appearing on the same page. And whatever the local bookseller (or librarian) may think, the ad in an important national medium is going to impress the author and his agent a lot more than any number of ads in small-town papers.

Cooperative Advertising. Assuming that you do want to advertise locally, you are more apt to do it on a cooperative basis

—sharing the cost with one or more local stores—than to place your ad direct. The reasons are obvious: in the first place, the dealer can buy space at retail rates which are much less than the rates charged for national advertising (but they are not subject to agency commission, therefore you or the dealer will have to prepare the ad at your expense). Second, arrangements for a cooperative ad are usually tied in with the purchase of additional copies of the book to be advertised, by the dealer, more than he might otherwise have ordered. Along with this, usually, the bookseller will agree to feature the book in his window, or inside the store. Everything, in other words, will be working for that title during that "promotion." Other local stores not desiring such an arrangement will also benefit to a degree, even though the ad is signed by a competitor.

The disadvantage of cooperative ads to the publisher is that usually his house name does not appear in the ad, only that of the store. But this lack of prestige and publicity for the publisher is unimportant if the resultant sales are substantial. Co-op ads also mean more trouble for the publisher than do the ads he places himself; one must watch, for example, that the store charges the publisher only for his proper share of the cost. The store should be required to submit to the publisher a tear sheet showing the ad as printed, as proof that it ran on the date and in the size specified; it should be willing to let the publisher inspect the original bill it received from the publication, but stores often neglect to take these actions promptly and in some cases are reluctant to disclose their true costs. Publishers are understandably reluctant to press the stores on this point, but the advertising department (rather than the sales department) should do it as a matter of routine.

Co-op advertising is of course essential when the store is having an autographing party for a particular author.

Also useful—but also a bone of contention at times—are the

many group ads and catalogues produced by stores, notably at Christmas time, in which publishers are invited to participate and to share the cost.

Whatever co-op advertising he does, it is most important for the publisher to bear in mind the stringent rules of the Federal Trade Commission, under the Robinson-Patman Act, which, among other provisions, forbids any arrangements that would tend to favor one dealer above another in the same trading area. Comparable cooperative arrangements must be made available to all competing dealers "on proportionately equal terms," and must furthermore be brought to the attention of competing dealers through some affirmative act such as notices by the published to affected dealers, in time for them to take advantage of it if they so desire; or a reasonable substitute must be offered in good faith. A similar policy must also be applied to wholesalers.

That is the law, and most publishers are careful to have their proposed co-op ads and "deals" looked over by their attorneys, or actually cleared by the F.T.C. before making them known to dealers. As this is being written, the F.T.C. is taking steps to bring about a better understanding of the regulations among publishers, and at the same time to insure a greater degree of compliance.

Some publishers' advertising managers take a dim view of the greatly increased use of cooperative advertising in recent years. They recognize the advantage of being able to buy advertising space at as much as 40 or 50 percent less in some cases, than what they would have to pay themselves if no store were involved; furthermore whatever the cost of the ad, it is supposedly split between store and publisher—on a 50–50, or more usually a 25–75 basis. (There is nothing to prevent the publisher bearing the entire cost of his customer's advertising, if he thinks it worthwhile doing so.) But the ad manager may have extreme reservations about co-ops for special reasons. For one thing, a disproportionate amount of such advertising, relatively, seems to be concentrated in a few large cities and over the signatures of a few stores, which quite naturally tends to make the smaller stores elsewhere unhappy—in addition to raising serious Robinson-Patman Act problems.

(Cooperative advertising is not the only area in which the book advertiser might well have the guidance of the firm's lawyers. The perils of libel are obvious; where a book itself is held libelous, quoting from it or even restating material taken from that book in an advertisement might also be libelous. In addition, advertisements for books have in recent years been introduced as evidence—generally to prove intent—in F.T.C. hearings and in a Supreme Court decision on obscenity. This subject is treated more fully in the chapter on The Publisher and the Law).

The ad manager is also concerned that the co-op program may get out of hand and—in effect—displace other forms of promotion which he considers essential. Other things being equal, the ad manager would prefer to have as free a hand as possible in spending his available ad money on his national campaigns, and in any case, on the titles he thinks need help, rather than to find too much of it already committed to co-op advertising by the sales department. (As a rule, co-op money tends to go to support the firm's top titles, to the neglect of lesser known authors and "dark horses.") It is best, therefore, to establish at the start of each season, what co-op offers the house will make, and to establish if possible an overall dollar limit for all such arrangements.

TV and Radio. Television and radio are very little used on a commercial basis in the selling of trade books, mainly because of the excessive costs of time and talent in relation to the publisher's limited budgets. This is true of network radio, and obviously even more so of TV, where a minute commercial on a coast-to-coast network would probably cost more than the entire amount of your budget for most books. Even if you could afford the cost, moreover, there would be obvious waste in paying for a large audience of which a high percentage is probably allergic to reading in any form.

This may seem paradoxical, when one considers that "name" authors are often sought after for guest appearances on quiz shows and discussion programs, and that a plug by a popular entertainer for a book on his own program has been known to start a run on the stores. You can't buy such plugs. All you can buy (possibly) is commercial time on or adjacent to a particular program, and (unless you own the whole "show") there is no way for you to control its content. TV appearances therefore belong under the aegis of the publicity department, not the advertising, and will until the costs involved are a lot less than at present.

Therefore paid TV advertising for books is apt to be limited to occasional "spots" bought on a local basis; or to "participation programs," where the cost is shared by a number of advertisers. At this writing, the only TV participation programs exclusively devoted to books are operating on the West Coast and would probably not be nearly so attractive to the participating publishers if they did not automatically insure the cooperation of booksellers in the area.

In contrast to TV, books have had a fair amount of paid advertising time on radio, whether by way of individual "spots," or participation in regular shows.

There are several syndicated book programs, such as "Assignment People" and "Inside Books," in which the publisher pays for inclusion of one or more of his titles in a "canned" (prerecorded) interview, or in a mimeographed review sent out for free use by stations who have agreed to use it. But since there is no formal guarantee that the material *will* be used—or at least by any definite number of stations—such programs should perhaps more properly be classified as promotion, than as advertising. The cost, however, will be charged to the ad budget.

STRATEGIC CONSIDERATIONS

When to Use Coupons. Occasionally you may want to run a coupon in your ad so that you can gauge responsiveness of a special audience to the book you are advertising. However, it is a mistake to assume that merely adding a coupon to a display ad automatically makes it into a mail-order ad. Coupons *are* being used more and more in special pre-pub offers.

You can nevertheless use coupons in general (display) advertising when you wish to test the effectiveness of a particular magazine, or when you have reason to believe that many potential readers of the book do not have access to a bookstore. Only when you have a book which is obviously a made-to-order mail-order "natural" with an inherent appeal to millions of people who might never in their lives visit a bookstore (self-help or self-improvement books are obviously in this category) will you go all-out in a direct mail or coupon-ad effort, to the exclusion of display space.

Selling by mail is a whole subject in itself; in this space we can merely indicate some of the possibilities. There have been great successes in this field—from such classic ads as "DO YOU MAKE THESE MISTAKES IN ENGLISH?" and "DR. ELIOT'S FIVE-FOOT SHELF" (*The Harvard Classics*), on. But there is great risk too; therefore the mail-order advertiser tests his book (and various copy angles) on small, representative lists of book buyers, or with ads in only one or two places (sometimes the regional issues of national magazines) before investing in a full-scale national campaign. If you want to try mail-order you must be prepared to test, test, then test again—until you have hit upon an offer (or a copy appeal) that is successful, or else you abandon the project and try again with another book.

Much of the mail-order selling is done today through book clubs, or specialist mail-order organizations, who have built up lists of people known (through repeated test mailings) to be interested in certain types of books. These organizations can usually spread the costs by offering several books to appeal to a particular audience, rather than a single title.

At the same time, remember that any advertising you do, even when it appeals frankly for direct orders, is apt to help the bookseller as well. Simon and Schuster found that their mail-order ads for the Lasser *Income Tax Guides* doubled their sales in retail outlets, in addition to paying off on a direct coupon return basis; almost all other publishers have had similar experiences.

When To Advertise——Timing is all-important. Most book campaigns can be broken into four parts:

1. Trade advertisements—which generally appear from six weeks to three months before the book's publication. This is apart from the list ads which most publishers take in the seasonal announcement numbers of the *Publishers' Weekly* and of other trade papers including wholesalers' organs, and in announcement numbers of the *Library Journal.* These seasonal announcement numbers are usually regarded as catalogues, used for reference purposes primarily. The major trade advertising of the firm's "big books" can appear either before or after these routine listings, or both.

2. Prepublication consumer advertising—especially where there is to be a special "pre-pub" price offer: that is, an opportunity for the public to place orders in advance at a saving. Less often, ads before publication are used simply to whip up

interest and focus attention on a book before it is officially "out"—in the same way that feature movies are sometimes promoted before the premiere.

3. Announcement ads—which usually appear on, or a few days after, publication day; or the publisher may decide to hold off his "big guns" for several weeks to give the reviews a chance to do their work in getting the book known and talked about.

4. Follow-ups—these may either be planned as part of a consistent and continuing campaign using the publisher's own words and prepared in advance of publication, or they may be held until there are enough (and sufficiently favorable) reviews to furnish the copy for "quote" ads.

From there on the publisher must play it by ear. The publisher (or its advertising agency) must be alert to take advantage of whatever "breaks" occur: sales success ("Fifth Large Printing," "The New No. 1 Best Seller," etc.), endorsements by important opinion makers, a Pulitzer Prize or National Book Award, tie-ins with headline news, a sudden flurry of sales in unexpected parts of the country, and so on. But whatever new advertising is planned must be based on the sales figures as they expand, since the wary advertising manager never lets the expenditure for a book get too far out of line with his "percentage formula"—unless his top management knows, and is willing to take, the gamble.

Each new burst of advertising should be thoroughly merchandised to the trade, if possible, before it appears, so that booksellers can order additional stock and take advantage of the additional sales impetus.

——*And When Not To!* Not all books should be advertised. A few books are published purely as prestige items—or to keep the author on the publisher's list. Some books are so special and have so limited an audience at best, that the publisher necessarily depends on reviews in the technical or scholarly journals, or on the enterprise of specializing booksellers, to reach the people for whom the book was written.

Another group of books that should not be advertised is that for which the advance is so small as to justify only very small advertising appropriations. If your estimates show that you can afford to spend only $600 to $700 on a new novel, it is far better to list it in trade and library publications and let it go at that, than to try to make an impression on the public with a totally inadequate sum.

There is an old saying: "Never whip a dead horse." There is no point in keeping on advertising a book which—after being given an adequate initial push—simply fails to respond. Advertising can build good sales into big sales; it cannot possibly sell the book which no one wants to read.

The same holds true for books which may have enjoyed a healthy sale for a considerable time but which have now started to slip. It is important to know when to stop advertising—and when continued efforts may revive a lagging sales curve.

PLANNING THE CAMPAIGN

The preparations for a book campaign begin many months before the actual appearance of the ads themselves—and in many cases, even before the manuscript goes to the printer. Usually as soon as a book is definitely accepted for publication and the contract has been signed, the editorial (or in some cases the sales) department will make up a "title information sheet" (which might run to several pages), giving tentative publication date and price, physical specifications, a synopsis of its plot or contents, something about the author (what he has written previously, where he lives), and some indication of possible markets. This information sheet is duplicated and circulated to all those responsible in any way for the future promotion of the book, including the advertising personnel. In addition, wherever possible—certainly in the case of all major books—the advertising copywriter will read the book itself either in manuscript or galley form, in order to develop one or more good "copy angles" as early as possible.

As the time for the sales conference (or the publication day of the book itself) approaches, headlines and basic copy are worked up by the ad agency, with suggested layouts for ads of various sizes; these are usually submitted not only to the advertising manager, but through him to the editors and the principal persons charged with selling the book, for their approval or revisions. Any artwork which is being prepared for the book—either jacket art or illustrations—is made available as rapidly as possible to the advertising department and to the agency so that the latter will be able to incorporate into the finished ads any art which seems appropriate. One of the most useful devices in advertising is the development of a "symbol" which can be used throughout the campaign, and usually this symbol is lifted or adapted from the jacket art.

While the ads so prepared may not appear in print until long after the sales conference, it is important to have as many as possible ready at that time, at least in rough form, to show the salesmen exactly how the house intends to push the season's books. Often photostats of the major campaigns are furnished to the salesmen to carry with them on the road and to show to the dealers they call on.

WHO DOES WHAT?

The Publisher. The publisher's advertising department may consist of few people or many, depending upon the type of publishing being done and the scope of responsibility assigned to the department. A study of eight typical trade houses revealed that on an average they employ one person in advertising and promotion for approximately each $300,000 of yearly volume. The advertising department of a typical medium-sized house might include: an advertising manager; his secretary (who may also keep the records of advertising costs, returns from direct mail campaigns, and the like); and an assistant whose chief duties might be the writing of catalogue and jacket blurbs, writing copy for circulars and sales letters, etc.; plus one or more typists. The department may also include the publicity person and the person in charge of sales promotion material; or these people may be independent of the advertising department and work directly under the sales manager or the head of the trade book department. The library promotion people will probably be a separate department in most houses, but may work with or through the advertising department in formulating the programs of advertising in library publications.

The number of people in the department is likely to be proportionately larger in a house which specializes in technical, scientific, or educational books having special markets, and in those which do a great quantity of direct mail advertising, than it would be in the case of a publisher of a general line of fiction and nonfiction sold primarily through retail outlets. The larger houses are also likely to have their own art staffs, which have the double duty of designing books and jackets, and laying out booklets, circulars, and other promotional material.

In any event the advertising manager (or an equivalent person, whatever his title) is responsible for directing the work of the entire department; for liaison with the advertising agency; for recommending the appropriations on individual books; for the writing of jacket blurbs and the production of all advertising matter which originates inside the house; for overseeing sales material produced by outside firms (such as special mailings and point-of-purchase displays); and for seeing that the views of the editors, sales department, and "top management" toward a book are accurately reflected in the ads and in all sales material prepared. In the last analysis, too, he is the one who must answer to the accounting heads for keeping the total money spent in all forms of promotion within the percentage limitation established by the house policy.

The Advertising Agency. Until the 1920s, practically all American publishers prepared their own advertising, and used an advertising agency (if at all) merely for "placing" purposes. Today only two or three major houses, at the most, still cling to this system; the majority have found it advantageous to retain the services of an advertising agency for the specialized services it performs. The staffs, resources, and functions of the various book advertising agencies vary widely; but in the main, all of them are expected to advise the publisher on the best ways of allocating his advertising money, and to suggest the most appropriate media; to submit detailed schedules of advertising space, with indicated costs; to write the copy and make layouts for each ad, and to submit these to the publisher for approval; and after such approval, to see to the necessary mechanical steps which have to be gone through to translate the artist's layout and the typed copy into a finished ad, which it then forwards to the newspaper or magazine in the form either of a complete plate or of a "paste-up" for reproduction (technically known as a "mechanical").

Just as the advertising manager is the chief liaison between his house and the agency, the channel through which the agency's work is delivered to the publisher is the account executive or "contact man" of the agency. He and the publisher's advertising manager work closely together, through almost daily contact; and in some respects the agency account executive is in all but name an integral part of the publisher's own advertising department.

Behind the account executive is the agency staff: copywriters; artists; production men; the media director and his assistants, who work up schedules and figure costs; the traffic department, which follows up on the other departments to see that deadlines are met; and finally the billing and accounting department, which checks and measures each ad after it has appeared, and which also sends tear sheets taken from the publications in which the ads have appeared to the publishers, along with the bills for space and production costs. The agency also interviews the hundreds of "space reps" who are eager to sell space in their particular publications; and most agencies carry on continuous research to keep abreast of changes in population, reading habits, and periodical circulations in markets from coast to coast.

PRODUCTION PROBLEMS

Book advertising creates special problems for the publisher and for his advertising agency, calling for a kind of service which would probably appall the average non-book agency (that is, one handling cigarettes, soap, automobiles, or what-not). Each book published is in effect a "new" product, demanding special care and thought—and most often carrying a total budget which most general advertisers would consider inadequate even for a test campaign. Short cuts in production are a necessity. Only rarely can the book advertiser afford to buy specially drawn art, or have photographs specially taken, with models, props, etc. For reasons of economy (as well as for better identification of the book with the ad) the art in an ad, if any, is usually derived from the jacket. Type set for one ad is frequently picked up and used in other ads for the same book.

(It is perhaps unnecessary to point out that reproducing a picture or design derived from the jacket art does not necessarily mean photographing the *entire* book and showing the whole front cover, plus one or more edges, in perspective. If reproduced in fairly large size, a photograph of the entire book *may* be a good way to display the title and have it closely identified with the accompanying art. But the art on many books is so meaningless that a photograph of one book in perspective is apt to look pretty much like the photograph of another, especially when both appear postage stamp size!)

Most ads are made up in the form of "repro copy," that is, a mechanical with type, art, and all other elements fully assembled and pasted into place ready for the camera. Making a single complete engraving from such copy is faster and cheaper in most cases than making separate engravings for each element in the ad, locking these up with the type, and making an electro; in addition more and more publications are being printed by offset, for which metal plates would be of no value, instead of by letter-press; in such cases the repro copy will be sent to the publication instead of a plate.

An occasional ad may be "pub set"—that is, you submit your copy and a layout to the publication, which sets the type (as a rule without charge) and sends proof for correction. But ads produced in this manner are not likely to be very pleasing in appearance; special effects are impossible, and the publication's printers usually have only a very limited selection of types available. You would use pub-set ads only when the space cost is so low as not to justify the extra expense of having your ad specially set by a typographic composition house at your own expense. In any event, allow extra time for the ad to be set and proofs submitted; the publication may hold your ad for days or weeks before setting it, and possibly there will be a number of errors in the proof when you finally receive it.

The publisher can assist his agency materially to keep down costs by supplying firm publication dates, editorial information sheets, artwork, and reading galleys as far in advance as possible, in order to avoid last-minute, "hurry-up" preparation of ads which invariably invites mistakes and type corrections. The publisher can also save money by "grouping" his ads—making a single ad do for several media instead of requiring each one to be produced as a separate job.

TYPES OF ADVERTISEMENTS

When you come to actually laying out and writing the ad, there is no set pattern you can or should follow. Each ad may bear a certain resemblance in style and typography to others in the series (for continuity and better identification of the house sponsoring it)—but apart from this, there are no rules as to what you should say or how to say it. As each book is different from others, each ad must be designed to accomplish a specific objective. In the course of a single season, you might be impelled to use large "one-shot" ads, in an attempt to establish a book quickly. Or you may rely on the slower (but less risky) plan of running a series of smaller ads, relying on the cumulative effect to establish the book's identity and give the title recognition value.

Some books may merely be included in "list" ads, or tacked on to the bottom of large ads primarily devoted to some other book, thus giving the secondary books (at small added expense) a chance to appear in important publications which would not otherwise be available to them because of the high space cost. And you may want to run, occasionally, a "reader" ad, taking the reader behind the scenes of the publisher's editorial offices. Such ads usually have neither special headlines nor artwork other than the masthead. Simon and Schuster's

"Inner Sanctum" and Doubleday's regular "Editor-at-Large" columns are excellent examples of this last-named type—but anyone attempting this kind of ad should first be sure he possesses a chatty and readable style, and has something to say that will really interest readers. "Reader" ads are usually based on the supposition that readers are interested in how books get written and published, as in fact most of them are. The key therefore is the "soft sell"—and sometimes what is called "disarming candor"!

BASIC INGREDIENTS

There are almost as many books on advertising theory and practice as there are products to be advertised; but no book can do much more than indicate the general principles underlying good advertising, and point out the things that should be avoided. Particularly in the realm of copy, it is probably true that the very successful practitioners have broken as many rules as they have followed. But everyone concerned in preparing book advertising should be able to make at least a simple rough layout, and should know the processes of mechanical reproduction; in addition, it is well to have a nodding acquaintance with marketing and media research, and here the standard textbooks will well repay reading. For the creative person, the uses of type can be fascinating; the best "teacher" here is a study of the type specimen books put out by various printers.

An ad should above all be easy to read, with body type no smaller and lines no longer than can be readily absorbed by a person with average vision. Off-beat headlines and startling art treatments are double-edged weapons; they may defeat the purpose of the ad, by drawing attention to themselves and *away* from the book and what you want to say about it.

The same is true of humor, especially that involving a play on words. Use with Caution! Your advertisement should have a simple, uncluttered look; it is the message, or the dramatic idea, conveyed by the ad that counts, not how "interesting" it looks, or how many trick effects and typefaces you managed to work into it.

The basic ingredient of a good ad is unquestionably the idea it contains. It is amazing how many ads appear that have really nothing to say, other than that there is a new book by So-and-So, called Such-and-Such; or that the book is a "National Best Seller." So-and-So may have a big following, but there may be many others who *may* not have read him before, so why not try to whet their interest too? (So-and-So may also have produced books of uneven quality in the past, anyway, so even his established audience shouldn't be taken for granted; assume that they, too, have to be sold on *this particular* book.)

As for that "best-seller" tag, if you can truthfully say that your book is No. 1 on the list, that is undoubtedly news and worth saying. But merely being *on* the best-seller list seems not to be a very compelling argument in istelf for the reader to rush out and buy it. Think of all the vaunted "best sellers" you yourself never got around to reading (and perhaps didn't want to.) At best, prominence on the best-seller list may rouse curiosity about the book; something more is needed to transform curiosity into action.

Finally, running a lot of favorable quotes from reviewers can help create an aura of "success" for a book, provided the reviewers quoted are really well known and say specific and interesting things about it. But a generalized plug that says only "this is a notable achievement," or "a work of great promise" or "I sat up until 2 a.m." (maybe the guy has insomnia) will hardly be persuasive to the man or woman who fails to find anything else in the ad to interest him or her. This type of advertising may please the author and, presumably, his agent, yet fail to impress the book-buying public.

In the words of a distinguished co-practitioner, now retired (one of the first to try to make book advertising make sense): "Why not let them in on it?" (What the book is about, that is.)

Try to visualize the natural, or potential, audience for the book or books you are going to advertise. Then, talk to members of that group in language that will interest them. And if there is anything unique about the book, try to let them know what it is.

If you do that, you will quite likely have an effective ad.

FOR FURTHER READING

Of the many books on advertising, only a few deal directly with the advertising of books. However, those listed below will be helpful to people in book publishing who want a wider knowledge of advertising principles and techniques. The School of Journalism, University of Missouri, Columbia, Mo., publishes an interesting and suggestive pamphlet "100 Books on Advertising" (eighth edition, 1965).

"The Ayer Directory" an annual published by N. W. Ayer & Son, Inc., Philadelphia. The media man's "bible," listing every periodical published in the U. S. and Canada, with information about markets. (Standard Rate and Data Service, Inc. Skokie, Ill. publishes a monthly service covering print media, radio and television, with detailed information about rates. Available only on yearly subscription.)

Baker, Stephen. Advertising Layout and Art Direction. New York, McGraw-Hill, 1959.

Caples, John. Tested Advertising Methods. Rev. ed. New York, Harper & Row, 1961.

Duffy, Ben. Advertising Media and Markets. 2d ed. Englewood Cliffs, N. J., Prentice-Hall, 1951.

Kleppner, Otto. Advertising Procedure. 5th ed. Englewood Cliffs, N. J., Prentice-Hall, 1966.

Schwab, Victor O. How to Write a Good Advertisement. New York, Harper & Row, 1962. Common-sense advice about copy by a famous mail-order expert.

Stanley, Thomas B. The Technique of Advertising Production. 2d ed. Englewood Cliffs, N. J., Prentice-Hall, 1954.

Wright, John S. and Daniel S. Warner. Advertising. New York, McGraw-Hill, 1962. A good basic text.

8

BOOK PUBLICITY

By LOUISE THOMAS

CONSULTANT ON PUBLIC RELATIONS,
DOUBLEDAY & COMPANY, INC.

❋

SOMEONE once said that the difference between printing a book and offering it for sale and really *publishing* it lies in the quality of the job done by the promotion, advertising, and publicity managers.

Sales promotion is the term, in book publishing, applied to all efforts to help the retailer at the point of sale. This includes displays, posters, circulars, and other materials supplied by the publisher to attract attention to titles in the store

Advertising is a direct approach to the public in newspaper or magazine space or air time purchased by the publisher to "sell" his wares.

Publicity involves informing the public, generating interest, and creating favorable public opinion. When a title receives extensive and commendatory notice in the press and on the air, not only is the current sale increased, but the potential motion picture, television, and reprint rights are enhanced, as well as the author's prestige. Telling one's story through the various forms of publicity is an accepted method of modern communication carried on by both business and government. No longer can newspapers send reporters to cover the multitude of events happening every day, so editors frankly rely on publicity managers for leads and information. The publicity manager is the link between the publishing house and established news channels. Attention is given to a book or an author because newspaper and magazine editors or radio and television directors are persuaded that their respective audiences would be interested. This attention is *free*—free of cost to the publisher and free of commercial taint in the mind of the public.

BOOKS ARE NEWS

Happily, books are news in many places. Some three hundred daily newspapers in the United States carry book reviews, as do many of the most influential magazines. Their editors are as eager for news of books as the publicity managers are to send it. However, to increase attention to books and constantly create new interest where it is not ready-made is the job of the person whose responsibility it is to "spread the word" and "tell the world."

THE PUBLICITY OFFICE

In most publishing firms today, publicity is a full-time job for one person with a secretary-assistant. In the largest houses extensive publication lists demand a department of six or seven people who divide the areas of publicity responsibility. In small houses the publicity is done in odd moments by the advertising manager, or even an editor. Such a firm often engages an outside publicity agency, either on an annual basis or for a special campaign on a single title.

However organized, the publicity office must have contact with all other departments of the publishing house, working most closely with those of editorial, sales, advertising, and sales promotion. Publicity should be coordinated with advertising and promotion and should supplement the efforts of those departments.

REVIEW COPIES

Sending out review copies and gathering reviews is the first responsibility of the publicity department. A publicity manager should know all the possible reviewing outlets and know them well. A basic list is to be found in the annual *Literary Market Place* (Bowker), an indispensable tool for all publicity departments. A checklist may be sent with each seasonal catalogue to all persons who mention books with any regularity. The response to this list gives an indication of what titles most interest a particular individual. Experience teaches the publicity manager to add to some requests and cut down on others. Watching the book pages and checking with the sales department is the only way to be sure that the free review copies are inspiring sales.

Review copies of every book should be sent to all the book trade publications well in advance of publication. These are: *American News of Books, American Library Association Booklist, The Library Journal, Publishers' Weekly, The Book Buyer's Guide, Virginia Kirkus Service, Inc.*

It is important to know the deadlines of various publications so that galleys may be supplied to book review editors who work many weeks or months in advance. Every publication expects to receive review copies at least a month in advance, giving the editor time to assign the book for review and allowing the reviewer sufficient time to read and write. All advance copies should carry a release slip indicating the publication date when the review may be released (so as to coincide as nearly as possible with the book's on-sale date in the bookstores) and asking that two copies of the review be returned to the publicity department. (It is customary for the review medium to send two copies of a review in exchange for the free book.) One clipping is kept in the publicity department as part of the book's record. The other copy is for the editor, who can forward it to the author. Many writers have said that they have benefited from reviewers' criticisms.

Although the sending of review copies is a fundamental routine, it should not be just routine. In addition to the lists of regular reviewers (which should be checked at least once a year), every publicity department should have specialized lists—women's page editors, garden editors, reviewers of religious books, and so on. Furthermore, many specialized media will mention a book of particular interest to their readers. A book on decorating, for example, will be reviewed in an interior decorating magazine which is not concerned with other books. A local newspaper, daily or weekly, will invariably report on a book by a native son, even if there is no regular book review page.

The number of review copies sent out may range from 25 for a high-priced, specialized book to 1,200 for a "big" book for which saturation coverage is wanted. Doubleday's average sending is 150 copies allotted among newspapers, magazines, the syndicated services which carry book reviews (Associated Press, United Press International, Saturday Review Syndicate, etc.), radio and television programs, and individuals who talk about books. Obviously, large circulation media are most important, though sometimes a single personality can influence sales in his area more than any other factor.

PUBLICITY TECHNIQUES

Releases, Special Stories, Planted Material, Pictures. A release is the term applied to news material sent out by the publicity department. The word comes from the custom of sending information to newspapers covered by a "release date" (in upper right-hand corner) so that all users will break the news at the same time. Releases should be written in a direct, newspaper style, starting with "who, why, when, where, and how," giving all the facts without elaboration. The object of the publicity should be interpolated early as an integral part of the story. Newspaper editors cut copy from the bottom up. Therefore, for example, in a release concerning a trip made by Justice William O. Douglas, it was important to place the title of his latest book in a way which would insure its inclusion when the story appeared.

The publicity manager's name and phone number should be on all releases or other material sent from the publisher, so that further information may be obtained easily and quickly.

When a story is sent to more than one section of a newspaper this should be indicated. A release on a timely political book might be sent to editorial writers, the city desk, and the book editor. A biography of an actor or actress will be of interest to drama and book sections.

Besides news releases, the publicity department should prepare and send out any other information which will be of interest to the public or useful to someone writing for the public, such as biographical notes about an author, facts about his research, the publishing background of the book, and so on. Special releases are directed to special individuals, bearing in mind the ultimate use of the material. A news story about a political book directed to editorial writers, "opinion makers," or news commentators should be short and crisp. A release on a child care book intended as a feature story on women's pages should be written so that it can be used as such. Material for use on women's radio and television programs should be chatty and informal.

It is customary in most publishing houses to ask an author to fill out a questionnaire, giving biographical information and notes on his writing habits, his other interests, the background of his current book, and all the towns where he has lived or where there might be a "local angle." The skillfully designed questionnaire, like a skillful interviewer, can draw out interesting material from the author for use in writing releases and suggesting stories.

Authors should also be asked to supply clear, reproducible photographs of themselves, preferably in an interesting setting. (Photographs of the author at his typewriter or smoking his pipe have become too commonplace.) Sometimes the publisher arranges to have the author's picture taken. Sometimes a sketch is more interesting than a photo. Frequently, a paper asks for an "exclusive" picture so it is well to have several on hand. If no good photo of the author is available, the jacket art can sometimes be used. Reproduced in glossy prints with a caption attached, pictures are sent to the press about the time review copies are sent.

A questionnaire to book editors will produce a list of those who can use pictures.

Suggested Stories. When an author's career has reached a point of recognized literary achievement and a book of stature is forthcoming, it may be the time to approach some of the magazines with the notion of comprehensive articles about him. Six or eight months in advance is not too early to start. An anniversary may be an appropriate time for articles on an author's work. H. L. Mencken's seventy-fifth birthday brought forth dozens of expressions of appreciation. Herman Wouk was the subject of a cover story in *Time* upon the publication of *Marjorie Morningstar.* His big best seller, *The Caine Mutiny,* had brought international fame to a relatively young and unknown writer. His next novel was the "news-peg," the event of the week which made it appropriate to discuss Herman Wouk. "News-peg" means the news reason, or even the excuse, for running an article or story. Most large-circulation publications want to feel that they are bringing their readers something fresh and new. Articles on worthy subjects are occasionally published on their own merits, but an editor is apt to feel better if at least part of the story relates to current news.

An "angle" is what the publicity man racks his brain to find. It is the out-of-the-ordinary thing which might interest a newsman. For example, when Doubleday published *The Thorndike-Barnhart Comprehensive Desk Dictionary*, many angles were suggested. The one which appealed to the editors of *Life* and which was the basis of an article done by a *Life* writer was the complex job of making a dictionary. Another angle for a story was the number of new words which come into the language each year and where they come from. Another, suggested to *The English Journal*, was a history of dictionaries starting with Samuel Johnson and coming down to the newest, *Thorndike-Barnhart.*

The Local Angle. Names make news and so does the local angle. Most small-town newspapers would rather give space to a local resident or even a former resident than to some momentous action in Washington. A local angle release should be specially prepared, including the local name and address prominently. Also, send a photograph, although quite likely the paper will do its own interview and photograph of a local author. The names of all U.S. newspapers with their circulations can be found in *N. W. Ayer & Son's Directory of Newspapers and Periodicals* and the *Editor & Publisher International Year Book.*

Columnists. Writers of daily columns of news and gossip depend almost entirely on publicists for their material. They want the kind of item which fits the character of their column and they want it exclusviely. There is some doubt as to the impetus given to sales by these mentions, but such tidbits are part of any saturation publicity campaign. They add to the general talk about the book or the author in question.

Notes and Fillers. An energetic publicity person can add greatly to the number of times his books and authors are mentioned by sending out brief notes, which furnish material for persons reporting on the publishing scene, and fillers which can be used anywhere to fill space. For example:

The word *run* has 39 different meanings, the most of any single word in the language, according to the newly published Thorndike-Barnhart Comprehensive Desk Dictionary.

Tie-Ins. Tremendous amounts of enthusiastic energy have been expended on tie-ins with other products. If there has been any benefit it may have been the tone loaned by a book to a non-book product. Certainly few people buy a book because it is associated with something else. To tie in with a motion picture may make sense. There essentially the same content is being sold. Some movies help book sales tremendously; others, which may be very successful films, inexplicably do not inspire people to buy books.

Often the author can provide valuable lists of special interest groups. *Take One Step* by Evelyn Ayrault—a personal story of overcoming cerebral palsy—is being sold largely through organizations dealing with handicapped people.

In most publishing houses the publicity department is responsible for submitting books for prizes and awards and special listings—the National Book Awards, the Pulitzer Prizes, Catholic Booklist, etc. These available honors for books are catalogued in *The Literary Market Place.*

Radio and TV. To have an author sympathetically interviewed about his book on a network television program is the greatest boost to sales a publicity department can achieve. I use the word "sympathetically" because it does little good to have an author on a program which is devoted to light entertainment and only mentions his book glancingly as he is introduced. Important television programs are always more interested in talking to the author of a nonfiction book than to a novelist. They fear running out of material. Sometimes it is possible to overcome this reluctance. When Arthur Hailey's best seller *Hotel* was published, the publicity department asked him to write down some of the fascinating things going on behind-the-scenes in hotels which he discovered while doing his research. These provocative notes intrigued program directors and resulted in invitations for Mr. Hailey to discuss *Hotel* on one network and two local television shows, twelve radio programs, plus two newspaper feature interviews in New York City alone. This approach worked equally well in Philadelphia, Chicago, and Los Angeles. Another way of being sure that the book is an integral part of a TV show is to provide props. When Doubleday published Professor William Howell's *Back of History*, the author could offer anthropological treasures to illustrate his points before the cameras. Obviously, "how-to" books are fine for television: a book on interior decorating, flower arrangement, or a title like *Training You To Train Your Dog*." Blanche Saunders, author of the latter book, made many very successful TV demonstrations assisted by two French poodles.

A number of radio programs discuss books and/or interview authors regularly. They should be on the publicity department's lists to be sent books and releases just as any book reviewer.

Needless to say, author interviews on radio and television are effective only if the author is a good interviewee, quick-thinking, and articulate.

Press Conferences. If the author is newsworthy, or if the subject of his book offers material for a news or feature story, a press conference or mass interview may be arranged. This is done by sending telegrams not more than two or three days beforehand to all papers and news magazines, radio and TV news desks, inviting them to send a representative to meet your author at a specific time and place. The best time is the day before publication, so that the stories will appear on pub date, when the books are being put on sale in the stores. Usually a release or "hand-out" is prepared for distribution, giving the author's name and credentials, the book's title and publication date, and the highlights of what is the news, and any pertinent background information. This may be planned to provoke questions at the meeting or to help later with the final story. There should be time and convenient conditions for photographers to get the shots they want. Remember that television cameras and tape recorders are large, clumsy equipment, and the technicians will arrive well in advance of the announced time.

Whether or not copies of the author's book are given away at the press conference depends on how much it might prove valuable to the reporters when they are writing their stories.

A press conference may be called to launch a new series. When the first two volumes of *The Anchor Bible* were ready and others sufficiently well along to be discussed, Doubleday held a very successful press meeting with the two general editors and as many of the scholars who were working on the Bible as could come.

Authors on the Road. All authors should be instructed to let their publishers know well in advance of any trips they are planning so that the sales and publicity departments can take advantage of their presence in various cities. It can take several weeks to alert the local salesmen, have them call their stores for an order of extra books, process the order, and ship the books for arrival before the author's arrival. Too often effective publicity is arranged and customers flock to the stores only to find them out of stock.

An author may be going on a trip of his own initiating, a research trip or lecture tour, or he may be sent by the publishing house to visit bookstores. In the latter case the close cooperation is essential between publicity and sales promotion departments. In all cases, publicity mails copies of the book, pictures, and biographical material about the author to the newspapers and radio and TV stations in each town suggesting author interviews and stating when and how he can be reached.

Autographings at bookstores should be planned by the sales departments, advertised by the store (with or without help from the publisher), and publicized by the publicity department—unless the store prefers to handle its own publicity.

Book and Author Luncheons. The American Booksellers Association and the New York *World Journal Tribune* have for many years sponsored a series of luncheons in New York which draw a large audience from the metropolitan area. Outside New York some of the big newspapers, department stores, and local women's clubs have arranged similar series, in, for example, Washington, Cleveland, and San Francisco. The time, effort, and traveling expense must be balanced against the sale of books at the event and the publicity carryover. The more professional the sponsoring organization, the better.

Publishers' Parties. There should always be sound, rational reasons for a publishers' party. Frequently, it is necessary to explain to an eager author that the money could be more wisely spent in other ways. A party is justified if:

The reviewers and critics will be really interested in meeting the author—someone like Robert Graves, whose work has long been admired but who has not often visited this country; an author who is saying something newsworthy either in fiction or nonfiction; an author the booksellers would be interested in meeting—either a well-known literary man, or a celebrity, such as Bob Hope, who has a new book on the market.

In some cases the most productive arrangement is a small luncheon of not more than eighteen or twenty seated at a single table where the author can talk informally and answer questions and where the interviewers can take notes.

Public Relations. The publicity department is the channel through which news of the activities of the publishing house are made known. *Publishers' Weekly* and other book trade media should be continuously supplied with the plans of the sales promotion and advertising departments. When the advertising department has put on a spectacular campaign this itself can be publicized in business media. Personnel notes about changes, appointments, or new assignments of any importance are of definite interest within the industry and should be sent to the trade media; and when an editor is made a vice-president, all the press should know of his increased prestige, but especially the journals for writers.

The publicity department acts as the voice of the publishing house. Because the publicity manager must constantly work with the press, it is well to have him the person to handle all press inquiries. Whenever two people talk with the press two versions of a story appear, not necessarily because either is incorrect, but because either the question or the answer was misinterpreted. It is important to cooperate with the press, for even a story which is bad publicity is likely to be less damaging if the reporter feels he has been treated politely.

Sometimes public relations means keeping things *out of the newspapers.*

The Publicity Department as Custodian. The author's biographical questionnaire should be brought up to date with each new book. Add to this information the files of reviews of each book and copies of all interviews and articles and the publicity department becomes the custodian of each author's literary history. Scholars, critics, and students frequently consult this repository. Reprint houses and foreign publishers call on the material to plan jacket copy, promotion, and advertising for their own editions. Sometimes the publicity manager may wish to do a short biographical sketch in printed pamphlet form suitable for reviewers, libraries, and booksellers.

A CASE HISTORY

Perhaps publicity techniques can best be illustrated by a case history, indicating what can be done with an individual title in addition to the basic publicity done on every title.

The Columbia Historical Portrait of New York, by John A. Kouwenhoven, was published by Doubleday in 1953, inspired by the bicentennial of Columbia University. It is a handsome and unique picture book telling the history of New York City from the point of view of its photographers and artists. The book was expensive to make, and, although it sold for $21, there was little left in the budget for advertising. Much depended on the publicity department.

A year in advance the announcement story, indicating the scope of the research and the distinction of the author, was made jointly with Columbia University, relating the project to the bicentennial celebration. The publicity department of Columbia was kept supplied with information to pass on to alumni publications throughout the year. Six months in advance, the trade publicity was begun with releases and special articles concerning the magnitude of the project, the rather unusual manufacturing procedure, and the publication plans. The publicity department then began to try to interest the large-circulation magazines in the book. In doing publicity, one always starts at the top and tries everything. A story in

Life would of course have been the biggest break, but *Life* turned the idea down because of an Americana article of its own, already started. The largest newspaper syndicate was approached with the idea of a one-page picture story with several paragraphs about the book. This worked. Then came the job of sending a *different* story to the cities not reached by the syndicate. No editor wants a competitor to have an identical feature story.

Articles on the production of the book were prepared for the printing and manufacturing journals. Because the rotogravure printing was done in Philadelphia, local stories on this product of the Beck printing plants were arranged.

Many of the historical pictures showed the early buildings of businesses still in operation. The pictures with captions were sent to the house organs of these companies. Review copies were sent to all publications concerned with history, to the art magazines, and to photography journals.

Dwight D. Eisenhower was in the White House, but he had been president of Columbia University when the book was proposed. A copy was presented to the President by the author and the publisher before reporters and news cameramen. Later a copy was presented to the mayor of New York City, with consequent publicity.

CONTINUING PUBLICITY

When Amy Vanderbilt's *Complete Book of Etiquette* was published, a competing volume had held the top position in the etiquette field for many years. Doubleday's publicity department determined to make her name a household word and to establish her beyond question as *the* new authority. With many thoroughly researched releases which emphasized the sensible modern approach of Miss Vanderbilt (with many interviews and personal appearances) Miss Vanderbilt began to be noticed. Each season gave its occasion for an etiquette release: the opening of the Opera, Thanksgiving, Christmas (Amy Vanderbilt has definite ideas about personalizing Christmas cards). Spring brought forth her ideas about Mother's Day and Father's Day, and June, her definite rules about wedding etiquette. When the New York Transit Authority announced they were starting a "Be Polite to Passengers" campaign, Doubleday phoned and suggested that they invite Miss Vanderbilt to give a course to the bus drivers. They did, she did, and the resulting publicity sold books. When Amy Vanderbilt's *Complete Book of Etiquette* had sold a million copies, Doubleday gave her a press party and this seemed to bring the final conviction that indeed she was America's arbiter of social behavior.

GENERAL PUBLICITY

In addition to initiating ways in which his authors and their books can be brought to the public's attention, a good publicity man is constantly promoting books *in general*—keeping the public aware of writing as an art and reading as a recreation, as well as a source of information. An example of the sort of thing publicity managers have promoted collectively is the National Book Award, an annual Spring event sponsored by the National Book Committee and to which the American Book Publishers Council, the American Booksellers Association, and the Book Manufacturers' Institute contribute. The industry's oldest general effort is Children's National Book Week, sponsored by the Children's Book Council. National Library Week is now an annual activity in thousands of communities, and publicity managers cooperate by arranging for author appearances in most large cities.

Publicity has its conventional approaches, but it is not bound by them or confined to them. Actually, a lively imagination is of first importance, the ability to see beyond routine possibilities for coverage and comment. A book publicity job well done usually means that, for a time at least, a book, its author, and its publisher have lived interestingly and profitably in the public eye. This can be very satisfying.

FOR FURTHER READING

Baus, Herbert. Publicity in Action. New York, Harper, 1954.

Bernays, Edward L. Public Relations. Norman, University of Oklahoma Press, 1957.

Hall, Babette. The Right Angles. New York, Washburn, 1965.

Harral, Stewart. Patterns of Publicity Copy. Norman, University of Oklahoma, Press, 1950.

Loizeaux, Marie D. Publicity Primer. 4th ed. Paper. New York, H. W. Wilson, 1959.

Schoenfeld, C. A. Publicity Media and Methods. New York, Macmillan, 1963.

9

BUSINESS MANAGEMENT AND ACCOUNTING

By GEORGE P. BROCKWAY

PRESIDENT AND EDITOR, W. W. NORTON & COMPANY, INC.

❈

THERE ARE two simple principles by which the business thinking of a publishing house should be guided. They are: 1) Reducing costs by $1,000 has roughly the same effect on the profit-and-loss statement as increasing sales by $15,000; and 2) You have to spend a dollar to make a dollar.

PUBLISHER'S DILEMMA

The only trouble with these simple principles is that they point in opposite directions. They are the horns of the publisher's business dilemma, and the successful publisher is he who can grasp them and bend them both to point his way. It is not easy.

The first principle is a dramatic overstatement of the fact that profits after taxes in trade publishing as a whole are currently about 3 percent of sales. It is an accountant's overstatement; accountants are trained to believe that costs can be reduced without affecting sales, while sales cannot be increased without increasing costs *pari passu*. This combination of beliefs apparently flies in the face of logic. But it fits the facts in a regrettably high percentage of the cases, and the wise publisher will be constantly searching for methods of reducing his costs.

Costs should be everyone's problem since everyone helps run them up, if only by the amount of his salary. It is the unhappy fact, though hardly surprising, that costs come to be chiefly the concern of some one person, the business manager—his title varies from house to house. If everyone else were properly cost-conscious, this person would have little or nothing to do, and *his* salary, at least, could be saved. As it generally is, he has as safe a job as there is in the house. He should, however, paste this maxim in his hat: As a good lawyer tells his clients not what they shouldn't do but how to do what they want to, so a good business manager hunts for the factors that will help his associates do new things better.

In his efforts to control his costs, the publisher must be both historian and prophet. He collects information on his past operations to guide him in budgeting for his future operations.

Much of the information he needs is collected in the ordinary course of business. Thus he will have somewhere in his office all his receipted bills and payroll slips. But this information doesn't tell him very much in its raw state. All he knows from it is that he spent a lot of money. He will therefore try to organize this information in various ways to see what light it can throw on his business.

THE "GET OUT" OR "BREAK-EVEN" POINT

One thing publishers try to do is to calculate the "get out" or "break-even" point on each title or at least on representative titles; that is, the number of copies that must be sold before the book can start being a financial success. Here is one method of figuring a "get out":

First add together all the prime or inescapable costs of the edition:

Plant (composition and plates)
Manufacturing (paper, presswork, binding, jacket)
Advertising (including publicity)

Then subtract from the average net wholesale price the publisher receives for a book the sum of the costs that are incurred only as a copy is sold:

Royalty (usually a percentage of the retail price)
Direct overhead (shipping charges, etc.)
General overhead (which includes staff salaries and all other costs of doing business not charged under one of the previously mentioned heads; overhead is actually a fixed cost but is here stated as a percentage of net sales for lack of precise cost accounting).

The difference determined by this subtraction may be termed "unit amount available for prime costs and profit (if any)."

Finally if you divide this "amount available" into the prime costs, you will have as a quotient the number of copies that must be sold to break even.

It might work as follows in the case of an ordinary-length $4.50 novel with a printing of 7,500 copies:

Plant	$1,500	
Manufacturing	4,500	
Advertising	2,500	
Total		$8,500
Net price ($4.50 less 43%)		$2.57
Royalty (average)	$ .50	
Direct overhead	.14	
General overhead	.85	1.49
"Amount available"		1.08

8,000 "get out" (round numbers)
$1.08 / $8,500

Publishers have found figuring "get outs" in this fashion very depressing, because a publisher doesn't have 8,000 copies to sell out of an edition of 7,500. (Also, the novel that sells 8,000 copies is all too rare.) Rather than give up publishing altogether, some publishers use what they call a "cash" or "basic get out," which leaves general overhead out of the picture because general overhead—or practically all of it—would have had to be carried whether this particular book had been published or not. The "cash get out" shows the number of copies that must be sold to recover the out-of-pocket costs of publishing this particular book. In economists' language, "cash get outs" reveal marginal costs while "real get outs" reveal average costs.

Since general overhead is so high, removing it gives the "amount available" a tremendous boost—in our example from $1.08 to $1.93. And of course the "get out" is lowered, from 8,100 to 4,400.

But even 4,400 is a pretty large number of copies of a novel to sell—especially if it's a first novel. And also it's rather silly to print 7,500 copies if you have doubts (as you do) of selling them all. So since most publishers like to publish novels if they can, they may make the first printing only 5,000, making the manufacturing cost only $3,250. They will probably make the first printing from type rather than plates, thus saving $500 (in the regrettably rare case that subsequent printings are called for, they can be made by offset). They will probably reduce the advertising, too, making it $1,000.

So the "cash get out" looks like this (needless to say, no "real get out" is possible):

Plant	$1,000	
Manufacturing	3,250	
Advertising	1,000	
Total		$5,250

Net price		$2.57
Royalty (all sales @ 10%)	.45	
Direct overhead	.14	.59
"Amount available		$1.98

$$\$1.98\ /\ \overline{\$5{,}250}\ \ \text{2,650 “cash get out”}$$

When a publisher has to take comfort in "cash get outs" too often he is obviously not getting much comfort. A book that achieves a "cash get out" of course still represents a financial loss because it makes no contribution to the overhead costs that must be met. A publisher seldom attempts to allocate these costs with any precision to his different titles because such cost accounting would be more expensive than it would be worth. Yet it is recognized that some titles require more time and effort than others. If a temperamental author demands all of an editor's time for weeks on end, that author's book is a bigger drag on overhead than a manuscript that comes in to the office in final shape and goes to press without a hitch. Consequently a publisher can afford to indulge the temperamental author only if his books sell well enough to carry an extraordinary share of overhead.

All a publisher can say for books that barely achieve a "cash get out" is that he has not paid directly for the privilege of publishing them. He has paid indirectly, in his time and energy and that of his staff. He may also have been repaid indirectly, in prestige, attracting salable books by other authors, or in good will, attracting a salable book by the same author. (It is worth remarking parenthetically, however, that an author rarely thanks a publisher for publishing an unsalable book; the publisher is usually blamed for the failure, which results in ill rather than good will.) And he may have been repaid directly in the form of income from subsidiary rights.

It is now almost universally true that trade publishers have to look to income from subsidiary rights for most of their profit. Since it is seldom possible to foresee and plan for subsidiary income, and since a purely routine submission of proofs to a book club may result in large amounts of it, many publishers treat it as found money and carry it down on the bottom of their profit-and-loss statements, where it dramatically changes loss to profit. This may be no exaggeration of the financial importance of subsidiary income; but most publishers feel that if subsidiary rights ever become their main concern, they might as well desert the industry altogether.

A publisher can learn many things from a study of his past "get outs." He will probably become convinced that certain sorts of book are not for him (though his competitors may seem to do well with them). On the other hand, he will possibly discover that certain fields he had tended to overlook actually hold much promise. He knows of course that, as the industry byword has it, "every book is different," and that exceptional books make their own rules; yet he will, if he is wise, think at least twice before disregarding one of his self-discovered rules.

The "get outs" may also raise questions about certain costs. If a few pennies could have been shaved off the manufacturing cost, or if the advertising had been less, a failure might have been at least a modest success. But there is always the danger (deprecated by accountants) that a less attractive book, with less advertising, would have sold far fewer copies and consequently have lost even more money. There are no pat solutions to these problems, but editorial and production and sales and advertising personnel should be aware that the problems exist, and fresh solutions should be constantly sought.

The "get outs" will also probably set the publisher worrying about his overhead, which has to be carried somehow even if his new books don't seem to contribute much toward it. Can't it be cut back somehow, he will wonder, without damage to his business?

He may get some idea of where to cut by studying the reports of the Statistics Committee of the American Book Publishers Council. This committee retains a firm of accountants to gather and analyze statistics from all publishing houses. A publisher (if he contributes his own figures) can compare his figures with the industry averages and thus learn where he is less efficient than the rest of the industry and his segment of it. (Where he is more efficient doesn't count.)

BUDGETS FOR SALES AND ADVERTISING

"Get out" calculations are of assistance in deciding whether to add a certain book to the list. Once the book has been added, it becomes the subject of various sorts of budgets. In general, budgets are a confession of weakness; they are attempts to control statistically what one lacks the skill, knowledge, or time to control in detail. They are most necessary in houses whose editors pride themselves on their indifference to business, and whose financial people pride themselves on their hard-headedness. Well-organized houses, all of whose principals are publishers, can largely dispense with budgets and thus save themselves a great deal of time and effort and much wasteful wrangling about purely imaginary figures.

The first budget to be made is usually the sales budget, frequently initiated by the sales manager (who tries to keep it low so he can triumphantly break it) and criticized by others on the staff, especially by the editor (who tries to raise it so that any possible failure will be plainly the fault of poor selling rather than of poor editing). The intention is for the sales budget to be a realistic appraisal of the number of copies the book will sell in a publishing season if all goes reasonably well.

The advertising manager takes the sales budget and estimates how much money he will have to spend on each title to push it up to the expected sales figure. This advertising budget is initially made without regard to the amount of money he will really be able to spend. But sooner or later he must descend from his tower where advertising budgets are unlimited and must trim his plans to fit the formula used by his house. Most houses try to keep total advertising expenditures within 10 percent of total net sales. Even though this figure is roughly twenty times that used by General Motors, trade houses find it very difficult to stay within it. Some houses try to apply the formula to each title individually; but since some books need more advertising than others, it is customary to make the formula an overall limitation within which wide local variation is tolerated.

After the advertising manager brings his budget down to the house formula, he submits it to his colleagues. It comes as no surprise to him that no one feels his pet book is getting a fair shake; but eventually differences are compromised and the budget is approved and becomes a guide for the advertising department. It is, however, always kept flexible and constantly subject to revision, because some hoped-for best sellers die in their tracks, and occasional dark horses run away. The advertising manager should whip the living horse.

The sales budget is used by others than the advertising manager. The sales manager may use it himself to set quotas for his salesmen. And the business manager will study it to decide whether to expand or contract the staff, whether to prepare to ask the banks for a loan, whether to issue another memo begging the editorial department to get fewer and better books.

Especially in larger houses the business manager may prepare a budget of his own which will show the heads of the different departments, including editorial, what they can spend for various purposes in the forthcoming period.

All of this budget-making is exceedingly stimulating to the parties involved but it has a tendency to emphasize the dangers that lie in wait for the unwary publisher. In general, budget-making, when it serves any useful purpose, is a means of carrying out the cost-paring principle of publishing. The other principle—you have to spend a dollar to make a dollar—is harder to institutionalize but in a stable or expanding economy is far more important.

INVESTMENT WITH THE HOPE FOR PROFIT

It is this principle that makes possible most of the new and dramatic things that appear under the publishing sun. A new series of books or a single elaborately produced title or just an ordinary best seller may bring in considerable profits, but a considerable investment must first be made.

The big problem here, of course, is to make the dollar; spending a dollar is easy enough. Some publishers have been able to turn lavish book production into increased sales; others—mainly those whose interest in design is only intermittent—find that higher production costs don't, as they say, sell ten more copies. It is the same way with advertising and even with such seemingly irrelevant matters as office décor.

More often than not the real quarry is not a buyer but an author. The public is seldom aware of a publishing imprint, but authors are almost always aware. They may be misinformed about the imprint but they are aware of it, and consequently much of a publisher's activity is directed toward making authors favorably aware. This is one reason advertising tends to be concentrated in the New York *Times*, which all authors are presumed to read. An ad may not sell many or even any books; but if it impresses many authors (and their agents) it may be counted well worth while. Likewise an attractively produced book may not sell many more copies than a slovenly one, but it is likely to impress authors and agents, who are, after all, bookish people and like books for their own sakes. Outsiders, especially those who are accounting minded, find this aspect of the book business exasperating; yet good will has value and is to a large extent irrational and expensive in every kind of business.

CAPITAL REQUIREMENTS

Bankers comprise one class of outsider frequently concerned with and puzzled by publishing operations. Most publishing houses are closely held and undercapitalized; so banks are asked to finance rapid growth or exceptionally big projects even when ordinary operations are covered by a house's own resources. Bankers realize that a publisher's tangible assets may weigh less in the balance than his skill and experience. Much of a publisher's inventory might be scarcely worth the paper it was printed on in a forced liquidation; skillful management, however, can probably turn it to good account in a going concern.

The capital requirements of publishing houses naturally vary widely in relation to the sort of book published and especially in relation to the success of the books published. As will be seen from figures given above, the cash investment in even a run-of-the-mill novel will be not less than $7,750 ($6,250 prime costs of an edition of 5,000 copies, plus an advance to the author). Longer books, heavily illustrated books, and books with complicated typographical details will require much more. Dictionaries have taken sums above a million.

A modest program of fifteen titles in a six months' season will thus need roughly $120,000 to cover prime costs. It is true, of course, that a book published in January will have recouped some if not all of its investment by the time June titles have to be paid for. On the other hand, backlist titles constantly have to be reprinted. While a backlist may be profitable, it is ordinarily relatively slow-moving; so it ties up much capital in inventory.

But the $120,000 covers only prime costs. There are also salaries and rent and insurance and a hundred other items to pay for—items included above under the heading "general overhead." And the general overhead represents for the most part fixed costs, that is, costs that will have to be met whether any books are sold or not. A publishing house capable of issuing fifteen varied titles a season will have overhead costs in the neighborhood of $25,000 a month.

Assuming that this publishing house's list consists entirely of $4.50 novels, something better than 175,000 assorted must be sold every six months to cover the overhead. Until the house hits a best seller, or makes a juicy subsidiary rights sale, or establishes a back list, or expands its program dramatically, its overhead will be a drain on its capital.

Consequently it takes a fair amount of money to start a publishing house today. During the 1920s several brilliant starts were made with $10,000 or less. But in the 1920s, trade publishing, when it was profitable at all, was highly profitable, and the tax structure permitted successful firms to accumulate capital rapidly; so a combination of skill and luck could get a new house off to a flying start with only a couple of books on the market and only a couple of partners doing all the work from editor to delivery boy. Shoe-string starts or, indeed, starts of any sort have been rare in recent years.

While there have been few starts, there have also been few closings. Bankruptcies are rare for such a chronically sick industry. In spite of the heavy publicity accorded a relatively small number of cases, mergers are also rare, probably because the industry requires and fosters rampant individualism. It is possible that the book publisher is still the closest remaining likeness of the free enterpriser of classical economics.

ROYALTIES AND ADVANCES

Some of the publisher's working capital is comprised of royalties payable. It is customary to account for and pay royalties semiannually, and to make the payments from two to six months after the end of the accounting period. Consequently an author may wait until December for royalty on a book sold in January. On the other hand, a publisher frequently has substantial sums out in advance payments to authors. Thus, although the same authors may not be involved in the two sorts of transactions, there is, from the publisher's point of view, a sort of rough justice here.

Advances to authors have brought several promising publishing houses to grief, and have led others on to victory. Even the most successful houses, however, find that a goodly percentage of their larger advances is never fully earned off. Sometimes the publisher doesn't really expect it to be earned off but is forced to the high advance in competition with another house. Since royalty terms are substantially the same everywhere, the advance becomes the bargaining point. When an unrealistic one is paid, it is a high royalty in disguise.

BILLING, SHIPPING, ACCOUNTING

The billing, shipping, and accounting problems of a publishing house differ in degree and emphasis but not in kind from those of any other business. From this point of view, the leading characteristic of the publishing business is that it deals in a large number of nonstandard, noninterchangeable items which are sold in small quantities at low prices. This characteristic makes billing, shipping, and accounting both slow and expensive—doubly expensive, because when a book is selling, time is money. The public is little inclined to wait to get a book that's out of stock; so delays frequently mean lost sales. Both publishers and booksellers are aware of the problem but have so far been unable to find an altogether satisfactory solution. Special orders are handled at or below cost by both booksellers and publishers, and each blames the other for the loss. No one likes to handle special orders but everyone must do so, because without them the market would soon be left to a few best sellers, which would soon become the exclusive province of the book clubs.

Various plans have been advanced for regional warehouses, to give booksellers faster service, and for combining several publishers' billing departments, to simplify booksellers' ordering, and to lower publishers' costs. A few publishers—mostly educational publishers—do maintain regional warehouses or depositories; but the combined billing departments have not yet come to pass. They may, in fact, be illegal under the antitrust laws and, furthermore, not startlingly efficient under economic laws.

In recent years there has been a steady exodus of publishers' shipping departments from New York City. The reasons for this can be found in any text on city planning. Some publishers hire out all their shipping. There are several companies in the New York metropolitan area that specialize in this business, and some of them are prepared to handle a publisher's billing and statistical needs as well. There are also groups of publishers that operate their own combined warehouses. And large orders are generally shipped directly from the bindery to the customer without passing through the publisher's warehouse.

DISCOUNTS, RETURNS AND THE LAW

The antitrust laws, and particularly the Robinson-Patman Act, have an important bearing on publishers' relations with the book trade. Ever since Macy's won an antitrust suit against several publishers a half century ago, the industry has been understandably cautious in joint action that might be held a conspiracy in restraint of trade. Consequently there are as many discount schedules, returns policies, and so on, as there are publishers.

Trade discount schedules are of two sorts: those that attempt to segregate customers into different classifications, and the so-called "uniform" schedules which offer the same discounts to all comers.

The classifications ordinarily used are "jobber" and "retailer." Until a recent ruling of the Federal Trade Commission, many publishers also had "semi-jobbers." And some still treat college stores differently from the rest of the trade. There is some doubt as to the legality of these classifications since it is questionable whether there are any groupings in the industry that are mutually exclusive.

The point where the whole industry flows together is the institutional market. Estimates vary for different kinds of books, but it is certain that library purchases, including purchases for army and navy libraries, account for a very large percentage of all books sold. And all segments of the industry compete for this market. Libraries buy from publishers, and from retailers, and from jobbers. The latter, in fact, do upwards of three-quarters of their business with libraries. Since a library is an ultimate consumer, some think that no valid distinction can be made between retailers and jobbers.

Because of doubts and confusions in this area, many publishers have adopted uniform discount schedules, which ordinarily apply to anyone who orders a book for resale. Such a schedule provides different discounts for different quantities or assortments or kinds of books. The permutations are endless.

Returns policies must likewise be the same for all competing customers. Almost all publishers now have liberal policies. Usually booksellers are permitted to return unsold books for full credit after they have been held for at least three months and before they are a year old. Again the permutations and conditions are endless.

The handling of returns is expensive both for bookseller and publisher. It is also one of the few expenses that can be precisely pinpointed; hence accountants like to talk about the problem (the talk doesn't seem to make it go away). Yet the publisher accepts the expense in order to give his books a chance in the market place, and the bookseller does so to keep from being swamped by unsalable inventory. For the trade business as a whole, returns have recently run as high as 15 percent of sales.

KEEPING AN EYE ON ALL DEPARTMENTS

The successful publisher will be continuously reviewing the practices and procedures of all his departments. A publishing business, like any other human enterprise, gains a momentum of its own; and a function of momentum is inertia. No matter how frequently he looks into things, he will find motions that are gone through merely because they have always been gone through. He will find other things that are not done merely because the specific order to do them was never issued. And he will find that some of his most competent department heads (as well as some of his least competent) are empire builders at heart.

Nor is it surprising that one of his most inert empires may be that very accounting department that is so prolific of reports revealing the weaknesses of the other departments. Accountants love statistics, as editors love books, and they will squirrel them away even when they cost a great deal to collect and there is no conceivable use for them. But this weakness should be relished even as it is rooted out, for it proves that even accountants and business managers are human.

FOR FURTHER READING

Annual reports from ABPC, published for members, summaries available: Operating Ratio Surveys; Trend of Sales reports, Annual Meeting reports reprinted in pamphlet form from *Publishers' Weekly*, including discussion of trends and figures. New York, American Book Publishers Council, One Park Ave., New York 10016.

Bound, Charles F. A Banker Looks at Book Publishing. New York, Bowker, 1950.

Bowker Annual of Library and Book Trade Information, statistical sections. Annual. New York, Bowker.

Other general titles listed at end of Chapter 1, especially Cheney, An Economic Survey of the Book Industry, and Unwin, The Truth About Publishing.

Publishers' Weekly, Annual Summary numbers, latter part of January each year, review of trends and statistics.

10

ORDER FULFILLMENT AND OTHER SERVICES

By SEYMOUR TURK

TREASURER, SIMON & SCHUSTER, INC.

❄

ORDER FULFILLMENT

IN BUSINESS the process of providing the customer with the merchandise he has requested is known as "order fulfillment." It is a fulfillment of the customer's request for merchandise. Although specific procedures vary from business to business, the basic steps in filling orders are similar. In the publishing industry these steps are as follows:

Receipt of Order. The order can come from a jobber, who in turn sells to bookstores, or directly from a bookstore, or from a customer who responds to a mail-order ad. At present we will consider only bookstore and jobber orders.

Order Review. All orders are given a preliminary review so that any orders requiring special consideration or attention may be separated from the rest. ("Rush" orders, for example, might be put aside for special handling).

Credit Review. Orders are checked to prevent shipment of books to any customer who has not met prior obligations to the publisher. (This step may be combined with the initial order review noted above).

Order Processing. Pertinent information is entered on the

order so that an invoice can be prepared. (The amount of discount, for example, might be noted on the original order).

Invoice Preparation. The invoice is typed or otherwise written up, one copy of which will be the document from which shipment will be made. Invoices can be prepared by hand, typewriter, or high-speed printer tied into a computer.

Shipping of Merchandise. The merchandise specified on the invoice is selected and packed and subsequently delivered to the post office for mailing, or for delivery to any other commercial carrier employed by the publisher or the customer.

Customer Accounting. The customer's bill is recorded. Monthly statements are prepared and payments from customers are recorded.

Other Account and Statistical Reports. Sales are analyzed by titles, by customer types, and by other information that will enable company managers to make profitable plans for the future based on past experience.

Previous chapters in this book have dealt with creating the manuscript (editorial); making the finished book (production); creating bookseller demand (sales promotion); and creating public demand (advertising and publicity). In dealing with order fulfillment, this chapter covers the process that actually consummates the act of publishing—getting the book from the publisher into the hands of the customer.

The publisher's expenditure of time, energy, and money can be returned profitably only through sales of the book (and/or through licensing of rights). Therefore, the efficiency of order fulfillment procedures is essential so that the main publishing objective can be realized.

A STANDARD PROCEDURE

The steps involved in order fulfillment are tailor-made to fit each publisher's peculiar requirements. The following detailed elaboration of these steps is based on a standard procedure applicable to most trade publishers.

Accounting machines, electronic calculators, high-speed data-processing machines are in common use in publishing, particularly in the large companies that must handle thousands of orders in one day.

The order fulfillment process must start with an order written by a salesman or a customer. The order can be written on a preprinted order form (preferable), or on any paper. To meet urgent requests, a telegraph or telephone may be used, or even a visit to the publisher's office. When the order has been written and mailed, the customer has completed his job. Now the publisher must act—quickly and accurately.

Incoming mail of all kinds is delivered to a single location, where it is sorted. The mail representing customers orders is forwarded to the fulfillment section to begin its processing cycle.

Order and Credit Review. The vast majority of orders received by a company can be processed in routine fashion. However, there are unique situations which require special consideration and handling. These are removed at the "filtering" or order review stage. The orders most commonly removed at this stage usually require the authorization of the credit department before further processing can continue. Obviously, unless customers pay for their purchases, the publisher will not be able to meet his own obligations. Therefore, efforts must be made to sell to the customers in accordance with their abilities to meet their obligations.

Judgment of credit is made by a person trained to analyze financial statements submitted by customers, as well as to evaluate information received from independent credit organizations (e.g., Dun & Bradstreet). Publishers also exchange information with each other through their trade association, the American Book Publishers Council.

Two main functions of a credit department are: 1) to establish accounts for new customers—this requires the setting of the maximum amount which should be owed to the publisher at any one time; 2) review accounts of customers to make sure that all customers adhere to terms of purchase and properly meet their obligations promptly and completely. In reviewing orders these two questions will be evaluated accordingly.

Determination of credit takes into account many factors. Among them are the customer's location and facilities, his reputation, *his* customers, and *their* methods of payment.

Because of audit procedures, governmental agencies take a greater length of time to pay their bills than regular commercial accounts. Therefore, if a credit manager knows that a particular customer sells exclusively to governmental agencies, he sets up a payment schedule to conform to the times his customer receives payment.

A successful credit manager encourages rather than discourages the distribution of books.

Order Processing. All orders that have passed through the order and credit review stage are now ready to be processed. Order processing will include all the steps prior to actual invoice preparation.

The following information is needed to prepare an invoice:

1. Where the books are to be shipped.
2. Where the invoice should be sent.
3. The title of each book ordered and its retail price.
4. The quantity of each title ordered.
5. Which titles are actually available at the warehouse for shipping.
6. What the customer shall pay for those books (price less trade discount).
7. Terms and method of payment.
8. Delivery instructions, if any.

Only if the order can contain clearly all the above information will the actual invoice preparation go smoothly and accurately.

Publishers spend money and effort to encourage the use of preprinted order forms to expedite the processing of an order. The order processing clerk refers to master lists of the publisher's titles to obtain the most current information relating to stock availability and retail price.

Best sellers and wide customer acceptance of a trade book are difficult to anticipate. Very often a book with a modest initial printing becomes a sudden best seller, and orders for the book far exceed the available supply. The availability of stock for filling an order is noted on the master card file, so that the invoices prepared include only those titles on which stock exists at the warehouse. Those titles on which stock is not available must be "back ordered." The customer, without having to repeat the title on a new order, will receive all the books ordered as they become available.

Trade books are most often sold for resale at a price quoted as a discount from the retail price (cover price, list price). Discounts may range from 20 percent to 49 percent, depending on a number of variables. Among them are whether the customer is a retail store or a jobber, the quantity of books ordered, and whether they are backlist or current titles.

Backlist titles include all those titles already published as distinguished from titles to be published, known as "current" or "front list" titles.

Invoice Preparations. The customer's order now contains sufficient information to prepare the invoice. Since the information on the invoice must be used for many purposes (packing slip, customer's copy, and statistical use), the invoice is actually a set of invoices bound together.

The billing clerk enters on the invoice:

1. The customer's name and address.

2. The quantity, title, retail price, and discount allowable for each title ordered.
3. Extension—the figure actually to be paid for a title. Each line is extended by use of accounting machines, computers, or possibly a prepared chart containing the most common extensions.
4. The total amount for each invoice is determined.
5. The invoice is forwarded to the warehouse.

Warehousing and Shipping. The warehousing and shipping functions may be performed at the manufacturer's, a publisher-owned warehouse, cooperative warehouses established by two or more publishers, or a private independent shipping service. It appears that the current trend among trade book publishers is to perform their own warehouse and shipping functions at the same location at which their order and fulfillment services are performed.

Warehousing includes the many functions involved in the receiving and storing of merchandise sent by the manufacturer. Books must be protected so that the book the customer receives is in a clean, salable condition. Periodic inventories, under the supervision of the accounting department, are also taken by the warehouse. The warehouse must be planned so that it can handle the order for a single copy from a small bookstore with the same ease and efficiency it gives a jobber with a 5,000-copy order for a best seller.

Shipping includes the many functions involved in selecting from shelves and bins those books listed on customers' invoices, in packing them for shipment, and in getting the book's transport under way.

Invoices are received from the order fulfillment section.

Controls are established to evaluate warehouse performance. In other words, many warehouses recheck an order before it is cartoned to make sure the order was filled properly. Often the checking is done on a random sampling basis by quality control people.

Invoices are given to warehouse employees who select from the various bins and shelves the quantities of each title called for by the invoice. The books are usually placed in prefabricated containers so that a complete order is kept together.

The books are transported by moving belts or trolleys (thus reducing unnecessary human labor—labor represents in excess of 50 percent of the direct costs of a warehouse) to the packing station where experienced packers select the proper size carton in which to pack the order and the books are placed in the carton. Before the carton is sealed, the packing slip is removed from the invoice and included in the carton, to be used by the customer to confirm the actual contents of the package received.

Poor packing will result in damaged books. The jacket and the corners of a book are the most susceptible to damage. A damaged book cannot be sold and if a customer returns a book damaged in transit, it is costly to both the customer who has lost a sale and to the publisher who has incurred an expense without completing a sale. Cartons of sufficient "test" strength must be packed properly to protect the valuable contents.

After the carton is packed, it is put on a scale and weighed. The majority of trade books are shipped via U.S. mail. If the weight of the carton falls within the limitations of "Fourth-Class Mail—Books," postage is affixed from a postage meter. Because sending books this way means that the package may be handled many times before it reaches the customer, many warehouses have U.S. Post Office substations on their premises, staffed with postal employees. Cartons, sorted by destination, are put in mail sacks and delivered to depots to be put on trucks or trains. This bypasses heavily congested local post office facilities, offers possible savings in the shipping time from warehouse to customer, and involves less handling, thus reducing the incidence of damage.

Purchasers of trade books usually pay the transportation between warehouse and their place of business (terms of sale, FOB WAREHOUSE). "Fourth-Class Mail—Books" is the classification under which most trade books are sent.

Parcel post rates are calculated by weight of package and distance between point of shipment and destination. Thus (as of early 1966) the cost of a parcel post shipment of two pounds from New York to California (72¢) is greater than from New York to Boston (40¢).

"Book post" is calculated on weight only. At this writing, the cost is 10¢ for the first pound and 5¢ per pound in excess. Therefore, a five-pound package will cost 30¢ (10¢ plus four pounds at 5¢ each), whether it goes from New York to Boston or from New York to California. There is a probability that book post rates will be increased along with other postage rates to meet the deficits of the Post Office Department.

Publishers' representatives are currently working with air freight specialists to develop overnight deliveries to West Coast customers at reasonable rates.

Department stores located outside the New York—New Jersey area may engage a single freight company to consolidate *all* merchandise—books, soft goods, etc., from East Coast suppliers to their stores. Larger freight shipments result in a lower cost per hundred pounds.

In the event the package is turned over to a freight company, the usual procedure is for the freight company to collect its fees directly from the customer. "Freight Collect" is the term used to indicate that the customer will pay the freight bill. "Freight Prepaid" indicates that the publisher has paid the bill and will add it to the customer's invoice.

On the invoice set, the warehouse employee marks the postage paid, the date the shipment was completed, the total weight of the package, and the number of units shipped.

Order fulfillment represents a multitude of separate steps required to meet a customer's request. In a successfully managed organization, the fulfillment manager responsible strives to have all the individual steps blend into each other smoothly and effectively.

In any business, mistakes do happen. The objective, however, is to keep them at a minimum. In the event that mistakes do occur, efforts are made to rectify them immediately. Hopefully, the customer receives the merchandise he ordered, promptly and in perfect condition. Again, hopefully, the merchandise is bought by an interested customer for reading or gift giving. Booksellers are usually permitted to return unsold inventory for credit. This is costly to both publisher and customer.

Customer Accounting. Now the invoice set, minus the copy kept by the shipping department to document the shipment, is returned to the order processing department.

1. The postage noted on the invoice by the shipping department is added to complete the invoice.
2. A copy of the invoice is mailed to the customer for payment.
3. A copy of the invoice is given to customer accounting to be entered on each customer's account record.
4. The remaining copy of the invoice is used for statistical purposes—to compute royalties and salesmen's commissions, to determine sales by territory, and to get the many other statistics required to give facts on which proper decisions can be made.

We have set down the series of steps followed by publishers in order fulfillment. The individual steps are more apparent in this description than in actual practice. Publishers traditionally have spent large sums of money perfecting their order fulfillment service to reduce to a reasonable period of time the lapse between receipt of a customer's order and the customer's receipt of the books.

MAIL ORDER FULFILLMENT

During recent years there has been an ever increasing use of the mails to sell books. Publishers have found in the mail order a successful way to sell books to the consumer who may find it inconvenient to get to where books are sold.

The mail order differs from the regular order in the following ways.

1. Solicitation by mail rather than by salesman.
2. Difficulty in ascertaining financial responsibility of mail-order customers.
3. The fact that mail-order customers are seldom "repeat customers" except when the offer provides for a series of purchases over a period of time, e.g., book clubs. There is no need to keep a detailed history on a customer who buys a single item.

When a customer purchases by mail, it is an impulse sale. It is a common practice to offer the customer fourteen days to examine the book, at the end of which time he is obligated to pay for it or return it. If a customer pays for the book with his order, the publisher pays the postage and handling. The customer still has the privilege of returning the book and getting a refund. The customer who asks to be billed is charged for postage and handling in addition to the price of the book.

The term "mail order" is used to describe two similar but different methods of sale.

Direct Mail. As it implies, this term describes the mailing of a solicitation for an order directly to a named individual. Direct mail solicitation usually includes the following: outside envelope, brochure, letter, order card, business reply envelope.

A list of names can be rented that is made up of individuals whose "profile" indicates probable interest in the book offered. For example, subscribers to a chess magazine will be likely purchasers of a new book about chess. The names on the list can be printed directly on the outside envelope or they can be printed on a gummed label which is then affixed to the envelope.

A code number is printed on the order card which indicates the specific list to which certain pieces are directed. When the card is returned by the customer, this makes it possible to keep records of the number of responses to each mailing and to evaluate the success of a particular list.

Coupon Space. In advertising his book, the publisher attempts to place his advertisements where they will do the most good. Most advertisements are placed in book review sections of Sunday newspapers. A reader of a book review section is interested in books and should be a good target for advertisements selling books. Or advertisements are placed in publications whose audiences would be most apt to respond to the particular book offered for sale. Again, an advertisement for a chess book would attract most attention in a chess magazine.

When space is bought in a magazine or newspaper, a coupon is sometimes included in the advertisement. The customer who is interested fills out the coupon and mails it to the publisher.

Coupons often carry a department number to which the coupon must be addressed. Each insertion is given a different number, and this helps evaluate the ad's success. Early knowledge of this success enables additional use of similar space.

As with general order fulfillment, the function of mail-order fulfillment is to execute fully the mail-order requests from customers. The publisher must handle the original order promptly and efficiently, and then bill the customer promptly to insure collection of money due. Every delay reduces the percentage of orders for which payment will be received.

The following is a simple procedure used by publishers to handle mail-order fulfillment.

1. The order is received in the mail center.
2. Since mail is very likely to contain currency, when the envelope is opened, precautions are taken to reduce loss.
3. Orders are counted by key numbers and the success of the list or coupon is evaluated.
4. If the order contains a remittance, the remittance is removed and a label stating the customer's name and address is prepared.
5. If the customer asks to be billed, an invoice is prepared which contains the following parts: customer's invoice, label and shipping department's copy, order department's record, statement to customer, past-due follow-up, and final notice.

This permits the addressing of the whole billing cycle at a single time. The typist enters the customer's name and address on the invoice as well as the book ordered and price (including postage and handling).

The customer invoice with label and shipping department copy is forwarded to the shipping department. The invoice with return envelope is placed in the package. The label is placed on the package. Postage is affixed and the package is delivered to the post office. The rest of the invoice set is given to the collection department.

If the customer pays from the original invoice, the remittance is deposited and the rest of the invoices are destroyed. However, if, at the end of a predetermined period (usually three weeks), no remittance is received, the "statement" is removed from the invoice set, placed in a window envelope, and mailed. Each follow-up notice containing the publisher's request for payment is sent in the sequence determined by the fulfillment manager.

A small percentage of orders are never paid for and it is usual procedure to engage professional credit agencies to collect from these hard-core "dead beats."

Firms with a large mail-order volume use computers to process their orders and to follow up customers for collection. The names of people who have paid for books ordered is a valuable source of additional income. These names can be rented to other mail-order advertisers and successful lists are a good source of continuing rental income.

There are a number of organizations specializing in mail-order fulfillment. They provide full-range services to those publishers whose volume does not warrant setting up a separate fulfillment department. Larger firms usually have their own facilities to handle this type of sale.

OFFICE MANAGEMENT

The office manager is responsible for the administration of the various duties necessary to keep an organization running smoothly.

Telephone service, mail room, reception desk, purchase of office supplies and equipment, repairs to office equipment, are the sorts of things that fall under the supervision of an office manager. It would be inefficient and costly to permit each employee to order supplies and services individually. In small firms, the office manager may be responsible for the complete order fulfillment service.

PERSONNEL DEPARTMENT

In smaller publishing companies, the personnel function is usually handled by the office manager. Larger companies usually find it to their advantage to have a separate personnel department, often with a director who is professionally trained in personnel work.

The personnel department does the following:

1. Coordinates departmental needs. One department may be overstaffed, and another understaffed. Without coordination one employee would be discharged and a new, untrained employee hired.
2. Hires new employees. Using public and private employment agencies, newspaper advertising, school employment offices, the personnel director seeks out qualified help. The personnel manager interviews and tests prospective employees to review qualifications.
3. Keeps personnel records. All records of past and current employees are kept by personnel department. Many inquiries are received regarding past employees who are seeking new employment. In addition, current employees seeking to establish personal credit responsibility give their employer as reference. Personnel records are also involved in the administration of benefits such as insurance, vacation privileges, and so on.
4. Salary review. Periodic reviews of an employee's performance are made by the personnel department in collaboration with department heads and other executives. Salary adjustments, when deserved, are made. Personnel coordinates salary information with department supervisors and the payroll department.

There are many positions in trade publishing, technical in nature, that are usually filled by the individual departments. Editorial and production department positions are usually filled by the executive editor and production manager directly with approval by the general manager of the company.

OTHER SERVICES

Publisher's Library. Most publishers keep at their editorial offices a library of all their previous publications. This library can be used for the following purposes:

1. To provide the references needed when licenses for subsidiary use of the publisher's property are requested by others. Information relating to copyright dates and ownership must be readily available.
2. To facilitate the sale of rights and permission by having in one place the actual book available for license.
3. To provide the production department with copies of a publication to photograph so as to make plates for a new edition.
4. To enable editors to review previous publications when considering ideas for new projects.

Other Library Collections. An increasing number of publishers find a need for a trained librarian in a large firm, or for several, to maintain a special library of reference and source materials. At any rate, someone has to keep track of the great number of trade, consumer, and professional periodicals that the personnel of a publishing house must both read and refer back to. Someone must be assigned to maintaining a current collection of specialized books that a particular house or department may need. And someone—for example, in the art and production department of a textbook house—has to apply a professional touch to the job of organizing and keeping accessible the elaborate files of source materials that editors and art directors may need.

These services are organized differently in different firms—sometimes in a central library, sometimes departmentally. Sometimes they are organized hardly at all, but many firms have found that efficiency calls for a degree of formal arrangement and direction.

Thus there are many careers open to those who want to work with books but not necessarily in the editorial, production, or sales and advertising departments. The visible portion of an iceberg represents but a small portion of its overall dimensions. The areas of editorial, production, and selling are to the whole publishing process as the visible portion of an iceberg is to the whole iceberg. Many people have made careers for themselves in the order fulfillment and other business areas of publishing.

FOR FURTHER READING

American Book Publishers Council. Annual Reports. Also reports of Business Methods Committee. New York, American Book Publishers Council.

Other titles listed at end of previous chapter.

11

SUBSIDIARY RIGHTS AND PERMISSIONS

By JOSEPH MARKS

PUBLISHING CONSULTANT AND FORMERLY VICE-PRESIDENT,
DOUBLEDAY & COMPANY, INC.

SUBSIDIARY RIGHTS are those assigned to a publisher by the author or his agent apart from the primary right to publish the book. They are called subsidiary because they are subordinate to the publisher's prime obligation to do the best job he can of publishing the book and giving it the widest possible distribution. When the publisher acquires these subsidiary rights from the author, he also assumes the obligation to exploit them. Not so long ago, they were a source of extra income, not large, but always welcome. In recent years, as the picture has changed in publishing economics, the successful exploitation of these subsidiary rights has become a very real necessity, often representing the difference between an unsuccessful and a successful operation. It has become increasingly difficult to publish a book profitably merely on its trade sale (see chapter on Business Management), and more and more publishers are finding that a book which would have shown a loss otherwise has been made profitable by the sale of subsidiary rights.

Let us consider these rights in their proper sequence, i.e., in the order in which they can be exploited.

PUBLICATION RIGHTS

First Serial Rights. First serial rights cover publication of all or part of the book in a newspaper or magazine before book publication, or at least beginning before book publication.

This right is almost invariably withheld for the author by the author's agent. When the author deals with his publisher directly, it is handled by the latter, of course. The market for first serial is rather clearly defined. The popular magazines, such as *The Saturday Evening Post*, *Ladies' Home Journal*, *McCall's*, and *Good Housekeeping* are important users of condensed versions of books in anything from two to eight parts. The preparation of a book for serialization is done by the staff of the magazine. Fees paid by the magazine to the author for this kind of use are quite high, frequently ranging up to $100,000, depending on the author, the book, and the magazine. There is a strong feeling among publishers that first serial use by high-circulation magazines adversely affects the trade sale of the book, but this has not been clearly demonstrated. However, the profit to the author undoubtedly outweighs any reduction of the trade sale.

There are important magazines of smaller circulation such as *Harper's* and *Atlantic Monthly*, as well as magazines of specialized interest, that use chapters or sections of books before publication. Their fees are naturally more modest, ranging from about $300 to $4,000 or $5,000.

There is also one-part magazine publication, known popularly as "one-shot." This is a condensation of the whole book which is used in a single installment before it is published as a book. Magazines such as *True*, *Look*, *Life*, and *Redbook*, in addition to those already mentioned, frequently use books in this form, the fees ranging from $2,000 to $15,000 and in some instances much higher. The effect of this use on the trade sale is debatable. It is generally felt, however, that in the case of nonfiction titles, the trade sale is helped, since the reader's interest is undoubtedly increased so that he wishes to read the entire book and own it in permanent form. There seems to be enough evidence that when the book involved is a work of fiction in which the plot is of prime importance, a mystery novel, for example, the trade sale is impaired. But there seems to be no adverse effect when the mood or style is more important than the plot.

First serialization in newspapers is less frequent than serialization in magazines. As a rule, books of wide political or historical interests are used—for example, *Crusade in Europe* by General Eisenhower, the books about President Kennedy and Eisenhower's White House memoirs. Frequently books of regional or topical interest are used by newspapers. Sometimes the book might be related to a purely local point of interest, e.g., a book on conservation reflecting a local problem, or a book about a local celebrity.

Books serialized in this manner are usually cut into twenty to thirty installments by the staff of the newspaper, and book publication usually takes place either as the installments are ending or soon after. It is felt that serialization over this period of time (i.e., three or four weeks) increases the trade sale of the books probably because their stature makes readers want to own them. To repeat, first serialization of an important book, or indeed of any book at all, in a newspaper is very unusual and very few publishers ever conclude such contracts with a newspaper. However, the astute and knowledgeable publisher should not neglect to look for such uses. The rewards are often considerable and gratifying. In some instances in recent years, arrangements have been made with the author by the newspaper, magazine, and book publisher, acting cooperatively.

When the sale of first serial rights is handled by the publisher, the latter's share varies from 10 percent to 25 percent of the proceeds.

Book Club Rights. There are about eighty book clubs operating in this country, ranging in interest from limited specialized subjects to the broadest kind of general reading. Book clubs are organizations whose members have obligated themselves to buy a minimum number of books a year; in return, the book club supplies them with its own editions of the books it has selected, at prices somewhat lower than the publisher's list price. Relatively few books are published that cannot find a place in one way or another on the list of one or more book clubs. Books are usually submitted to the larger clubs in galley form, sometimes even in manuscript form if an extra copy is available. The smaller clubs, whose distribution usually follows trade book publication by several months, are able to make their selections from the finished books. Book club royalties range from 4½ cents a copy to as much as 10 percent of the club's selling price, with guarantees based on sales of a few hundred copies to 400,000 or 500,000. Fees paid by major book clubs frequently amount to $150,000 to $200,000. Generally speaking, the publisher supplies the necessary plates of the book to the book club, which then has to make its own arrangements for manufacture. Some of the larger book clubs, the Book-of-the-Month Club, for example, or the Literary Guild, distribute books to their members almost simultaneously with trade publication. Smaller clubs distribute their selections three or four months after trade publication. The clubs also purchase from publishers the rights to issue special editions as premiums or dividends. In recent years, these premiums have become rather elaborate, in the number of books offered as well as in their size and scope. Premiums are offered to prospective members as an inducement to join, and dividends are offered at intervals as inducements to continue buying. (See also chapter on Mail-Order Publishing.)

A development of a few years ago is the condensed book club, notably the Reader's Digest Condensed Book Club, which issues condensations of four or five books in a single volume. Membership in this club has quickly grown to 2.5 million and guarantees are made on this basis.

The sale of book club rights is invariably handled by the publisher, and the proceeds are usually shared equally by the author and publisher.

Translation and Foreign Publication Rights. Translation and foreign rights involve the licensing of publishers outside this country to publish a translation of a book or, in the case of an English publisher, to publish a title in the British commonwealth market. Preparation of the translation is undertaken by the foreign publisher who acquires the right, which encompasses a language rather than a territory. For instance, a French publisher acquiring the French language rights would acquire these rights for the whole world and could sell his edition anywhere in the world. The Spanish language is sometimes an exception: a Spanish publisher may acquire the rights for Spain only, while a Latin American publisher acquires the Spanish language rights for the Western Hemisphere. Books are submitted to publishers abroad in book form as a rule rather than in galleys and through agents rather than to publishers directly. Virtually every publishing center throughout the world has one or more agents, who represent one or more publishers exclusively or work on a free-lance basis. Some of these agents have been established for many years and most of them are highly capable people. Through them, most American publishers are in close touch with the publishing programs of their foreign colleagues, and very many of the books published in the United States are translated into foreign languages.

Besides the agents, some foreign publishers have employees permanently in the United States to buy American books, and some send principals or employees to the United States at frequent intervals to purchase rights. Some American houses maintain representatives in foreign countries to sell translation rights.

The fees paid for the foreign translation rights to a book vary so greatly from country to country as to make it pointless to discuss this here. Much depends on the book, the author, and the country. Generally speaking, starting royalties are rather low in order to enable the foreign publisher to absorb the cost of translation. Once cost has been covered, however, royalty rates approximate those usually paid in this country.

Not only are the book rights sold for foreign translation but also the serialization rights. In many instances, book publishers abroad are publishers of or associated with publishers of magazines and newspapers, and these rights are often acquired at the same time as the book rights. When this is not the case, however, and the serialization rights are sold to a newspaper or magazine publisher, the closest control has to be established in order to avoid a conflict of interests. The publisher's share of the foreign rights' proceeds varies from 25 percent to 50 percent. (See also chapter on the distribution of American Books Abroad.)

Second Serial Rights. Second serial rights differ from first serial rights in two respects: second serialization begins after book publication; and its market is largely in newspapers rather than in magazines. Special editing is necessary to prepare a book for newspaper publication. It must be cut and divided into the required number of parts, usually eighteen to thirty. Special headings for each installment have to be written as well as bridging material, where necessary. Art work must also be arranged for, when required. Since this demands special technical knowledge, as well as special knowledge of the market, virtually all publishers deal with newspaper syndicates rather than with the newspapers directly. There are many syndicates, frequently connected with newspaper publishing organizations, that sell feature material including columns, comic strips, cartoons and book installments to newspapers. Frequently, a book of wide public interest is serialized in a hundred or more newspapers. It has been rather clearly demonstrated that serialization in a newspaper, after book publication, materially increases the trade sale, even though the newspaper uses the book many months, in some cases years, after publication.

A very clear example of this occurred some years ago when two books by Fulton Oursler, *The Greatest Story Ever Told* and *The Greatest Book Ever Written* were serialized in a large number of newspapers long after book publication. It became quite obvious that as each newspaper started to do these series, not only did its circulation rise, but sale of the books in local bookstores picked up immediately. The fees paid by the newspapers vary, naturally, depending upon the importance of the book and the size of the newspaper's circulation. The syndicate's charge for preparing and distributing the material is usually 50 percent of the proceeds. The cost of preparation and distribution is absorbed by the syndicate, of course.

Reprint Rights. The reprint right is one that entitles the publisher to license another publisher to issue an edition of the book that is usually less expensive. Up to a few years ago, reprints almost invariably took the form of lower-priced hardbound editions, and distribution was effected through the usual book channels and through numerous drugstores. Now, since the advent and growth of low-priced paperbound reprints, hardbound reprint sales have fallen so much that they no longer are a very important factor in the subsidiary rights market. The reprint sale of a book is invariably handled by the publisher. Reprint rights are ordinarily not sold until two or three months after trade publication. No rule can be set up since many factors determine when the book is sold and when it is released for reprint. Indeed, there have been recent instances where the reprint rights to a book have been sold before the existence of the manuscript. But this is rare and is accompanied by great amounts of publicity and cash.

The reprint royalties on mass market paperbound books are usually 4 percent of the cover price on the first 150,000 and 6 percent thereafter. However, in the case of books greatly sought after by reprint houses, royalty rates of 10 percent to 20 percent have been paid. The royalty guarantee varies widely, ranging from $1,500 to $100,000 and sometimes much more, $3,500 being a fair average. One should not be misled by guarantees, since repeated reprintings and continued sales amounting to millions of copies are not unusual. There is no close relationship between trade and reprint sales. Low-priced reprints are sold, for the most part, through channels that do not handle books, their distribution closely resembling that of magazines. They are usually found where magazines are sold: on newsstands, in drugstores, etc. But they are increasingly sold in general and college bookstores and in specialized paperback bookstores. A substantial number are sold through schools or for student use. (See chapter on Mass Market Paperbacks.)

Softbound reprints of scholarly works and books of high literary merit, selling at 85¢ to about $1.95 and sometimes higher, have achieved an important position in the book trade. While these books, under such imprints as Anchor Books, Harvest Books, Vintage Books and others, are not selling in the same quantities as the low-priced, mass-appeal paperback books, their sales are rather impressive, 150,000 copies of a title being not at all uncommon. These reprints are sold mainly in bookstores as are regular trade books. There are some 400 houses issuing either low-priced or higher-priced paper-covered books totaling over 4,900 reprint titles in 1965, in addition to over 4,400 new books. The reprint royalties are, almost without exception, shared equally by the author and the publisher though there is pressure to increase the author's share.

PERFORMING RIGHTS

Radio and TV Rights. The radio industry has never been a major consumer of books as a basis for radio programs and consequently has not merited very close attention. But with the rapid growth of television, with its apparently insatiable hunger for literary material, the publisher has had to keep in close touch with the changing picture in the television industry. Television rights can be utilized in many ways. The simplest way is: the television producer adapts a book or story for a "live" television performance which is then put on tape so that the program may be shown in parts of the country in different time zones. As a rule, this utilization is limited to thirty or sixty days. Though there are no standard prices, $500 to $750 per half hour is an average fee. There are exceptions, however, depending on the author, the book, and the program. In a somewhat more complicated case, the program is first put on film or tape and then shown on various stations over a period of time, sometimes as long as seven years, for a flat fee. In other cases, additional fees are specified for additional showings of the film. Occasionally, merely an incident from a whole book or story is used, a twist of the plot, or even the title alone. In some instances, a character taken from a short story has been developed into a series of programs. The fees charged by publishers for the sale of radio and television rights vary from 10 percent to 25 percent of the proceeds. Each of these cases calls for special negotiations; within certain limits, the fees paid depend upon the astuteness of the negotiators.

Motion Picture Rights. A publisher rarely handles the sales of a book for use as a motion picture since the author usually handles this himself, either through a literary agent or an agent who devotes himself to this special field. However, there are instances when the publisher finds himself with the obligation of selling these rights. Motion picture companies maintain story departments or scouts in Hollywood, New York, and sometimes in Europe, for seeking out and acquiring literary property. Sometimes the entire book is sent on to the principal, but more frequently only outlines are used.

The publisher's important function at this point is to see that news of likely books and the books themselves are available to those people who make decisions about their use in motion pictures. Until a book seems to have motion picture potentialities, there is little more that the publisher can contribute. But if the motion picture company decides to use it, the publisher plays a most important role in negotiating the contract. The intricacies of motion picture contracts are too numerous to discuss here; the publisher must be fully aware of the potential of the book and the probable trends in the motion picture industry. Many years ago, for example, long before television had reached its present development, a publisher insisted on reserving television rights to a series of books for the author. Many years later, as a result of the publisher's foresight, an entirely new source of income was available to the author when the television rights were exploited.

Fees paid for motion picture rights vary widely, ranging from $10,000 to $200,000 or more, involving various kinds of profit participation, and depending not only on the usual factors inherent in the book itself, but on the very many unpredictable features operating in the motion picture industry. Release of a motion picture based on a book appears to increase the sale of a book; perhaps this applies only to its paperbound edition. The publisher's share of the proceeds from motion picture sales varies from 10 percent to 25 percent.

Dramatic Rights. Dramatic rights give the right to use a book as a basis for a play, with or without music. Occasions for exploiting this right arise even less frequently than in motion pictures; as a rule, the producer seeks out the book. The royalty paid to the author by the producer varies, depending upon the kind of play. In a musical play, for example, the adapter, the librettist, and the composer will all have to be paid out of the total royalty. The payments to each of these contributors vary according to their importance in the theater. Here again, the publisher's share of the royalty proceeds is usually between 10 and 25 percent.

Permissions. Permissions involve extracts, anthologies, and abridged versions of books. An important market exists in various periodicals, such as digest magazines and the men's magazine market, usually adventure magazines, which publish not only full-length condensations but also excerpts. Also, children's magazines are a market for complete stories. It is not uncommon to find many chapters of a single book sold to several magazines. There is no overall pattern of payment; price for single use of a book or part of one by these magazines ranges from $25 to $10,000. Frequently, portions of a book are included in an anthology. Fees for the use of portions of a book in an anthology are not very high, but they are important to the author since they may be a mark of recognition or may lead the reader to the author's other work. The publisher's share of the proceeds is usually 50 percent.

Commercial Exploitation. Commercial exploitation is a right that can be used so infrequently that it is hardly worth mentioning. On the rare occasion when it can be sold, the rewards and excitement are both high. Sometimes, cartoons in a book suggest possibilities for use on ashtrays, drinking glasses, fabrics, or any one of a number of gadgets. Perhaps the most extensive commercial use of a character from a book in recent years has been that of Hopalong Cassidy, who was a character in some of the books written by C. E. Mulford.

The profits and excitement coming from the conscientious and successful exploitation of the subsidiary rights we have just considered give an added zest to an already exciting business.

FOR FURTHER READING

All titles listed at the end of the following chapter, "The Publisher and the Law."

Wincor, Richard. From Ritual to Royalties: An Anatomy of Literary Property. New York, Walker, 1962.

"Rights and Permissions," weekly column by Paul Nathan, in *Publishers' Weekly*.

SECTION IV

FURTHER MAJOR CONCERNS

THE PUBLISHER AND THE LAW

By HARRIET F. PILPEL, LL.B.

MEMBER OF THE LAW FIRM OF GREENBAUM, WOLFF AND ERNST

and NANETTE DEMBITZ, LL.B.

JUDGE OF THE FAMILY COURT OF THE STATE OF NEW YORK

"NO MAN is an Iland, intire of it selfe"—and a book publisher soon finds out from his lawyer that he must carefully review what he proposes to publish from a number of angles if he is to avoid legal difficulties and penalties. What is the law that determines the publisher's rights and obligations? Can he publish what he proposes? Will the government, other publishers, authors, or even entirely unknown persons attempt to jail him or collect damages from him if he goes ahead with his project?

THE PUBLISHER'S LEGAL FRONTS

To begin with, the publisher and his lawyer must keep their eyes on a number of fronts and possible legal battlefields. The publisher, like the rest of us, has to worry about both federal and state laws, not to speak of the minor laws administered by the governing bodies of small subdivisions of the state such as counties, cities, and villages. A publisher obtains a copyright to protect his book from plagiarism after its publication, by registering it in the Copyright Office maintained by the federal government in Washington. Such copyrights are governed by federal law that is uniform throughout the whole country. On the other hand, there are separate laws in each state on a great many matters affecting publishers, such as contracts, libel, or obscenity—all of them in turn subject to the federal constitution. Indeed, if a publisher fears a libel suit will result from a book, he would do well to consider the varying libel laws of all the states where the book may be distributed.

When a case is decided in either a federal or state court, the judges may apply a statute that has been enacted by the Congress or by the legislature of the state. Or if there is no statute on the subject, the judges have to decide on the basis of past decisions, and whatever they think are the applicable principles—in other words, there is judge-made law. Then, too, the publisher, like the rest of us, should be aware that he may become enmeshed in both criminal and civil suits. He is subject to criminal punishment by jail and fine if he engages in conduct considered so dangerous or so immoral from the general social standpoint that the federal or state governments have made it a crime—for instance, the publishing or selling of obscene literature. On the other hand, if a publisher merely refuses to honor a contract he has made or if he infringes someone else's copyright, it is ordinarily no crime, and he suffers the consequences only in that the person he has injured can bring a civil suit against him to restrain further publication or to collect damages. As in other businesses, the publisher's usual concern with the law arises not because he is involved in a court case, but because he wants to conduct his affairs lawfully so that he will stay out of court.

A FREE PRESS

What a book publisher has for sale is ideas—some lofty, some sordid, some expressed in poetic imagery and some in slang or profanity—but still ideas. So, one fundamental principle that lies beneath the surface, even when it is not right out on top, of all the law affecting publishers is our basic Constitutional guarantee of a free trade in ideas. The theory of our Constitution is, as Justice Holmes put it, "that the best test of truth is the power of the thought to get itself accepted in the competition of the market." One might ask how this idea applies to such literature as some so-called comic books, or books which are obviously misleading or perverted in viewpoint and from which no great truth could possibly be learned. The answer is that once freedom to publish and read is abandoned as a general principle, and once government officials are given the power to decide what is or is not worthwhile to read, no reading matter is safe.

Even so, we do not permit absolute freedom to publish. Words are weapons—they can sting, shock, humiliate, injure a reputation, destroy a business, or incite to violence. So, though the objective of a free press always stands as a touchstone in deciding whether the publisher's rights should be restricted, the law strikes a balance between the interest in freedom and the injuries some types of publications cause, by imposing some limitations on freedom of publication.

PRE-CENSORSHIP

The guarantee of a free press is most strictly observed when it comes to attempts to suppress a book or other writing in advance of publication. Though a publisher may be punished or may have to pay damages because of something he has published, it is ordinarily only in exceptional cases that the government can stop the publication beforehand. Thus, there has never been in the United States an official censorship system as there is in Ireland, where a board must read and approve all books before they can be distributed. The courts have slapped down the sporadic censorship attempts that have been made here, pointing out that the main purpose of the First Amendment guaranty of freedom was to "prevent all such previous restraints upon publications as had been practiced by other governments." One of the most famous Supreme Court decisions in this connection was the case of *Near v. Minnesota.* Under a Minnesota statute the courts there were given the power to issue injunctions against the continued publication of newspapers which habitually published false and scandalous matter. The law carried penalties of fines and imprisonment of the publisher for disobedience of the order. A state's attorney went to court to get an injunction against a political scandal sheet called the *Saturday Press.* It was alleged to be habitually lurid and violently anti-Semitic, in that it charged such things as that "we have Jew gangsters practically ruling Minneapolis. . . . Practically every vendor of vile hooch . . . and embryonic yegg in the Twin Cities is a Jew." Nevertheless, the Supreme Court of the United States held that under the Constitution, the right of expression and criticism must be upheld, and the state could not close down the publication.

This same principle comes into play whether the effort to pre-censor is made by a government official or by a private person who believes a publication will injure him (with one worrisome exception established in some recent right of privacy cases discussed below). As to libel—traditionally, the courts will not prevent publication of a libel. The principle was reiterated a few years ago in connection with one of the litigations arising out of the controversy among doctors and others about the alleged cancer cure, krebiozen. Some doctors connected with the University of Illinois supported the claims for the drug, but the former president of the university, who was highly skeptical of its curative powers, wrote a critical book called *Krebiozen: The Great Cancer Mystery*, for a Boston publisher; he called the drug worthless and its promoters unethical. After the book was set in galleys, a suit was brought to try to prevent the final publication and distribution of the book. Though it certainly seems true that the doctors and supporters of the drug would be tremendously and unfairly damaged if the charges in the book were false, the Massachusetts Court would not prevent its publication. A cure for cancer is a matter of great public interest, so the Court supported the publisher's contention that "the truth or falsity of the [doctors'] . . . claims shall be tried and tested in the crucible of the fullest and freest public discussion"; the Court agreed that no judge should "assume the awful responsibility of stifling such discussion before its birth."

If the book, in fact, made false statements about the drug which destroyed its and the doctors' reputations unjustly, is there no remedy? Yes, despite the principle of a free press, a publisher is responsible for damages for publishing a libel; that is, a false statement which injures the reputation, or as the cases say, holds a person up to shame, ridicule, or obloquy. Indeed, he may even be punished criminally for a libel, though these criminal libel actions are rarely instituted by prosecuting attorneys. Doesn't the fear of punishment or damages cause a publisher to think twice or thrice and perhaps abandon publication, with just about the same result as if a Court issued an order to prevent publication in advance? There is something to this; still it is important that the courts maintain their firm stand against advance restraints on publications even if they contain false and injurious statements for which punishment can be imposed afterwards. As Zechariah Chafee, professor at Harvard Law School, an outstanding expert on communications and the press, has said: "A damage action for libel comes after publication. . . . The public still has a chance to read what is said. . . . One may ask, 'What is the value of letting people read false statements?' That is not quite the whole story. . . . Along with the lies and distortions may go a good deal of truth, which the public ought to read and will never read if the publication is prohibited. . . . If the judge could suppress the whole publication because of his opinion about a few items, he would be a sort of censor. One man's judgment is not to be trusted to determine what people can read."

PUBLISHERS AND CRIMINAL LAWS

Some types of publications are considered sufficiently evil in their effect on society so that anyone publishing them is punished with criminal penalties. From way back, in old English law—which was the mother of American law just as England was the mother country of the United States—seditious, obscene, and blasphemous publications were criminal. Though the states still have laws against blasphemy, religious disputes do not have the importance they had in early England and blasphemy has rarely been prosecuted here. Still, as in early England, and in every other country in the world, we do take measures against seditious publications, that is, publications that threaten the government by advocating its overthrow, or interfere with national safety in wartime by obstructing recruiting, and the like. So that freedom of political criticism will not be unnecessarily impaired, however, the

Supreme Court has evolved the rule that expressions of seditious opinion cannot be punished unless they cause a "clear and present danger" to the body politic.

Obscenity. The only criminal offense for which even the most reputable publishers sometimes find themselves in the clutches of the criminal law is obscenity. The laws punishing publication and distribution of obscene literature, which exist in just about every state of the Union, do not just apply to the "dirty postcard" kind of thing; on occasion they apply as well to works of acknowledged literary merit.

Along with the change in standards of physical modesty over the years has come a drastic change in the law applicable to publications touching on sexual and physical functions; the old orthodox test of obscenity, borrowed from the English, was whether the book has a "tendency . . . to deprave and corrupt those whose minds are open to such immoral influence and into whose hands a publication of this sort may fall" (the so-called Hicklin rule, stated by Lord Chief Justice Cockburn in 1868). However, in 1957, the United States Supreme Court declared, in what has since become known as the Roth case, that the same First Amendment guarantee which called forth some years later the nationally applicable libel rule enunciated in the New York *Times* case (see below), a nationally applicable constitutional test of obscenity. This test has since been elaborated. And in one aspect, perhaps it has been limited—in the case arising out of the prosecution of Ralph Ginzburg for publishing the magazine *Eros* and a book called *The Housewife's Guide to Selective Promiscuity*. Basically, the standard of obscenity is three-pronged. For a work to be condemned as obscene, it must (a) appeal to prurient interest; (b) be patently offensive in the light of contemporary community standards; and (c) be utterly without any "redeeming social importance." Applying this test, the Court has found *Tropic of Cancer* by

Henry Miller and a magazine apparently addressed to homosexuals, etc., not obscene. It has also made clear that no one can be found guilty of obscenity unless the prosecution proves that he not only sold a work, but also had knowledge of the contents of the work which is the subject of the prosecution. And it is equally well established that a work may not be banned as obscene because of its effect (or supposed effect) on children. To permit this type of ban, Mr. Justice Frankfurter said, would be "to burn the house to roast the pig."

As of this writing, the most recent pronouncements on the subject of obscenity by the United States Supreme Court were in the Ginzburg case and the two cases which were argued at the same time. The Court appears to have held—probably without modifying the basic three-pronged test of obscenity—that when works are promoted with "the leer of the sensualist" they may be held obscene, i.e., the Court will judge them in the light of the claims made about them, even though the works in and of themselves might have passed muster.

Though the Supreme Court has upheld the statute making it a crime to send obscene matter through the mail, the Court came to the rescue of freedom of the press when the Postmaster General attempted also to restrict the mailing of matter he thought was "morally improper." The Post Office has the very important power to grant or deny to publishers the privilege of mailing their magazines at the cheap second-class rate; in the case of the magazine *Esquire*, which the Postmaster General tried to bar from the privilege, it was found to be worth a saving of $500,000 a year in mailing costs. The Postmaster General's ground for denying the privilege to *Esquire* was that it contained matters "in that obscure and treacherous borderland zone where the average person hesitates to find them technically obscene, but still may see ample proof that they are morally improper and not for the public welfare and the public good." The Court held that at least as long as a publication was not actually obscene, the Postmaster had no power to consider its merits in determining the rate to which it was entitled. He was not to consult his artistic, literary, or moral predilections, but had to allow the second-class rate to any publication that technically qualified as a newspaper or magazine.

The Post Office at one time got into quite a muddle over its seizure and refusal to deliver to a bookseller an imported copy of Aristophanes' play, *Lysistrata*, the classic satire of Greek women withholding their favors from their husbands to coerce them to end the Peloponnesian Wars. The Post Office backed down and released the book when an appeal from its ruling to the courts was threatened. No doubt Postal officials were correct in foreseeing that no Court would uphold its ban on this centuries-old classic. How severe we should be on the classics was also the question in another Customs case. Customs officials had prevented an amateur archaeologist's receiving from abroad a portfolio of prints showing vases and lamps from many centuries ago decorated with erotic scenes and designs. When the would-be archaeologist went to court, the Court upheld the Customs officials, because of "the hands" into which the portfolio would fall. The Court recognized that similar collections of prints were in circulation and that "most normal men and women in this country would approve ownership of such a publication by a museum, library, college, or other educational institution where its use could be controlled." However, the Court held, the collection should not be put at the disposal of amateurs or unsupervised members of the public. The Court here, though, does not have the last words; the collection might still be admitted under an amendment to the Tariff Act passed in 1930, which gave the Secretary of Treasury discretion to admit a book for individual use, even if obscene, if it "is a classic or of recognized and established literary or scientific merit."

There is no question but that the obscenity situation has turned in the direction of virtually complete tolerance in regard to books and pamphlets written in a serious vein on the subject of sex education. Dr. Marie Stopes' dignified work *Married Love* was barred from the mails for many years, and in 1938 a Boston distributor was convicted and fined $500 for selling an issue of *Life* magazine containing a dignified treatment of a "The Birth of a Baby." Now, however, such books are freely sold and sent through the mails, including the Kinsey Institute's unprecedentedly detailed studies of sex behavior.

Though control of obscenity has been an issue in Anglo-Saxon law for hundreds of years, there is still confusion about just what is our objective in this field of law. And the many concurring and dissenting opinions in each of the leading United States Supreme Court cases makes clear that the line in this field is very much in the process of "becoming" clear but has as yet not achieved intelligible clarity.

LIBEL SUITS FOR DAMAGES AGAINST PUBLISHERS

Like other businessmen, publishers are not as much concerned in their day-to-day operations with the criminal law and with the possibility of the government's prosecuting them as they are with the possibility of private suits against them for damages by individuals who claim to be injured by their publications. Before letting the presses roll, every publisher must consider whether he may end up on the receiving end of a libel suit. Libel is a recognition in the law that he who steals my good name steals what I most hold dear.

A libel is any false statement in writing communicated to another individual—just one other is enough—that injures someone's reputation, or "holds a person up to shame, ridicule, or obloquy." When a book is factual or biographical, it is routine for the publisher to scan every word carefully before publication to determine whether it may give rise to a libel suit. Even in a novel, he must give thought to whether the supposedly fictional characters might be identified with any real persons, and if so, whether the characterization might falsely damage their reputations. Suppose a novel paints an unflattering picture of a character it terms Mr. A, and there are so many similarities between the fictional Mr. A and a real Mr. B, that Mr. B's acquaintances assume it is a thinly disguised characterization of B; B may be able to recover for libel. However, if it is really true that the resemblance is "purely coincidental," the Courts will find a fair way out of the situation. Thus, when an author coined a name for a gangster in a novel and, purely by coincidence, this turned out to be the name of a real and reputable person, the Court held that authors and publishers could not be expected to go through every city directory in the United States to be sure they were not using the names of real persons; and no damages were awarded.

Printing a libel is no light matter for a publisher; once it is out, the amount collected by the injured person in damages can run into large figures. Repeated suits may be brought for the same libel in all the places and against all the various people responsible for distributing it—author, publisher, bookseller. Thus, Representative Martin Sweeney brought seventy-odd different suits for libel against newspapers printing a syndicated column by Drew Pearson, which he claimed libeled him. And the victim of the libel can, in contrast to the victim of an automobile accident or practically any other kind of injury, collect damages without proving any items of actual loss. The Courts will presume that damage in the form of injury to reputation results from a degrading charge. Of course, if the victim can show any actual pecuniary losses resulting from the libel—such as loss of customers if one is in business—he collects this too. Beyond this, if the victim shows that the publisher has either purposely or recklessly published the falsehood, the publisher of the libel will have to pay exemplary or punitive damages as a sort of punishment and warning against heedlessly destroying a reputation. When author Quentin Reynolds brought suit because of libels against him in a newspaper column by Westbrook Pegler, the jury awarded Reynolds $175,000 in exemplary damages.

Libel law also is strict in that it doesn't help the publisher to say "I only *suspect* John Jones may be a thief," or "someone told me so," or "he has that reputation," or even "I *don't* think it's true that John Jones is a thief." Libel law recognizes that people reason, "Where there's smoke there's fire," and that even if the charge is put somewhat obliquely, it casts a doubt and a shadow on reputation.

What sort of statements hold a person up to shame, ridicule, or obloquy and damage his reputation? Sometimes the first step is to determine what charge the publisher was intending to make. Thus, in the Sweeney cases, Drew Pearson had charged that Sweeney was opposed to the appointment of a certain man as a judge because the man "is a Jew and one not born in the United States." Some of the Courts sitting in the many suits brought by Sweeney thought this statement charged Sweeney with being anti-Semitic, and some thought it did not and merely charged him with considering political expediency. There was also disagreement about whether the charge of being anti-Semitic would in any event be damaging to Sweeney's reputation.

In the Quentin Reynolds case the Court had no doubt that the statements made about Reynolds were libelous. The charges complained of and found to be untrue were, the Court thought, obviously injurious to the reputation; and it didn't have to go into any refinements of libel law. Sometimes, however, whether a statement damages the reputation depends on the time and place. In England at one time, it was held damaging to call a person a Papist, and at another time an anti-Papist; in Georgia it has been held defamatory to call a white man a Negro; during World War II, you could sue for libel if you were called a "Jap lover"; and it is now held clearly injurious to a person's reputation in this country to call him a Communist. Sometimes more than the prevailing mores and general circumstances must be considered. A publisher who was putting out a book dealing with extremists among Protestant clergymen had to consider whether a statement that a particular clergyman was a "fundamentalist" might injure his reputation in the particular groups of concern to him—other Protestant clergymen and his parishioners. One wrinkle in libel law is that some courts hold that only statements in special categories (charging commission of a crime, unchastity in a woman, a loathsome disease, or relating to business or professional conduct) will be treated as libelous *per se*, i.e., that only in the case of such charges will the Court presume damages without proof that any actual damages were caused. If an action is brought in these more rigid courts for any other charges injuring the reputation, the complainant must go through the sometimes difficult task of proving his damage in order to recover.

If the charge is true, the publisher is not liable. However, it is the publisher who must show in a libel suit that the statement is true. The complainant need not show it is false; his side of the case is only to prove that the publisher communicated a statement injurious to his reputation. The publisher must worry about the practical difficulties of establishing the truth of whatever he is publishing if he fears a libel suit.

Besides considering whether anyone's reputation would be

injured by the statement, and whether he would want to undertake to prove its truth if challenged, the publisher will consider whether he would have any special excuses or defenses if he were sued for libel. Because of the public interest in freedom of discussion, there are in some circumstances special privileges to print libels, no matter how damaging and untrue.

During the past several years, there have been two major developments in libel law which make the publishers' lot an easier, if not a happier, one. The United States Supreme Court has held that no libel judgment may be obtained against federal officials on the basis of statements made by them in connection with their official duties. And conversely, the Court has held that public officials—state and federal—may not recover for libels directed against them in connection with their official acts unless they can prove that the libelous statements were made "with actual malice." The Court has said that by "actual malice" it means that the person making the libelous statements must be shown to have known that the statements were false or to have recklessly ignored whether they were true or false. This rule that public officials may not sue for libel unless they can prove actual malice was first enunciated by the Supreme Court in an action brought by an Alabama official against several clergymen and the New York *Times*, and is referred to as the "New York *Times* Rule." As of this writing, the full meaning and implication of the rule is being developed in a series of cases involving such questions as who is a public official for the purposes of the rule. In addition, some cases have held that the rule applies to public figures who are not public officials. It has, for example, been successfully invoked against former General Edward Walker who has been in the forefront of public controversy.

A publisher also has a special privilege and defense, again for the sake of public information on matters of public interest, when he publishes a report of official proceedings, such as those of courts or legislatures. Sometimes, of course, it is difficult to see any public interest served by printing accounts of some court proceedings, such as lurid divorce cases reported for sensational purposes. Still, these reports are permitted because, as a general principle, the public has a right to know what is going on in its courts, and this public airing can be a valuable corrective to maladministration of justice.

Some question has been raised in recent years about use of the privilege to report official proceedings in connection with Congressional hearings, and a case on this point was brought against the publisher of the book *Red Channels*, which had allegedly been used to blacklist entertainers in radio and television, quoting statements from Congressional hearings indicating the Communist affiliation or sympathy of various performers named before Congressional committees. Undoubtedly the recital of this testimony in the official committee reports is privileged even if it is false and would be libelous if first printed in an ordinary publication. No doubt, also, the charges can be quoted as part of a fair and true account of the proceedings directed merely at informing the public as to the content of the hearings. John Henry Falck won his case against *Red Channels*. However, the extent of this privilege of quoting official proceedings is still unsettled, not only on the question of motive, as in the *Red Channels* case, but also on the question of what type of proceedings are important enough to be included (what about city council debates, for example, or board of education hearings as opposed to proceedings of Congress or state legislatures which are clearly privileged?). How far the privilege extends will depend on how the Courts come out in their continual weighing and balancing of the harm flowing to individuals from false charges on the one hand and the public interest in freedom of information on the other.

THE RIGHT TO PRIVACY

Libel isn't the publisher's only worry if the book deals with a living person. The publisher must also be concerned with whether he is violating the right to privacy.

While most legal rights can be traced back to the manor courts in feudal England and other early origins, the right of privacy is in effect a creature of the twentieth century. In 1890 Samuel Warren and Louis D. Brandeis, later Justice of the Supreme Court, attracted attention to the need for protecting a person's desire for privacy, with an article in the *Harvard Law Review:* "The press is overstepping in every direction the obvious bounds of propriety and decency. . . . The intensity and complexity of life, attendant upon advancing civilization, have rendered necessary some retreat from the world . . . so that solitude and privacy have become more essential to the individual; but modern enterprise and invention have, through invasions upon his privacy, subjected him to mental pain and distress, far greater than could be inflicted by mere bodily injury." With this article for a starter, many of the fifty states (including New York by statute) by now have recognized the legal existence of a right to privacy—in most states by judicial decision.

Essentially, the right to privacy is, the Courts say, the right "to be let alone—a right directed against the commercial exploitation of one's personality." Contrary to libel law, a publication can invade the right to privacy without being in any way either discreditable or false; for example, by making an unauthorized commercialization of a person's statement or picture for advertising purposes. Quite often, however, right to privacy actions involve the situation with which Warren and Brandeis were more concerned: exposure and publicization of a person's experiences or life-story. Here the Courts, as in the libel cases, constantly are trying to draw a line between the individual's desire to be let alone and the public interest in information. Certainly spot news accounts in the daily press about persons of current interest must be permitted whether or not the subject wants the publicity. How much farther can publishers go, to feed the public's appetite for information or entertainment, at the expense of the individual? In the case of the symphony orchestra leader, Serge Koussevitzky, the conductor tried to stop publication of an unauthorized biography revealing some unflattering details of his career. The biography stuck almost entirely to Koussevitzky's musical career and had little to say about his private life. Though a biography is certainly not in the category of news, the Court believed the career of such a prominent musician was "well within the orbit of public interest and scrutiny." As long as there was no attempt to shock and sensationalize, Koussevitzky's sensitivity would have to yield, the Court concluded, to the public interest in freedom of information.

The Courts' emphasis on the public's right to information as against the right to privacy came out even more in a case involving a former child prodigy, William James Sidis. The *New Yorker* magazine carried a biographical sketch of him titled "Where Are They Now?" Until the *New Yorker* sketch, Sidis had purposely and painstakingly managed to avoid public attention for some twenty years. Though the Court recognized that the article was "a ruthless exposure of a once public character, who has since sought and has now been deprived of the seclusion of private life," it believed the subsequent history of a child prodigy was "a matter of public concern." Though it would draw the line at intimate and shocking revelations, unwarranted by the public's desire for information, the Court would tolerate some public curiosity about the private lives of public figures.

But, suppose the book is not straight biography, but an account that has been livened up by the author's imagination? The "case of the one red rose" concerned an aviator, killed in action in the war, who had willed that one rose should be sent every week to a woman he had admired from a distance. After the newspapers carried news of this bequest, a publisher printed an article playing up the romantic angle, the aviator's background, the woman's present situation as a happily married woman, and her surprise at the bequest. She sued the publisher for violation of her right to privacy. The Court sympathized with her embarrassment from the article and held she had a right to recover against the publisher if she could show the article was "a sensationalized version of facts embellished with matters drawn from the author's imagination." Generally, if the account seems dramatized and embroidered by fiction rather than a straight factual narrative, the courts are inclined to say the publisher is engaged in a commercial proposition violating the right of privacy. Of course, every book published is a commercial venture—but the courts emphasize its informative value to the public rather than its profitable angle to the publisher when it concerns a public or in some way newsworthy person and is written in a factual style. It is the style and approach that count; the courts do not decide in a privacy case whether the statements are in fact true or false, as they do in libel cases, but rather whether the tone and purpose of the work is "commercialized" and "fictionalized" as opposed to factual and informative.

Judges often also seem influenced to protect a person's right to privacy, even though he has played a newsworthy role, if they feel he has been unnecessarily exposed to hardship by the publication. This was not so in the Sidis case, but it often is. Thus, when a radio program reenacting true crime stories exposed a woman's past criminal conduct after she had been rehabilitated and had gained a reputation for respectability, she won a privacy action—not because, as in libel, the account was untrue, but because it was held an unnecessary violation of her privacy. Indeed, when a radio program reenacted a hold-up that had taken place some time before, and the victim, rather than the criminal, complained of her distress about the broadcast, she too recovered because her "right to be let alone was violated."

There is one situation where the name of a real person can be used fairly freely even in a book that is entirely fiction, and that is if it merely is used for local color. For instance, Lou Stillman, who is known for conducting a gymnasium in New York for the training of boxers and prizefighters, recently sued for violation of privacy because a fictional character in a non-documentary film spoke of going to "Stillman's Gym" and getting a punch-drunk fighter. The Court held there could be no recovery for such an isolated and incidental use of a name, which the author was not trying to capitalize on or exploit. This seems the right decision; and it would be unfortunate for the Courts to try to prevent references to real persons who serve only in effect as landmarks.

Occasionally there is a real person with personality and characteristics—or eccentricities, depending on your point of view—that make him interesting, though he has not accomplished anything special or become so widely known as to rise to that "indefinable" position of a public figure. When one author picked such a neighborhood character for a central figure in a novel, describing her in terms easily identifiable to her neighbors, the Court held the author had no license so to use her character and personality and awarded damages for violation of her right to privacy.

In 1966, privacy cases of great importance were confronting important courts. The great baseball pitcher Warren Spahn obtained an injunction and damages in New York against an author and publisher who had put out what he claimed was a "fictionalized"—although not unflattering—biography about him. He had refused to be interviewed in connection with the book, and, understandably, it contained some mistakes as well as, according to the lower New York courts, imaginary dialogue and surmises about his innermost thoughts and feelings. Concerned with the impact of the Spahn decision on freedom to publish, such organizations as the Authors' League of America and the Society of Magazine Writers joined the defendants in their appeal to New York's highest court—the Court of Appeals—alleging that the lower court's decision was an unconstitutional violation of freedom of the press.

In 1967, the New York Court of Appeals affirmed the decision in the Spahn case, and as of early 1967 an appeal was pending to the United States Supreme Court. Meanwhile, however, that Court has decided *The Desperate Hours* case on an appeal by *Life* Magazine from a decision of the New York Court of Appeals, holding that a picture story in *Life* presented the plaintiff in the case and his family as the true life bases of the play *The Desperate Hours.*

The Court reversed the injunction granted by the New York courts on the ground that only such violations of the right of privacy could be enjoined as were published with knowledge of their falsity or in reckless disregard of whether they were true or false, and the New York courts have not made a finding in this regard. The rationale of the decision, however, as the dissenters pointed out, is very threatening to our free press guarantees.

Until now, it has always been thought that there was a constitutional right to lie—as well as to speak the truth—subject, of course, to the law of libel. And while we all agree that we prefer the truth, we must be ever mindful that truth is elusive. One man may honestly believe what others are sure is false and if he gives it expression he may be unable to satisfy judge and/or jury that he really believed it, especially if he represents an unpopular or even hated point of view.

It is to be hoped that in further cases, the Supreme Court will delineate more clearly and more narrowly exactly what is comprised within a right of privacy that can be constitutionally made the basis of an injunction (and damages) against speech and the press. [In May 1967 the Supreme Court vacated the New York judgment for Spahn and remanded the case.—*Ed.*]

PUBLISHERS' RIGHTS

Copyright. Here we come to an old right, rather than a new one like the right to privacy, a right that descended to us from England where it was established before this country was founded. This is a right *of* authors and publishers rather than a right *against* them, a right protecting creative literary work —in a word, the right to copy. The major copyright protection in this country is provided by the Federal Copyright Act. No major revision of this Act has taken place since 1909, but after a series of intensive studies and meetings, the United States Copyright Office prepared a major revision bill which, as of early 1967, was pending before Congress. Without this statute the author would be entitled to the fruits of his creation only so long as he kept it to himself; once he exposed his creation to the public anyone could help himself.

The need for copyright protection was recognized by the U.S. Constitution itself, at the very founding of our government. The Constitution expressly gives Congress the power under which it enacted the copyright statute for the protection of literary and artistic works, as well as the patent laws which give similar protection to inventors. The Constitution declares: "The Congress shall have power . . . To promote the progress of Science and Useful Arts by securing for limited times to authors and inventors the exclusive right to their respective Writings and Discoveries." The purpose of giving this right to authors, one of the Congressional committees working on the copyright law later explained, was "not primarily for the benefit of the author but primarily for the benefit of the public . . . the policy is believed to be for the benefit of the great body of people, in that it will stimulate writing and inventions by giving some bonus to authors."

The copyright law rewards literary creation in this way: If the author or publisher gets a valid copyright on a book, he alone has the right to make copies, and he is protected against anyone else's copying the book without his permission, for a period of twenty-eight years. The copyright can be renewed for another twenty-eight years, but that is all. Why should not the creator of the work, or his heirs, or the publisher have the right to own a copyright for a longer period? The argument has been that in copyright, as in all other phases of the law of publishing we have been discussing, there is a public interest to balance against the individual's right and that the public interest is in the free use of literary and artistic creations. It was supposed to be sufficient encouragement to creation and publication of new creative works, if the author and his original publisher profited from monopolizing the creation for fifty-six years; after the fifty-six years the public was supposed to benefit from the opportunity for all publishers to reprint the book, without obligation to the original creator or publisher. The facts by and large demonstrate that this is not so, and the pending revision bill gives authors a better break and provides for a period of protection for the life of the author plus fifty years—which is the period of protection in most Western European countries.

The mechanics of getting a copyright are simply to publish

a proper notice of copyright at the place in the book called for by the Copyright Act. There is also a requirement that the title of the book and the name of the copyright owner be registered in the Copyright Office at the Library of Congress in Washington with the deposit of two copies of the book and the payment of a small fee. This, though, is just a mechanical procedure, and is not essential to the obtaining of a valid copyright. Failure to register will prevent suits for copyright infringement being entertained by the Court. But belated registration (even after years have gone by) cures the defect if the work was published with the proper copyright notice in the first place, and successful suit can be brought against infringements taking place thereafter. The Copyright Office does not ordinarily consider whether the person is entitled to the copyright before registering it. It is when one publisher or author sues another for copyright infringement that the question of whether the work is original and therefore validly copyrighted, or whether it is merely a product of copying, is decided by the courts.

Suppose Book A is published and copyrighted, and shortly thereafter Book B, which has many similarities to Book A, is put out by another publisher. Similarity between two books does not by itself show the second one is not original and was copied from the first and infringes its copyright. As long as each author has independently gotten the same ideas, no matter how alike they are, each is entitled to copyright. It is the individual act of creation which is entitled to protection, even though the author's mind may work in exactly the same groove as someone else's. As long as it is purely coincidental that two minds have but a single thought and manner of expression, the book that is the work of each is validly copyrighted.

One case, for example, involved an author who had written a novel called *Woman of Destiny* about a woman becoming

Vice-President of the United States, and on the death of the President succeeding to the Presidency. About ten years after *Woman of Destiny* was published and copyrighted, someone else came out with a novel on the same theme. The author of the first book did not recover. The judge decided that the similarities were "those which would normally occur in two stories dealing with a woman becoming President of the United States. . . . Similarity can, of course, occur from copying, but it may also occur by reason of the subject matter and setting with which both stories deal . . . it seems more reasonable that the many similarities that do occur are those which are almost compelled by political imperatives rather than to conclude . . . that they are the result of either reading or copying the story of the plaintiff." It is interesting that a jury in another case involving precisely the same question went the other way.

The Court may, of course, use other evidence besides the similarities and dissimilarities in the two books to determine whether the second has copied from the first. The second author may submit evidence that he never saw the first book and that he got his ideas from something that happened to him, or that he had been collecting notes for his book for years—in other words, circumstances about his composition showing he either didn't even have access to the first book, or at least didn't use it. On the other hand, the author of the first book, trying to prove that the second was in part copied from his, may show that the second author had a copy of his book, or had access to his manuscript, that the second author had no knowledge of the subject of the book which would have enabled him to write it without copying the first, and so on.

But even on the question of the right to copy during the copyright period, there is a play of conflicting interests. For the sake of the development of our literature and culture, we make some exceptions to copyright protection, and allow authors to some extent to build on the works of their predecessors, even while they are copyrighted. Thus, it is a standard expression in copyright law that ideas are free and that there can be no ownership of mere ideas. Even if the man who wrote the second book about a woman President got the idea of writing a novel on this theme from reading the first book, and even if this could in some way be proved, as long as he then developed this theme on his own, it would not be a case of copyright infringement. The locale, the theme, the general idea for a character—all these may be borrowed; it is only their development and the form of expression of ideas that cannot be. In one case, the author of a copyrighted article showing the Freudian concepts in the novels of Oliver Wendell Holmes sued the publisher of a later volume called *The Psychiatric Novels of Oliver Wendell Holmes* which developed the same theme. The Court held that the first author could not recover, though the second author used the same theme as she had, and even had relied on some of the same material. It would, of course, be very difficult for the first author to prove that ideas of this sort had been derived from his book rather than from the second author's own observations and speculations. In any event the Court did not need to pursue the question of proof, because "copyright does not protect mere ideas."

Because of this freedom of ideas, the author using historical material may find there is little protection for the fruit of the hours he spends in research. Thus, the author of a copyrighted book called *Wyatt Earp, Frontier Marshal,* which was a biographical narrative about a U.S. marshal of old Western days, sued for copyright infringement when a radio program on Wyatt Earp was produced. The Court agreed that the radio program used the same "sequence of claimed historical events and in a few instances the content of the dialogue" of the book. Nevertheless, the author lost the case, because, the Court said, the radio program "used neither the word order nor the expression or literary style of the copyrighted book . . . historical facts and events in themselves are in the public domain and are not entitled to copyright protection." In effect, the Court said, those who write history are adding to that storehouse of knowledge to which all may help themselves provided they don't steal the actual expression of the ideas set forth. The publisher or author of the first book must be able to show his work was used for a great deal more than general inspiration or background material to make out a case of copyright infringement.

Though authors and publishers frequently lose suits they bring for copyright infringement even when they think the later work is a "dead steal" from theirs, this doesn't mean that the first author never wins; indeed, in one case of semi-news stories, the author of the first won a suit for copyright infringement. After a series of copyrighted articles on the then-current submarine warfare had appeared in a newspaper, a similar series was carried in another. Certainly, the Court said, the facts of the news about submarine warfare were not protected by the copyright nor subject to exclusive use by anyone. Nevertheless, the later series of articles was held to infringe the copyright on the first series, because the second author had copied some of the "felicity of wording and phrasing, well calculated to seize and hold the interest of the reader" from the first series.

Moreover, the courts have begun to draw distinctions based on the reasons why copyrighted works are reproduced without permission. Thus, although news media liberally copied Martin Luther King's great speech arising out of the integration march on Washington, that was allowable because it was news. But copyright infringement was found when a record company put out its own recording of the speech without Dr. King's permission—that was not a news use. Similar reasoning is to be found in some of the cases involving speeches given by Admiral Rickover.

This is but one instance of the cutting down into the protection a copyright affords its owner, under the principle called "fair use." "Fair use" is the one complete exception to the rule against copying copyrighted material. The very manner of expression, which ordinarily is protected, can be copied; indeed, a verbatim copy can be used if the copying is appropriately limited and done for what the Courts determine is a legally approved purpose: a "fair use." Another "fair use," for instance, is scientific advancement or dissemination of scientific knowledge. Thus, a copyrighted scientific work showing the development, say, of atomic bombs, could be quoted at length in another scientific work or even in a popularized layman's account of how to make air-raid shelters. This doesn't mean that scientific material is fair game for copyists; it is the purpose that counts in "fair use." When a copyrighted scientific treatise on the throat was quoted in cigarette advertising, the Court held the advertiser could not shelter himself behind the doctrine of "fair use" of scientific works, and he had to pay damages for infringement to the publisher of the treatise.

There are a number of other literary or artistic purposes that have been held "fair use." However, the Courts have held that burlesque and satire is not a "fair use," where the parody uses too much of the original. Thus, though the purpose may be a "fair use," this does not mean that the copyrighted material can be used to an unlimited extent.

In the final analysis, the best all-round test of "fair use" which the writers have found is whether the alleged infringement could be used as a substitute in whole or in part for the original work. If so (and leaving aside for the moment questions of access), the chances are that the use is not "fair."

The protection against copying that a publisher secures by

copyrighting his book extends to use of it in various forms and versions. A novel or biography cannot be dramatized, whether for the theater, movies, radio, or TV, without the consent of the copyright owner, and on the other hand, it is a violation of copyright to convert a work published as a drama into a novel or other nondramatic form. If the author or publisher can show the book has been copied to an extent the Courts will agree fits that vague term "a substantial taking" —and of something more than mere "ideas"—it doesn't matter that the book has been put into another form or version. Indeed, copying a book into one of the other media is one of the most fertile grounds for infringement suits. It is true the author or publisher of the original book is often denied recovery, as in the Wyatt Earp case mentioned earlier, because there is only a similarity of ideas between it and the later work. On the other hand, there have been some notable recoveries by the first author, such as the case of a play called *White Cargo,* which was held an infringement of a novel called *Hell's Playground.* The judge pointed out: "A play may fairly be subject to the charge of piracy, if a substantial number of its incidents, scenes, and episodes are, in detail, arrangement, and combination, so nearly identical with those to be found in a book to which the author had access, as to exclude all reasonable possibility of chance coincidence." Applying this to the author of *White Cargo,* the judge said: "Without access to the book, I think it inexplicable that he should have incorporated into his play such a list of similar and parallel incidents, episodes, and scenes. In addition, many of them are presented in language that is hardly more than a paraphrase of the text of *Hell's Playground.*"

International Copyright. Besides translation into other forms, the copyright gives its owner the exclusive right to publish translations into other languages for the life of the copyright.

This brings up the question of whether a publisher copyrighting a book here will be protected against its being copied and published without his permission in foreign countries. He is given this protection by certain international agreements.

A most important and long-established treaty on copyright, which has been signed by a number of nations other than the United States, was originally drafted at Berne, Switzerland, and is known as the Berne Convention. It provides in effect for each of the various countries that agree to it to give copyright protection to the books published in the other signatory countries. It has been common and sensible practice for United States publishers, simultaneously with publication of a book in the United States, to put at least a token quantity of the same book on sale in one of the countries that is a member of the Berne Convention, such as Canada or Great Britain. This usually protects the book in all other Berne Convention countries. The United States has entered into treaties with some other nations, one at a time, under which our authors and publishers will get copyright protection in the other country with reciprocal protection in the United States for the authors and publishers of that country.

In 1953, after many years of international consultation, a new treaty on copyright called the Universal Copyright Convention was signed by representatives of forty-odd countries outside the Communist sphere, to enable authors and publishers to secure better copyright protection in a greater number of countries with fewer technical difficulties. The United States is a signatory to this convention, which provides in effect that an author or publisher of any country signing and ratifying the treaty will get copyright protection in all the other signatory countries merely by printing a simple copyright notice specified in the treaty in his book. As this treaty has been ratified by an increasing number of governments, it has greatly improved the copyright situation abroad for American authors and publishers. Up to now, they have had to go through a rather complicated procedure to get protection in some foreign countries, and in a few are unable to get any protection for their work.

If, as is to be devoutly wished, a copyright revision bill goes through, authors, publishers, and the public in general will benefit greatly in many ways worked out on the basis of the distinguished Copyright Office studies.

UNFAIR COMPETITION

A publisher has one possible source of protection when all else fails, and that is the protection the courts afford against "unfair competition." "Unfair competition" is a loose and flexible principle of law under which the courts try to remedy situations that offend current business mores and ethics when one businessman—in any business, not just publishing—seems to be unfairly profiting from or exploiting his competitor's investment or work, or in some other way unfairly undercutting him. The law of "unfair competition" may protect a publisher when the law of copyright does not. This issue frequently comes up in the publishing field in connection with titles. The title of a book is not included in its copyright. As far as copyright is concerned, anyone can use the title for another book or any other type of work. But if the second publisher uses a title that has become associated in the public mind with the previous work, he may come up against the law of unfair competition, and the first publisher may recover damages. The second publisher may be unfairly trading on the reputation, good will, and advertising investment of the first.

General principles of fair dealing and business ethics can also come up if someone comes to a publisher with an idea for a series of books or a promotion plan, or for some publication technique—in other words, with something to sell other than a manuscript. Thus, occasionally, a publisher will put out an anthology, only to have someone claim that he had originally suggested this collection to the publisher and that the publisher used his idea without paying for it. There are always two sides to such a story: the complainant's that the publisher is unfairly profiting from his ideas, and the publisher's, usually that he got the idea in complete independence of the alleged suggestion and that therefore there is nothing he should pay for. The result here will be a matter of evidence; the verdict will depend on how clearly the complainant can show his suggestion was in fact followed and that there was an understanding between him and the publisher in their conversations that he would be paid if his idea was used.

Contracts. How much a book is protected against use by others by the law of copyright and the law of unfair competition affects the terms of the contracts publishers make with their authors, as well as those they make to sell movie rights and other uses of the book. For the law in these fields determines how exclusively the author and the publisher will have the right to profit from the book, and how far it can be used by movie companies or others without contracting and paying for its use. For instance, a publisher of a how-to-do-it book will know that, despite his copyright, other publishers can take the general idea and bring out a similar book on how-to-do the same thing. This possibility will of course affect the original publisher's prospective profits and therefore the terms he will offer the author. Again, a movie producer will know that, despite copyright, he can without an agreement base a movie on the same general theme as a book. But he will also know that he could not use the title to a popular and advertised book without purchasing this right from the publisher or author, unless he wants to risk a suit for unfair competition. The law of copyright and unfair competition makes a real difference in dollars and cents.

FOR FURTHER READING

Ernst, Morris L., and Alan U. Schwartz. Censorship. New York, Macmillan, 1964.

—— Privacy. New York, Macmillan, 1962.

Kaplan, Benjamin and Ralph S. Brown Jr. Cases on Copyright. Brooklyn, The Foundation Press, 1960.

Nicholson, Margaret. A Manual of Copyright Practice, for Writers, Publishers and Agents. 2d ed.; rev. New York, Oxford University Press, 1956.

Nimmer, Melville B. Copyright Law and Practice. New York, Bender, 1963.

Pilpel, Harriet F., and Morton D. Goldberg. A Copyright Guide. 3d ed. New York, Bowker, 1966.

Pilpel, Harriet, and Theodore Zavin. Rights and Writers. New York, Dutton, 1960.

Wittenberg, Philip. The Law of Literary Property. rev. ed. Boston, The Writer, 1964.

13

THE DISTRIBUTION OF AMERICAN BOOKS ABROAD

By KYRILL SCHABERT

ASSISTANT MANAGING DIRECTOR,
AMERICAN BOOK PUBLISHERS COUNCIL

❋

SINCE 1957, when Mr. Jennison wrote the chapter on the distribution of American books abroad in the first edition of this volume, the world of books has undergone a revolutionary change. The rapid growth in world population, coupled with the emergence of new and independent nations in Africa and Asia, the establishment of new and pressing educational programs, and the firm establishment of English as the second language have all contributed to an upsurge in the demand for American books abroad that has surpassed Mr. Jennison's optimistic prediction of less than ten years ago.

In 1955 the officially reported import volume of books amounted to $31 million. This meant that the actual volume was nearer to $45 million, because the officially reported figures do not include shipments under $100 in value, which in the aggregate are a sizable factor in the export of books. Ten years later, in 1965, book exports, as reported by the Bureau of Census of the United States Department of Commerce, amounted to over $99 million which, if we allow again for the less-than-bulk shipments not reported, will bring the true figure for that year closer to $140 million, or more than three times the 1955 volume. The most recent figures for the first quarter of 1966 show a continuation of this trend with an increase of over 32 percent over the like period of the previous year, and with the continuation of the boom in book exports, the attainment of new record figures for 1966 becomes a certainty. Where the dollar volume of exported books represented a mere 7 percent of the total United States book production in 1957, the 1965 percentage exceeded 14 percent.

Today the export of American books accounts for over one quarter of the total volume of books exported by the fourteen major book producing countries. Especially significant is the fact that between 1962 and 1964, when the world export value of books rose from $26 million to $34 million, American publishers managed to record remarkable increases in their share of total exports to countries where neither Great Britain nor the United States have exclusive selling rights. The following table shows to what extent American publishers improved their export position in some of the countries where American books are sold in competition with books from the United Kingdom.

Country		*Total Million $*	*U.S. Percent of Total*	*U.K. Percent of Total*
Argentina	1962	1.4	16	4.3
	1964	2.5	47	5.3
Chile	1962	.7	55	3.1
	1964	.9	70	5.3
Colombia	1962	.5	42	8.0
	1964	.7	61	1.4
Peru	1962	.3	62	7.7
	1964	.5	80	4.9
Italy	1962	5.7	18	10.5
	1964	7.7	34	4.9
Sweden	1962	.15	4	13.2
	1964	.73	14	12.4

Country		*Total Million $*	*U.S. Percent of Total*	*U.K. Percent of Total*
Iran	1962	.18	46	16.3
	1964	.61	57	18.9
Lebanon	1962	.99	12	15.6
	1964	1.40	23	12.1
South Africa	1962	3.60	13	67.5
	1964	8.00	35	57.9
Liberia	1962	.15	67	13.3
	1964	.31	80	5.4
Japan	1962	3.80	45	16.4
	1964	8.10	64	10.7

The top ten importers of American books based on 1964 import figures for these countries are as follows:

Country	*Dollar Volume*
Canada	$37,000,000
United Kingdom	13,319,000
Australia	6,062,000
Japan	5,402,000
Brazil	3,391,000
South Africa	2,846,000
Italy	2,715,000
Philippines	2,233,000
Mexico	1,917,000
India	1,810,000

It is also of worthy of note that in the first quarter of 1966 books represented the major category of all exports from the United States, amounting to 43 percent.

HOW BOOK EXPORT VOLUME IS DIVIDED UP

Text, technical, medical, scientific, scholarly, and reference books account for more than 60 percent of the total volume of books exported. This estimate does not include editions that a number of larger firms today manufacture abroad in order to make cheaper texts available to students in countries where, because of the relatively high price of American books, they would be out of reach of the students' pocketbooks.

As a rule the American textbook publisher does not license English language editions to a foreign publisher, preferring to control selling rights himself. He is more likely to make an agreement with a publisher abroad for the translation of a work, and where the demand for a foreign language edition of a textbook is sufficiently large, as it might be in Spanish, he will assume the translation and the distribution instead of making such an arrangement with a foreign publisher.

While roughly 60 percent of yearly book exports is derived from the sale of textbooks, the remaining 40 percent consists of exports of hardbound trade books and paperbacks. Trade books, that is fiction, nonfiction, and art books, are not a large factor in the export volume. Hardbound editions in this category are usually too high priced to be in great demand abroad. The foreign publication rights for works of this nature are generally separately concluded between the author or his agent with a British publisher, with the result that the American edition of the book may not be sold anywhere except in open market territories, that is, countries not included in what is known to be the "British publishers' traditional market," which with a few exceptions, includes all the countries that constituted the British Commonwealth and empire as of January 1, 1947. For practical purposes this reduces the sales territories for the U.S. edition to the nonexclusive, non-English–speaking countries, where American books have to sell in competition with the considerably lower-priced British editions.

Although U.S. paperbound books are handicapped by the same restrictions as far as sales territory are concerned, and also must compete with the lower-priced British paperbacks, their export has risen sharply in these open-market territories. Modern merchandizing techniques and eye-catching cover designs, added to the American publishers' ability to supply titles not available in the British paperback editions, enabled these publishers to maintain themselves against the stiff British competition. Unfortunately, unauthorized infiltration into territories exclusively reserved to British books has led to complaints that American selling methods are overly aggressive and that territorial rights are often willfully ignored. In defense of American paperback publishers, it must be stated that even the most meticulous observance of territorial rights cannot always prevent their violation, as there are too many roundabout ways by which books can be illegally imported without the knowledge of the offending imprint.

Although the amounts derived from the sales of territorial and translation rights are not included in the export figures, and are therefore omitted from this discussion, such sales are an important part of the literary commercial traffic. The sale of these rights is usually negotiated by the author or by his literary agent, and American publishers seldom participate in the proceeds.

EXPORT MECHANISMS AND REQUIREMENTS

Depending on the firm's size and the potential export value of its books, there are basically three avenues by which an American publisher will bring his books to the foreign market. The large firms maintain their own export divisions or international sales departments. Such a division is staffed by an export manager and his assistants, who either maintain a direct contact with their foreign accounts or effect their distribution throughout the world, not only to call on the retail and wholesale booksellers in foreign lands, but also to confer with agents and government officials.

Because of the highly intricate nature of book exports requiring highly trained and specialized people, most medium-sized publishers prefer to handle their foreign sales through companies specializing in the export of books. There are three large firms in the United States representing the majority of publishers on a commission basis. A number of university presses are grouped together in a separate organization for the sale of the more scholarly university press books in foreign countries.

Lastly, some of the domestic jobbers supply the foreign markets with American books; a not inconsiderable portion of book exports is derived from unsolicited orders received by these jobbers or by the publisher direct.

Ideally, the export manager should bring to his task an extraordinary combination of talents. In the first place he must be conversant with the basic facets of publishing economics. He must know American sales techniques and merchandizing methods and the extent to which they can be applied abroad. He must have a knowledge of the business climate of each country, its currency restrictions and customs regulations. He must be aware of national idiosyncracies and able to distinguish between the sincere promoter of his books and the literary mountebank. The importance of textbook sales requires a familiarity of educational curricula, especially in the developing countries, and the ability to recommend to the editors of his firm how a text may be adapted to conform to a particular country's teaching requirements. He should have something of the diplomat in his makeup in order to ingratiate himself with foreigners, and he must know the ways of a skillful politician to make an idea acceptable to his supervisors.

The commonly held notion that linguistic excellence is one of the prime prerequisites to the job dates back to the time before English became, for most countries, the second language. The ability to address a foreign customer in his native tongue is certainly appreciated; more essential than anything is the understanding to appraise the needs of the foreign country and the ability to create a sales organization to handle the many intricate details connected with the export of books.

Only a few of the major publishing houses maintain regional offices where the foreign buyer can visit display rooms. In most cases the buyer must rely on the information contained in the catalogues from U.S. publishers although sometimes publishers' representatives will call to show them samples of jackets and discuss the contents in the same manner as they do in the home market. Trade journals and reference works carrying advance information—for example, *Publishers' Weekly*, the Publishers Trade List Annual, the *Library Journal*, Books in Print, and Wilson's Cumulative Book Index—are air-mailed to the subscriber, but even with the most modern communication, the necessary information is slow in reaching the bookseller abroad.

In order to give the foreign book trade an opportunity to have a preview of books published by foreign publishers and negotiate for the acquisition of translation rights, book fairs have become increasingly popular. The most famous, largest, and most international is the Frankfurt (West Germany) Book Fair, which in 1966 played host to 2,500 publishers from 51 nations.

UNITED STATES GOVERNMENT BOOK PROGRAMS

Like other major governments, that of the United States encourages book exports and recognizes that books promote an understanding abroad of the nation's character and general outlook. Moreover, with world peace and long-range trade benefits in view, American policy emphasizes help to the development of indigenous publishing in "new" and emerging countries.

Since 1962, book industry leaders have taken part in the State Department's Government Advisory Committee on International Book Programs, a consultative and coordinating group. Government activities in international book programs are many. Two of the principal agencies under which these activities fall are the U.S. Information Agency and the Agency for International Development.

The USIA for many years has purchased U.S. books for the U.S. Information Service libraries abroad, and has bought even more to distribute to foreign libraries and educational centers —often on a pilot basis to encourage direct purchase in the future. It underwrites some books especially intended to present American policies or describe the United States—an activity that has been debated. It puts the major part of its book funds, however, into translated editions published abroad, including low-cost paperbacks and simplified editions. This may involve help in the purchase of rights from the original U.S. publishers, and assistance in securing translators.

AID's use of books abroad includes: extensive backing for translation and publication locally and in local languages to aid in technical development and education; help in producing and distributing low-cost textbooks in the countries assisted; the provision of information about books in specific, crucial subject areas; and use of a special fund for demonstration programs in book distribution and library development abroad.

At the same time, the Franklin Book Programs, a cooperative, quasi-public effort, with locally managed offices in many countries, has been strengthening local book industries, with U.S. advice.

The thrust of these programs and others not mentioned here is both to serve the country's broad national interest and to increase the international flow of books and scholarship, which is in the interest of all the countries involved. In the latter connection, a long step forward was made in 1966 when the United States revised its laws so as to take part in the UNESCO treaty known as the Florence Agreement on the Free Exchange of Educational, Scientific, and Cultural Materials. By this agreement, tariff and customs barriers to books and scientific materials are virtually wiped out among the countries signing.

Important and stimulating as the government programs are, they represent a minor fraction of U.S. book trade abroad. Leonard H. Marks, director of the USIA, said in 1966 that "as a result of the efforts of American publishers, the export of books today is estimated at 30 to 50 times the number sent abroad by government agencies."

REFERENCES AND FURTHER READING

Bogsch, Arpad. The Law of Copyright Under the Universal Convention. New York, Bowker, 1964.

Books and Libraries in the Americas. English and Spanish. Washington, Pan American Union, 1963.

Cassell's Directory of Publishing; Great Britain, The Commonwealth, etc. 4th ed.; rev. New York, International Publications Service, 1966.

International Literary Market Place. Annual (Addresses). New York, Bowker.

Publishers' World. Annual (Export-import reference data). New York, Bowker.

UNESCO. Books for the Developing Countries: Asia, Africa. New York, International Documents Service, Columbia University Press.

UNESCO. International Directory of Educational Publishers. New York, International Documents Service, Columbia University Press.

SECTION V

SPECIAL AREAS OF PUBLISHING

14

THE CHILDREN'S BOOK DEPARTMENT

By JEAN KARL

VICE-PRESIDENT, CHILDREN'S BOOKS,
ATHENEUM PUBLISHERS, INC.

PEOPLE who deal with children's books are providing materials for one of the most eager and responsive audiences available to book publishers. In spite of everything that has been said or written about children's reading problems, the fact remains that there is a vast number of reading children. And there is another great number of younger children who cannot read but who continually plead, "read me a story." These children are hungry for books and consume them at a great rate, first of all because books give pleasure, but also because they give a wider view than the children might otherwise get of the many worlds they live in—themselves, their families, their schools, their country, the world, and the universe.

Children who read are eager to explore in all areas, often one area at a time, with an intensity that takes them, for example, first through all the "horse books" they can find, then through all the "electricity books," then through all the science fiction, and so on. The patterns of interest vary as much as children themselves vary. And because their demands are so different, only books, which can be handled on an individual basis, can really meet the needs of all of them.

THE SCOPE OF CHILDREN'S LITERATURE

To serve these readers, books must be published in all corners of interest. People who work with children's books find themselves dealing with picture books, "young novels," and books of nonfiction that take them into any area on which anything is known at all. Once there were written and unwritten limitations on what kinds of information were suitable for and acceptable to children. Today there are almost none.

To work with children's books is to work with important ideas. One author of fiction books for "middle age" children (approximately eight to twelve) says that her friends ask smugly, "When, now that you have written so many children's books, are you going to settle down and write an adult book?" She says she thinks about it sometimes, but always decides finally that she can say more in a children's book. Children's fiction can be profound. At its best it deals with some of the deepest truths of human experience and human relationships; true, those within the grasp of children, but nonetheless real and valid, too, for adults.

In nonfiction the same is true. Nonfiction authors, particularly in science, agree that unless they are writing for college students in their field, children understand more of what they have to say than adults do.

Artists feel that the children's book is one of the few areas left free for exploration and experimentation in the graphic arts.

Children's books are the universe and all that is in it. Children's books are knowledge, challenge, and delight. And they will exist and increase as long as children exist and man's knowledge and understanding expand.

STRUCTURE OF THE DEPARTMENT

The job of producing and distributing children's books is not one to be taken lightly, nor is it one always to be accomplished between 9 and 5, Monday through Friday. Be forewarned. What was once, at least in the memory of some, a gentle, calm, easygoing center of work, has in the last decade or two become a hectic hive of productivity, with a minimum number of workers producing a maximum amount of material. And this is work to which all involved must give all of themselves, not just a part. It demands everything one can give, tiring, but satisfying to those willing to be involved.

The departments or individual people, whichever the case may be, needed to accomplish the task are roughly: editorial; copy editing, and proofreading; production and design, including art direction; publicity, promotion, and advertising; and sales. In other words, the operations needed to produce children's books duplicate all of the operations a publishing house normally has.

Once it was customary for a children's book department to be almost an autonomous entity, including within itself all of the people involved with children's books, except sales. The department was small, and sometimes a children's editor and her secretary did everything there was to be done. This is still almost true in some places. In small houses the children's editor may still be head of a relatively small department that handles everything but sales. In very large houses, too, the children's book department may be a single entity, with many people to carry out the various functions, all coordinated by the children's editor or a department manager. At the other extreme are large companies where each operation is completely separate. The children's editorial department supervises most of the work done on children's books; it selects the books and oversees their progress. But copy editing and proofreading, production, design, publicity, promotion, and sales are all handled in separate departments that handle these functions for the entire company. They work with the children's book department and are subject to varying degrees of control by it.

EDITOR, AUTHOR, AND MANUSCRIPT

In between these two extremes are many other combinations. In general, editorial, proofreading, copy editing, art direction, and design are the functions most likely—though not always—to form the core of the department. In many cases these are joined by one or several people doing publicity and promotion, especially school and library promotion. Whatever the local structure of a publishing house is, however, the jobs tend to be about the same. The work that must be accomplished does not vary greatly.

In all but a few houses, the children's editor heads the children's book department, supervises whatever it consists of, and tries to achieve the very best possible results from the departments that are not directly under her control. In the few houses where the editor herself (the feminine is used because women tend to predominate, though more and more men are entering the field) does not manage the department, a department manager or supervisor coordinates the efforts of the editor or editors, the other divisions in the department, and the functions not carried out in the department itself.

Essentially the editor in most houses is responsible for securing and accepting manuscripts, working with authors, deciding upon illustrators (with or without the help of an art director), determining overall formats for books (with or without the help of a designer), working with illustrators, dealing to some extent at least with publicity and promotion, having something to say about advertising, and perhaps even dealing with subsidiary rights. No children's editor, mercifully, is expected actually to sell books, that is solicit orders, from wholesalers and bookstores.

Her strictly editorial functions do not differ greatly from those of other editors. She probably does not herself read all the manuscripts that come in. The department will probably have a first reader who reads and makes comments on each manuscript, comments which the editor examines before the manuscript is returned. If the department does not have a first reader, this responsibility may be shared by several people in the department, including the editor herself. In any case, those manuscripts with potential are separated from those without, and those without are eventually returned.

In no children's book department is there a dearth of manuscripts, if quantity in itself is of any value. To many people, writing for children is a training ground, a simple approach, to the matter of writing. Other people have mistaken ideas of what a children's book is. These people supply stacks of bad manuscripts. But mixed with the bad ones are always some worth considering. It is because the latter do come in that all manuscripts must be recorded, read, and evaluated with care.

Possible or publishable manuscripts come from many sources. Unsolicited manuscripts (those that do not come from authors' agents or through friends) are still a source of published books in children's book departments, while in most adult departments this is very rarely the case. Agents are a larger source of children's books today than they were before the early 1960s, however. This is probably because children's books are selling better than they ever have, more children's books are being published, and more accomplished authors are finding it not only respectable but somewhat "in" to write a children's book. The writing of children's books has also become a more profitable venture than it once was. Other sources of manuscripts include authors previously published, friends of authors, and friends of people in the house.

But the editor cannot be content with just the manuscript that arrives unasked. She also talks with agents about the kinds of books she is looking for so that they will know what to send her; she gets in touch with writers' groups, with authors who have expressed an interest in writing a book on a given subject, and with people she thinks might write a good children's book. She consults with authors who have written books before to see what new things they have in mind, and she talks with people who are sent to her by friends or who make an appointment by some other means to discuss book ideas.

Once the manuscripts have come in, it is the editor's job to decide which will be accepted. Sometimes the decision is made substantially by the editor alone. Sometimes final decisions are made by a committee of people representing various areas in the children's book department or by a committee with representatives from sales and management.

Whoever makes the final decision, the contract is generally negotiated and prepared by the editor. Royalties, advances, subsidiary rights, and other matters must be settled between the publisher and the author or his agent, generally before production can begin.

A contract or lack of it does not hamper editorial work, however. The single most important job of an editor, probably, is to work with authors on manuscripts. Few manuscripts are perfect when submitted. It is the editor's job not to separate the perfect sheep from the imperfect goats, awarding one a contract and the other a rejection slip, but to look for what is good in all manuscripts and to know when it can be made good enough to publish. Ideally, the editor and author work as a team, the editor pointing out the places where things seem to slip and the author trying to see why the editor feels this way and what can be done to remedy the situation. Somewhere in the process, the book either becomes one the editor wants to publish or it does not become one. Most editors will at least encourage more books than they eventually publish. One of the rewards of being an editor is to help an author see what he can do to make his manuscript closer to what he dreams it is.

Generally, working with an author means letters or conversation. Sometimes it means copious notes on the margins of the manuscript. And occasionally it means actually sitting down and working through the manuscript, showing just how changes can be made. An editor hopes that an author who needs much help of this kind will slowly develop and need less and less help on subsequent books. Editors may give help and advice on everything from choosing a subject, plotting, characterization, developing background and using literary devices, to grammar, style, and organization of material. Editors may also be called upon to deal with all kinds of crises in their authors' lives.

Whatever the editor is dealing with—idea, manuscript, or the author's personal life—the key to the whole is knowing just how far to go. And knowing what and when to build up and what and when to tear down. Anyone with some literary knowledge can find flaws in a work. The secret of editing is to find the good and help it grow. And it is knowing when to stop editing, and when to stop an eager author from rewriting further. No book is perfect; but there is a point when a book comes as close to perfection as the author can bring it, and it is at this point that work on the manuscript must stop. To go beyond may bring technical improvement, but it will surely damage the life and spirit of the work, and these are the things that make it worth publishing.

When all the work that can be done is done, the editor may

think, especially if the book is nonfiction, that both she and the author would feel better about the book if the material were to be read by an expert in the field. So the editor may send it out to be read, in order that any small point of fact, missed by the author and by the editor, may be caught.

The editor may serve in somewhat the same capacity for an illustrator as for an author. There may be an assistant or an art director who sees artists who come by with their work, but ultimately it is generally the editor who decides which illustrator will illustrate a given book. Of course, the opinion of the author is also sought, if the author is someone who knows illustrators or who has specific ideas for illustrations.

The illustrator is usually chosen on the basis of the suitability of his style to the book in question. Once he has been chosen, he generally has considerable freedom in determining what he will illustrate and how. But the editor, or art director, will coordinate the artist's preferences with the book as a final product to make the whole a single entity. The editor also decides, on the basis of the number of pictures, the kinds of pictures, the budget for the book, and the author's contract, how much the illustrator will be paid and whether or not he will receive a royalty.

ASSISTANTS, ASSOCIATES, AND COPY EDITORS

All of these functions—the job of getting the basic components of the book ready and selecting those components from among the choices available—may be handled entirely by the editor. In a very small house or in a new department, they will be. But in larger or older departments, where the volume of sales can support more people, the editor will undoubtedly have at least one assistant and maybe many people working in many capacities. There is always a secretary in the department. Depending on the size of the department and the load carried by the editor, the secretary may or may not have some editorial responsibilities. If the department is very small, she will know everything that is going on, but aside from registering manuscripts, etc., may not have time for more than her secretarial duties. In a somewhat larger department, her scope of information may be more limited, but she may do some first reading of manuscripts. A secretarial job may actually be better preparation for other work in the department than any other kind of job, for a secretary sees everything an editor does.

Assistants in a children's book department may register manuscripts in and keep track of them until they are returned, read manuscripts, check factual material in manuscripts, see artists if there is no art director, see would-be authors who drop by without appointment but who just *must* read their manuscript to someone, actually work with authors and manuscripts sometimes, and do copy editing and proofreading. Their duties may be specific or they be required to do any of a great number of things, including some publicity and promotion.

There may also be assistant or associate editors in a department. They will assist the editor to select books, will see and deal with agents, will work with authors and illustrators and in general handle books just as the editor herself would, subject, of course, to some degree of supervision by the editor, at least surrounded by a certain amount of department coordination. In a department with several editors of this kind, they may specialize—one doing picture books, another science books or all nonfiction books, another "middle age" fiction, and so on, depending in part on the interests and backgrounds of the people involved and on the nature of the department in question. In a very large department, most of the actual editing may be handled by editors of this kind, while the editor herself may deal with only a few authors, spending most of her time managing and coordinating the efforts of the department as a whole.

Once a manuscript has been contracted for and is as good as it is going to be, the copy editor takes over. The copy editor may be one of a general pool that serves all editorial departments in the company, or she may be a part of the children's book department, perhaps given the title of copy editor or managing editor (in which case she may distribute the work to others and also be in control of all production schedules for the department), or perhaps she is listed as an editorial assistant or even as an assistant editor. In a few houses, copy editing is sent out to be done by a free-lance copy editor. The copy editor checks facts, grammar, punctuation, spelling, consistency of names and dates and other items, and aligns the material with house styling. If she finds major errors, she calls them to the attention of the editor. The copy editor may also check maps and charts for agreement with the text, bibliographies for accuracy and consistency, and any other addenda for whatever seems to be required. The work of the copy editor is particularly important in children's books because they, even more than adult books, must be as nearly perfect as possible in all respects. Because child readers do not have the background of experience to bring to their reading that adult readers do, children's books must be right in details as well as in substance. If there are few changes to be made, the manuscript can go from the copy editor to the production department. If there are a number of questions or corrections, the editor or the copy editor will probably consult the author before sending off the manuscript.

DESIGN AND PRODUCTION

The manuscript cannot go to the typesetter, however, until there is a design for the book. The children's book department may have a designer or an art director as a part of it, or the designer may be a part of the company's overall design or production department. If the designer is also the art director for the children's book department, he, or maybe even his assistant, sees artists and takes part in deciding who is to illustrate the book. In any case, when the question of design arises, in all but a few houses there is a designer who is consulted.

If he has helped choose the illustrator, he knows what the art will be like and probably something about the book. If not, the editor gives the designer the information he needs: the kind of story it is; the art it will have; the age-group that will probably enjoy the book; and how everyone involved, including the illustrator, sees the book. The designer then determines page and trim sizes and page layout and type suggestions. If the book has some unusual features that are likely to make it cost more or less than other similar books or if it is a kind of book totally new for the department, the designer or the production department estimates costs on the book—if this has not been done long before.

Once the design has been approved, the designer prepares helps of any kind necessary for the artist, including, often, for picture books, a complete dummy. He works with new artists to make sure their work will reproduce as they want it too, and will be exactly right for the overall design of the book. It is the designer's job to plan the setting for the text and pictures and to unite the two visually, from typography and illustration to binding and jacket.

When the designer has completed his task, arrangements for manufacturing the book can begin. The production department, which oversees this, may be one or two people in the children's book department, or it may be a separate department that serves the whole house. In the latter case, one person may be in charge of children's book production. In some houses the designer of children's books is also in charge of children's book production. Production and design must work hand in hand on children's books because the varieties of format, the large number of pictures, the unusual type sizes, the sometimes special paper requirements, all mean that each must know what the other is doing. Since production determines who the typesetter, printer, and binder will be, the designer must make his needs known, so suppliers who can fill his requirements will be selected. The designer must also take into account the cost of what he is proposing and must secure costs from production so that his final product is not so expensive no one will buy it.

The production department sees that material is set in type, galleys pulled, corrections made, and layouts verified. (Galleys will be read by authors, copy editors, proofreaders, and maybe by editors. They will also be used by illustrators and designers for paging, to determine where pictures can go, etc.). Later, the production department supervises printing, accuracy of color reproduction, and binding, making sure that everything is done to the editor's and designer's specifications. The production department also secures cost quotations, checks billings, and puts bills through to be paid.

REACHING THE MARKETS

Eventually, there is a finished book. But a book must have an audience or it is not really a book. So people must be made aware that it exists. This is done through publicity, promotion, and advertising. Exactly what and how this is done depends on the house and the market it wants to reach.

There are two basic kinds of children's books: books designed for mass market outlets, and books designed also for general appeal but promoted largely for use in public and school libraries, supplementary collections for classes, and also for sale in quality bookstores. The line between the two kinds of books can be a fuzzy one. There are books for the quality and library market that sell widely in major chain and department stores; there are mass market books of high quality that sell well to schools and libraries and in the "better" bookstores.

Mass market books are generally produced in large quantities—25,000 or even several times that number in a first printing—and are sold at low prices—25¢ to 50¢ in some storybook lines, $1.95 to $2.95 or $3.95, or more, in larger, more colorful editions. Highspeed multicolor printing and machinery and automatic binding equipment are keys to economical production of these books. The method of sale is another key to their success: they are "merchandised," that is, sold in quantity lots to retail outlets that display them as lines identified by the publisher's name or series name. (Incidentally, besides the two basic kinds of children's books just mentioned, it is important to note the "series" story books for children of various ages—books usually consisting of straight text with little illustration, and sold in chain and department store outlets. These are not to be confused with the hundreds of series produced to cover a great variety of subjects not only for mass market sale but for school and library use).

Compared with the mass market books, children's books for the school, library, and quality retail trade are manufactured in smaller quantities, in more varied, less standardized formats, and often have more individuality of content. They are sold more as individual titles than as "lines" to the bookstores, and especially to the wholesalers who in turn sell them to schools and libraries.

Largely because of the smaller press runs and the use of less highly automated equipment, and also because payments to authors and illustrators are higher, the library and quality trade books tend to be priced considerably higher than mass market titles. The prices and the lack of children's book specialists in all but a few stores tend to limit the retail sale of these books; still, some of them do have a ready sale in bookstores—for example, widely recognized, often award-winning books for older children, and some nonfiction on subjects that seem suitably educational to adults looking for books to buy as gifts.

Mass market publishers' promotion to retailers is of course somewhat different from the promotion done by trade and library book houses. The person who handles publicity and promotion for the mass market publisher works to establish the firm's trade name. Once he has done this, it is hoped, an adult (or a child) will walk into a store and ask for a "Golden Book," "Wonder Book," or whatever. Then the purchaser may choose on the basis of picture appeal. There may be no need to establish individual identities for the books in advertising. This is true in spite of the fact that some mass market children's books contain top-quality writing and color work and deserve a long life on their individual merits.

The publisher for the library and quality bookstore trade, however, deals with an item that may sell on the basis of quick appeal, but may be priced so high that only a purchaser's clear awareness of what is in the book will sell it to him. Few publishers can afford to advertise children's titles individually in such a way as to capture the attention of the buying public. Therefore, any attempts—with special exceptions—to sell books widely in bookstores are likely to be attempts to attract the attention of the bookseller, so that he will stock the book, become familiar with it, and inform his customers about it.

Probably because of the problems of bookstore selling (Christmas is almost the only time children's books sell, many retailers say), and because the public library and, in late years especially, the school library have been highly dependable purchasers, the promotion publicity, and advertising of non-mass market books has tended more and more to be channeled to institutional buyers. Why look over the fences to the bookstore, say the publishers, when we are already deep in the green library grass? This tendency has been, if anything, reinforced by the massive federal appropriations for school library literature following passage in 1965 of the Elementary and Secondary Education Act.

And so publicity, promotion, and advertising for children's books of all kinds, to the library market, has become an area of vast importance. It is in a very real sense the growing edge of the business. School and library promotion people may be a part of the children's book department, but in some houses they constitute a separate and very important department on their own, handling adult books as well as children's books.

Most children's book advertising is done in trade, educational and library media and is handled by the school and library promotion people. (Any newspaper or other advertising will also be handled by them for children's books, because the budgets for all media are generally figured together.) Catalogues and promotion pieces of all kinds are geared to use by libraries and teachers. Substantial amounts of money are spent exhibiting books at library and educational meetings, both national and local. And promotion people not only attend these, but travel to visit large school and library systems to create good will, to discuss what their house is publishing, and to get ideas for books that are needed. The bulk of the review and examination copies of new books sent out are sent to magazines that reach school and library buyers, to school and library systems that do their own reviewing before purchasing, and to examination centers that make books available to teachers and librarians who want to see books before they make their purchases.

The good promotion person knows his books well, knows

school and library people and their tastes, both collectively and individually, and tries to achieve a consistent, well thought-out, thorough approach to the market as he sees it, and as seems best for his particular house's products.

The school and library promotion staff may also do for children's books whatever newspaper and other publicity is done. If they do not, then a publicity person for the department, an assistant in the department, or perhaps, but not likely, the general publicity staff for the house will do it.

THE SALES MECHANISM

Some companies today have separate sales forces, some small but some quite large, that do nothing but call on schools and libraries. In some cases they sell package arrangements of new books. And in most cases they give special attention to books put in special bindings for the institutional market.

Most publishers rely on jobbers or wholesalers, however, to sell their books to most institutions and to many bookstores as well. The reasons for this of course lie in ease of billing and shipping and in discounts. The object in sales for these publishers is to see that the many jobbers carry adequate stocks of their books. Here again, the mass market publisher may sell by job lot, but the trade and library publisher must convince the wholesaler of the potential of each title. If a jobber does not carry a title or does not have an adequate supply, orders for the title may be unfilled and the sale lost.

Another market for children's books is the prebinder. He buys sheets, not bound books, and binds them in heavy library bindings, according to standard specifications of the Library Binders Institute, for institutional sales only. Initial sales to prebinders are made long before the books themselves are available, and sheet stock is allocated to these companies. Alternatively, they may buy hardbound books, rip off the covers, and rebind; or they may buy sheets when books are being reprinted. Some publishers hold books in sheet stock continually for prebind orders.

The sales department, even if it is a corps of salesmen selling directly to schools and libraries, probably is not an immediate part of the children's book department. Children's book sales may be a part of the company's general sales effort, or may be a part of a combined school and library promotion and sales effort.

This, then, is what happens to a children's book, from the author's conception to the eyes of the reader—either a bookstore customer or a library patron. And these are the people who do the work involved.

THE PAST AND THE FUTURE

Children's books have come a long way since they first began as moral tracts devoted to obedience and dying a good death, then blossomed into something more under Newbery in England, and finally came of age under such authors as Howard Pyle, Stevenson, and Lewis Carroll. Good books for children have been around a long time now. Children's book departments have existed in publishing houses in this country since about 1920. Since the 1950s, the number of books and the number of departments producing them has increased enormously.

What will happen in the future no one knows for sure. Certainly there will be many attempts, as there always have been, to make children's books didactic, mere teaching devices, reducible to computer programs. There will be continuing attempts to equate with children's books the cute, the coy, and the relentlessly comic—to the exclusion of depth, sincerity, integrity, warmth, and respect for the stature of children. But as long as there are children seeking truth and understanding, and discovering that true pleasure goes beyond mere entertainment, there will surely be authors, illustrators, and publishers anxious to be creative in their approach to the children's books they produce. And there will be those who find work with children's books the most rewarding work they know.

FOR FURTHER READING

Colby, Jean Poindexter. Writing, Illustrating and Editing Children's Books. New York, Hastings House, 1967.

Duff, Annis. Bequest of Wing. Paper, reprint of 1944 ed. New York, Viking, 1966.

—— Longer Flight. Paper, reprint of 1955 ed. New York, Viking, 1965.

Klemin, Diana. The Art of Art for Children's Books. New York, Clarkson N. Potter, 1966.

Mahony, Bertha E., and others. Illustrators of Children's Books, 1744–1945. Boston, The Horn Book, Inc., 1947.

Meigs, Cornelia L., and others. A Critical History of Children's Literature. New York, Macmillan, 1953.

Pellowski, Anne. The World of Children's Literature. New York, Bowker, 1967.

Targ, William, ed. Bibliohile in the Nursery. Cleveland and New York, World, 1947.

Also promotional guides and other publications from the Children's Book Council, 175 Fifth Avenue, New York 10010.

15

RELIGIOUS BOOK PUBLISHING

By EUGENE EXMAN

FORMERLY VICE-PRESIDENT OF HARPER & ROW IN CHARGE OF RELIGIOUS PUBLISHING; AUTHOR OF A HISTORY OF THE HARPER FIRM FROM 1817 TO 1853 ENTITLED *The Brothers Harper*

BEFORE any discussion of the publication of religious books is undertaken, it would be well to define what we are talking about. What, after all, is a religious book? *Publishers' Weekly*, that bible of the book trade, must know the answer; each January it reports the number of religious books issued during the preceding year—for example, 1,855 new books and new editions in 1965. Statistical information has also been put out by the U.S. Department of Commerce giving estimated sales of books in all categories. In 1964 the figure for religious books and Bibles was 86 million, something more than 6 percent of publishers' total receipts for all kinds of books. Statisticians must have a criterion for separating the literary sheep from the goats, but what is it? If a religious book is defined as a book on a religious theme, then many books known as trade books get wrongly classified each year, including such fiction as *The Devil's Advocate* and such nonfiction as *The Phenomenon of Man*. Likewise an increasing number of college textbooks deal with aspects of religion—historical, comparative, philosophical, and the like.

WHAT IS A RELIGIOUS BOOK?

Perhaps the best definition, though not altogether accurate, is a functional one: religious books are published by religious book specialists, reviewed and advertised largely in religious periodicals, and sold through religious book outlets to people interested in religion.

However, to define religious books is hardly to categorize them. There are many kinds and they serve many purposes. Perhaps the largest number might be called not religious books, but books about religion. Theological and philosophical books instruct and inform regarding the varied aspects of faith and belief. Theological books discuss the ideational element in religion, especially in regard to beliefs in God. Currently, biblical theology is a popular subject. Karl Barth, Rudolf Bultman, Karl Rahner, and Hans Küng are among Europeans whose theological works have been translated into many languages and are widely influential. The late Paul Tillich is more widely read than any other American theologian. His books and those of Dietrich Bonhoffer profoundly influenced Bishop James Robinson, and the latter's best seller, *Honest to God,* in turn popularized the work of these two men. Robinson also testified to the importance of Bultman and introduced many laymen to "demythologization," the effort, long known to scholars, to separate the positive content of the Gospel from a mythical world-view. The controversial Bishop James Pike has also written books seeking to interpret theological concepts to the lay mind. Currently a "God is Dead" theology is being discussed, proving, perhaps, that theology is not. A rising group of scholars, typified by Jaroslav Pelikan, show promise for vigorous theological writing for the years ahead.

Philosophical books with such names as Heidegger, D'Arcy, Eliade, and Maritain on their title pages discuss the ethical, teleological, and epistemological aspects of religion. Existentialism as a philosophical concept has its religious connotation; indeed, it arose largely through the religious writings of Kierkegaard, a nineteenth-century Danish thinker. Psychologists are also writing books about religion, although no one has yet done for our generation what William James did for his with *Varieties of Religious Experience*. One of the book clubs is the Pastoral Psychology Book Club, and often its selections are books on counseling.

Books about the church are another important kind of religious book. Historians of the church are turning out many books. The counterpart of Arnold J. Toynbee in the field of secular history is Kenneth Scott Latourette for the field of religion, with many volumes to his credit. Within the Roman Catholic fold there has been, in the 1960s, a growing interest in liturgical books, books on the papacy, on Christian shrines, religious orders, outstanding personalities, etc. Of late much attention has also been given to the synthesis of faith and science and of psychiatry and religion. There are also works on the reunion of the churches. The most significant recent event in the religious world was the Second Vatican Council. Its three sessions in Rome focused public attention on ecumenicity and inspired a spate of books. In contrast are the publications setting forth the claims of certain sects or denominations. There are also books on missionary endeavor, especially in the Far East and Africa. Stories of adventure and heroism—even martyrdom—experienced by modern evangelists have found a ready and expanding market. However, the word "missions," which implies a certain amount of paternalism, tends now to take on an ecumenical or world-wide connotation. Whatever the nomenclature, many books representing this phase of the work of the church are published each year. Finally, there are books that relate the church to social action. Partly through their books, men like Martin Luther King are arousing the public conscience to apply the tenets of faith to the necessities of racial equality.

A third type of religious book, somewhat allied to books

about the church, has to do with instruction or indoctrination. Such a book may be the testimony of a convert or it may be the learned treatise of a scholar. Courses of study published for church schools fit this category, as do books on theory and practice of religious education. Many new titles each year are bought by laity and clergy in order to enable the church to improve the religious instruction of both adults and children.

Books specifically written for clergymen make up a further classification. Although the reading of sermons is often eschewed by preachers, it is the clergy who buys most of the sermon volumes published. To clergymen and their younger brothers in seminaries go the flood of books on preaching methods. Several divinity school lectureships, such as the Lyman Beecher Lectures of Yale, add to the production of homilectical books each year, while the increasing use of radio and television calls forth an occasional volume. Clergymen, too, are the chief buyers of reference works, such as dictionaries, encyclopedias, and anthologies on religious subjects; probably the most extensive reference books in the field are Bible commentaries, such as *The Interpreter's Bible*.

In all the above categories books are often published with the college and seminary textbook market in mind. Courses in religion are given in most colleges and even in state universities. Textbooks are adopted for courses on the Bible, in church history, philosophy of religion, ethics, comparative religions, etc.

Finally, there are the large classifications of Bibles, devotional books, and inspirational books. Bibles are published in so many versions, type sizes, and bindings, that no one dealer could possibly display them all. Modern translations such as Moffatt, Goodspeed, Phillips, and Knox are widely read, but currently most popular is the new *Revised Standard Version*. From its publication, September 30, 1952, to the end of 1965, at least 15 million copies of the complete RSV were sold. The *New English Bible* promises to reach a similar figure. Only the New Testament portion has yet been marketed by the university presses of Oxford and Cambridge, with an estimated sale of 6 million copies. Devotional books include a steadily increasing number of books of prayer, or about prayer, and spiritual exercises. In the section of a bookstore handling devotional books will also be found the spiritual classics, as old as St. Augustine's *Confessions* or as new as Martin Buber's Hasidic legends. *The Imitation of Christ* and Thomas Kelly's *Testament of Devotion* are typical of devotional books. Still the most popular author of inspirational books is, in the mid-1960s, Norman Vincent Peale. The books of Emmet Fox also belong here as does that perennial best seller on Knopf's list, *The Prophet*, by Kahlil Gibran.

VARIETIES OF RELIGIOUS BOOK PUBLISHERS

Not only are there various types of religious books, but also various types of religious book publishers. As all literate persons know, the first book published in what is now the United States was *The Bay Psalm Book*. Obviously a religious book, its publication symbolized a type of publisher that has existed from 1640 until the present—the church publisher whose job it is to publish books for the propagation of a particular faith. In fact, the second oldest American publisher, in terms of continuous operation, is the Methodist Publishing House, founded in 1789. One of the most recent is Seabury Press, which publishes under the auspices of the Protestant Episcopal Church.

There are also independent publishers whose output of religious books does not come under denominational surveillance. Thus the Bloch Publishing Company issues Jewish books, Sheed & Ward and P. J. Kenedy & Sons are among the several outstanding Catholic publishers, the Fleming H. Revell Company is one of several prominent Protestant publishers—each specializing successfully in producing religious books.

Nearly every general publisher will occasionally add a religious book to his lists, and some, like McGraw-Hill, Meredith, and Scribners, have editors who specialize in religious literature. Among the houses that have organized departments are Doubleday, Harper & Row, Holt, Rinehart & Winston, Lippincott, Macmillan, Oxford, and World. Several of these departments have their own salesmen to represent them to the trade.

This increasing interest in religious matters has been widely publicized. No doubt the "return to religion" trend over the past couple of decades has stimulated the reading and increased the sale of religious books which, in turn, have broadened the base of the religious appeal. Certainly religious book publishers —whether church controlled, independent, or departments of trade houses—continue to take advantage of the trend. In order to increase the distribution of religious books, they are especially concerned about the effectiveness of three phases of their work: editorial, advertising and sales. Each of these aspects of publishing should be considered separately and in relation to trade practices.

EDITORIAL PROBLEMS

First, what particular concerns of an editorial nature do religious book publishers face? To answer this question it is important at the outset to know something about the authors of religious books. They are for the most part actively and professionally engaged in religious work. Many of them are clergymen; many others are college and seminary professors. Therefore, they write out of specialized knowledge, but unlike many trade book authors, they do not depend upon their literary output for their livelihood. Publication does carry kudos, even so, and the production of a book frequently means an advance in position, or in salary, or both.

It follows that the *average* royalty paid by religious book publishers for hardbound books is less than that paid by trade publishers. Percentages, according to 1964 statistics compiled by the American Book Publishers Council, Inc., were 13.4 and 15.4 percent of receipts, respectively. It should be noted that these percentages are not based on the retail prices but on the wholesale prices (approximately retail price less 43 percent). Thus a royalty of 15 percent of the retail price is less commonly found in religious book contracts. Sometimes, indeed, contracts call for a beginning royalty of less than the customary rate of 10 percent of retail.

This lower royalty rate is often agreed to by an author for reasons other than personal gain. He may be concerned that his book be as widely read as possible and consequently is willing to aid the publisher in keeping the retail price down to a lower figure. Nearly every author of a religious book is, so to speak, an evangelist. He believes in what he has to say and is eager for as wide a reading as possible. And lower retail prices do encourage wider sales, particularly to clergymen whose budgets are limited. Religious books are generally priced from fifty cents to a dollar less than trade books of comparable size and format. Even so, the average retail price of hardcover religious books in 1965 was $6.72 (nearly a 100 percent increase in a decade) and publishers face the dilemma of pricing books beyond what most buyers can afford, since inflation of costs always runs ahead of a corresponding increase in consumer's income.

Since few authors of religious books are professional writers, does it follow that the literary quality of religious books is less high than that of general books? It may well be so, although literary grace is not limited to the professionals, and some new religious books equal the best of trade books in style. However, it is probably true that most authors of religious books are more concerned with the content of their writing than they are with expression. The public for religious books might profit if authors should occasionally recall that St. Basil once wrote to St. Gregory, "What would be more blessed than to imitate on earth the rhythm of the angels?"

Although there is still much to be desired, literary standards are definitely higher in this field than they were a generation ago, and it is no longer possible for a popular clergyman to get his book published by a reputable house, irrespective of style, simply because he has a wide following. If a publisher is impressed by a large potential market, he labors with the author to rewrite and revise in order to achieve a happy marriage of style and content.

Finally, it should be noted that the religious book editor is alert to what is being written and published on the Continent and in England. Translation costs on books of mutual concern can often be halved if New York shares the cost with London. An offset printing or sheet importation lowers expensive composition for one side of the Atlantic, with advantages to both sides in lower production costs, and, most likely, in the feasibility of producing a smaller first edition in order to get a book launched.

PROBLEMS OF ADVERTISING AND REVIEWING

A second concern of the religious bookmen is to do an adequate job of advertising their output. As often pointed out, the problem of book advertising is how to spend a comparatively small sum on books with a "new model" being launched every publication day. As advertising budgets are necessarily based, at least in the beginning, on income from the sale of first printings, and as first printings are, for the average title, 5,000 copies, it follows that most new books will yield only a few hundred dollars for advertising expenditure. Suppose a publisher decides that he can spend 10 percent of his income from sales on advertising (and he may include circular costs as well), then on a $3.50 book (for which he receives $2) he has 20¢ a copy available, or a possible total of $1,000. It takes more than twice this amount to pay for a page in the *New York Times Book Review* or the *Saturday Review*. Even so, the linage rate in important book media such as these is more than equaled by some religious periodicals, whose charges may be fair in terms of circulation totals, but unrealistic in terms of book-reader interest. Among the best media for Protestant books are *The Christian Century* and *The Christian Herald*; for Roman Catholic books *America*, *The Critic*, and *Commonweal;* and for Jewish books *Commentary* and the *Bloch Book Bulletin*. Many denominational magazines are widely used along with those which are nonsectarian. Also important for the religious advertising man are periodicals that go directly to the clergy, for whom books are tools of the trade. *Pulpit Digest* and *Church Management* are typical of this group. Trade advertising is also important, and the media most often used are *Publishers' Weekly*, *Catholic Book Merchandiser*, and *The Christian Bookseller*.

Magazine publishers often plead that income from book advertising is necessary if they are to maintain sections of reviews in their periodicals. The argument makes sense if the rates are in keeping with the modest budgets that determine the amount of available advertising money, and if the reviews are intelligently presented. Not only do the religious periodicals do a much better job today, but so do the general media and the literary sections which in the 1920s were inclined to put religious books in the raised eyebrow department. The New York *Times* book critic, Eliot Fremont-Smith, has acknowledged (March 23, 1966) that the "critical silence about religion is only now lifting. . . . one can only welcome the trend toward open examination of what is, after all, a major part of many people's lives and touches all of us."

Competent critical reviews of books in important periodicals are, of course, essential. The publisher makes a wise investment when he distributes free books to good reviewers. A carefully classified list of periodicals that review religious books has recently been made by a committee of the Religious Publishers Group, which operates within the American Book Publishers Council, Inc. Religious books also receive a share of radio and television reviewing. Likewise they figure prominently in the news of books, for religious trends have increasingly broad news significance, and the content of a religious book is often good copy for a general editor or commentator.

DEVELOPING THE MARKET

The third concern of the alert publisher is to increase the market for his religious books. A generation ago this market was largely limited to denominational or other religious book stores. While the religious book stores still give the publisher his most productive acreage, he is steadily plowing new ground—new to him, at least—which formerly the trade salesman alone cultivated. This new development is due in part to the changing climate, for as general interest in religious questions has grown, so has the writing and reading of religious books. In the 1930s alert salesmen began to urge general bookstore and department store personnel to set up religious book sections with clerks who knew, for example, the difference between a divinity circuit and a circuit rider. Thus the customers learned where to go to get books that spoke to their spiritual condition. The religious bookstores may be either denominationally controlled, as is the important chain of Cokesbury Book Stores (Methodist), or they may be independently set up, as is the Morehouse-Barlow group. All religious bookstores are more dependent on mail-order business, however, than are the trade publishers. Thus, Carroll Whittemore Associates of Boston estimates that 85 percent of its religious book sales are made by mail. One reason for this important direct mail factor is the wide geographic distribution of clientele—clergymen, for instance—who buy from one religious dealer; another is institutional buying for church schools, adult seminars, and libraries.

Direct mail sales require direct mail promotion. Hence the preparation of circulars and other direct mail pieces takes its toll of time and thought in publishing offices. Sales conferences give consideration to their size and content. Experts in typography attempt to make them distinctive. Properly timed and mailed to the right lists, these circulars sell the books that help keep the religious bookseller solvent. An important phase of religious book promotion, for which publishers say a prayer of thanksgiving, is the "books and supplies" catalogue. All dealers use such catalogues at least once a year; if they are denominational bookstore managers they are using catalogues they helped prepare. If they are independent of church affiliation, they may purchase imprinted catalogues for their own use. Thus the evangelical Protestant groups will probably use the Moody Press catalogue or that of the Warner Press.

Since the establishment in 1927 of the Religious Book Club, many book clubs specializing in the distribution of religious books have been organized, with at least two dozen clubs currently operating—Catholic, Protestant, and Jewish. Some buy only a few hundred copies of a selected title; several regularly use 7,500 or more copies of a month's selection. Therefore, as in trade books, the importance of book sales in this category is high indeed.

RELIGIOUS BOOK TRADE GROUPS

No consideration of religious book publishing would be complete without mentioning groups that have been organized to better trade practices, and, without violating federal statutes, to share information among publishers. The Religious Publishers Group, mentioned above, is an outgrowth of the religious book section of the National Association of Book Publishers, now the American Book Publishers Council, Inc. Thus it has a history of forty years of activity. Mutual problems are discussed at regular meetings and once a year (March) there is a workshop. Another valuable religious book trade group is the Protestant Church-owned Publishers' Association, which serves the special needs of the denominational publishers.

At the beginning of this chapter a working definition of a religious book was attempted. The definition presupposed a specialized function and what followed has been a description of that speciality. Implicit in all that has been said are the factors of growth and of change. Books issued as religious books often deal with eternal truths but they live, move, and have their being in a temporal world of change. Thus what is adequate as a description of religious book publishing this year may be out of date a few years hence. "Everything," Professor Whitehead of Harvard, once said, "is in process of change. . . . Change is constant whether we measure it by minutes or millennia." Thus anything written about religious book publishing will have to be replaced within a few years by a "revised edition." And it will probably appear as an enlarged edition as well.

FOR FURTHER READING

Brown, Benjamin P., ed. Christian Journalism for Today. Valley Forge, Pa., Judson Press.

—— Techniques of Christian Writing. Valley Forge, Pa., Judson Press.

Glazier, Michael, "Catholic Publishing—Trends in the New Era," Catholic Book Merchandiser, January-February, 1966.

Library Journal, religious book numbers, January 1 and September 1 each year.

Oysteyee, Edith T. Writing for Christian Publications. Valley Forge, Pa., Judson Press, 1953.

"Profit or Loss in Religious Book Publishing," workshop report, *Publishers' Weekly*, April 13, 1964.

"The Scholarly Religious Book: Editing, Pricing, Marketing," workshop report, *Publishers' Weekly*, March 29, 1965.

Publishers' Weekly, religious book numbers, normally in February and September.

Transcriptions of Religious Publishers Group annual workshop meetings. New York, American Publishers Council.

16

TEXTBOOK PUBLISHING

By MAUCK BRAMMER

MANAGING EDITOR, AMERICAN BOOK COMPANY

TEXTBOOK PUBLISHING is only one area of specialization within the larger field of educational publishing. Performing a basic service to education, it functions as preparation for all other areas of book publishing, being largely instrumental in creating a reading public. While only a small part of the educational process, it is nevertheless a major area of the American publication industry, producing about one-third of the annual income from book publishing.

DEFINITION OF THE TEXTBOOK

The textbook is an exposition of generally accepted principles in one subject, intended primarily as a basis for instruction in a classroom or pupil-book-teacher situation. As it must be an embodiment of principles, the essential textbook or pedagogic character is pronounced in the elementary stages and is gradually replaced by the technical and scholarly at advanced levels.

Textbook publishing shows significant differences from other forms of educational publishing. This is noticeable in all phases of the industry—in author selection, manuscript preparation, production, promotion, distribution, and sale. But to the extent that the textbook character is replaced by the more advanced educational, these distinctions tend to disappear.

PLACE OF THE TEXTBOOK IN EDUCATION

The educational system in America is firmly based on the teacher-textbook-pupil relationship. In its beginnings, the teacher-pupil situation was necessarily centered about the only books available. Import of English textbooks followed, to be supplemented and then replaced over the next century and a half with imitations by American authors, who generally created their manuscripts without benefit of publisher, contracting with bookseller-printers for manufacture and distribution. After the appearance in 1783 of Noah Webster's first speller, the shift to indigenous American textbooks was rapid. The textbook publisher soon replaced the author-printer arrangement, and textbook publishing centers spread throughout the United States.

Starting in the 1820s, the growth of tax-supported free public education created a phenomenal demand for textbooks. By the late nineteenth century, the teacher's manual had appeared, to develop into the elaborate and largely free teacher's annotated edition and other accessories of the twentieth century. Standard test publication was greatly stimulated by military use in the selection of draftees for World War I. The consumable workbook, an elaboration of the earlier copy and exercise books, subsequently accelerated in popularity. The demand for audio-visual and three-dimensional materials developed only recently. All of this has created a current fashion for a packaged system of education, a system still, however, centered around the textbook. Growing rapidly to keep pace with a spiraling school population increase, textbook publishing is firmly established as a major area of book publishing.

SCOPE OF TEXTBOOK PUBLISHING

What is the relation of textbook publishing to publishing as a whole? An exact, up-to-the-minute comparison is not available. A recent (1964) estimated annual sale of textbooks, workbooks, and standard tests is $508,850,000 compared with about $1.3 billion for nontextbook sales through the various avenues of trade and specialized publishing.

What is the position of the textbook publisher in the overall financial structure of education? "It is surprising to find that an industry responsible for a product so vitally important to education," says the Committee on School Education, "plays such a small part in the nation's economic and business structure." Less than two cents of the school dollar are spent on textbooks. As may readily be understood, the salaries of the instructional staff represent the major share of the school operating expense.

How are the textbook expenditures distributed? The American Textbook Publishers Institute, representing most of the textbook publishers, has estimated textbook sales to schools, political divisions, and retailers in 1964 at $508,850,000.

This staggering sum has at last become slightly more than the amount spent annually on packaged pet foods in the United States! The expenditure of $508,850,000 for the youth of America seems large, but it becomes meaningful when related to the individual pupil consumer. It actually provides an average of only 2.42 textbooks and 2.74 workbooks yearly for the elementary-school pupil. At the high-school level, it furnishes only 3.3 textbooks and 1.23 workbooks. The college student, paying his own book bill largely, does better, with 9.52 textbooks and 0.79 workbooks. It is obvious that, with at least six subject cores—language arts, mathematics, science, social studies, vocational subjects, and the arts—to cover each year, textbook publishing is far from the ideal of providing a new text in each subject for each pupil each year.

How many textbook publishers share in this $508,850,000 annual income? *Literary Market Place, 1965–66* (Bowker), in its classification of publishers, attempts a complete listing. It shows a total of 172 textbook publishers. A breakdown of specialization by grade level lists these subtotals: elementary school, 62; high school, 78; college, 112; unclassified or general, 25. Of these, only eleven elhi publishers, according to the American Textbook Publishers Institute, boast an annual income of over $10 million and nine college publishers of over $5 million. Obviously most of the plums in the textbook pie are very small.

Where are the textbook publishers located? Most of the larger houses are centered in four great cities—New York, Chicago, Boston, and Philadelphia. A detailed survey shows, however, that geographical location is not a determining factor, for over a third of the firms are scattered in smaller cities throughout the country. While the movement to the Far West remains small, there appears to be a growing realization that location within a large city is a mixed blessing for the textbook publisher.

HOW TEXTBOOK FIRMS ARE ORGANIZED

Is there a typical textbook company organization, differing essentially from that of trade book publishing? There are differences, but they lie more in the basic economics, in the selection of authors, in the preparation of manuscripts, in the kind of competition, and in the methods of distribution than in technical organization.

Perhaps the most noticeable differences stem first from the

TEXTBOOKS, WORKBOOKS, AND TESTS SOLD IN 1964

Gradation and Type of Book	*Number Sold*	*Dollars Received*	*Average Net Price*
Elementary (Grades 1–8):			
Enrollment in Public			
and Private Schools, 31,734,000			
Textbooks (hardbound)	56,305,000	$121,620,000	$2.16
Teacher's editions (sold)	2,670,000	4,035,000	1.51
Textbooks (paperbound)	20,530,000	13,345,000	0.65
Workbooks	86,870,000	52,990,000	0.61
Standard tests	33,695,000	2,865,000	0.085
Manuals, etc.	—	1,745,000	—
Total	200,070,000	$196,600,000	
High School (Grades 9–12):			
Enrollment in Public			
and Private Schools, 12,813,000			
Textbooks (hardbound)	31,335,000	$102,470,000	$3.27
Textbooks (paperbound)	7,495,000	8,695,000	1.16
Workbooks	15,740,000	16,370,000	1.04
Standard tests	2,085,000	960,000	0.46
Manuals, etc.	—	605,000	—
Total	56,655,000	$129,100,000	

College (Grades 13 up):			
Enrollment in Public			
and Private Schools, 4,644,000			
Textbooks (hardbound)	30,710,000	$154,160,000	$5.02
Textbooks (paperbound)	13,530,000	21,915,000	1.62
Workbooks	3,670,000	6,900,000	1.88
Standard tests	—		
Manuals, etc.	—	175,000	—
Total	47,910,000	$183,150,000	
Grand Total	304,635,000	$508,850,000	

[For later figures, consult ATPI, or *Publishers' Weekly*, May 29, 1967, p. 28. Totals for 1966 show about 200,000,000 more copies sold and about $200,000,000 more received than in 1964.—*Ed.*]

uniformity in basic curricular needs and second from the strongly competitive character of the industry in meeting these needs. To issue books that will withstand severe competition, the textbook publisher must provide competent authorship, large editorial staffs for the "carpentering" of manuscripts, and large promotional, sales, and consultant staffs for school-to-school canvassing and service.

In spite of merger fever in the late 1950s and early 1960s, the greater number of textbook houses are separate and independent organizations exclusively devoted to textbook publishing. Among these, the largest are the elementary and the high-school publishers. A minority are branches of general publishing houses. The evidence of publishing history is that, outside the college area, textbook publishing is most successfully carried on by specialists who give full attention to this type of publishing.

The corporation is far more popular among textbook publishers than the partnership. Distribution of ownership in textbook corporations is wide, indicating a growing trend to public ownership, a departure from the individual and family ownership characteristics of the nineteenth century.

The financial resources of the textbook publishing corporation must be considerable. An elementary reading series, the most costly and potentially the most profitable of a textbook publisher's enterprises, may require from thirty to one hundred separate publications, many of them accessories given away to further the sales of the others. There is typically a time spread of four to eight years from the initial step toward publication to the first sales of the finished series. Since well over $1.5 million may be invested in preparatory costs alone for a reading series before a single copy can be printed and bound, the elementary textbook publisher must be able financially to assume large financial risks a long period of time.

The initial investment in plates for a single high-school history, workbook, manual, and accompanying tests may run to over $100,000. Even in the college area the investment in single publishing projects may reach $50,000.

With a million and a half to invest, a trade book publisher should be able to distribute his chances for a best seller about ten times more widely than the publisher of, say, elementary readers. And he can expect to receive the results on his investment in a considerably shorter time.

The textbook publisher must also maintain a greater inventory than the trade book publisher. With a large list of titles carrying on from year to year, with many separate copyright editions of the same title under adoption for extended terms, with sales concentrated largely into one-third of the year, with a growing need for alternate editions, and with bonded contracts guaranteeing delivery in state adoptions, the textbook publisher must carry as much as one-third of his total yearly supply for a full year in advance of sale. This is about twice the average inventory requirement for general business.

Education must go on, of course, whether in deflation or inflation, and the textbook business shows less violent ups and downs than trade publishing. With the current population explosion spiraling school needs, the trend is definitely up. Compared, however, with general business, the margin of profit is so small that there is little room for losses. Setting aside reserves for "retooling" with new publications requires considerable and continuous profits.

Textbook publishers vary greatly in their internal organization, but perhaps no more so than trade publishers. The prime source for the success of a textbook publisher rests finally in the making of a book that will be ordered and reordered widely in quantity, whether the responsibility for the publication comes from the author, the editor, the sales force, or the administrative official. In some form or other, each textbook house must perform four functions: diagnosing needs, creating manuscripts, producing books, selling them—and repeating the process.

EDITORIAL DEPARTMENTS

Textbook editorial departments or divisions tend to be larger than in trade houses. Manuscript writing by the house staff, involved and time-consuming comprehension controls, wide subject matter, and full grade-level coverage make it necessary for a textbook publisher to provide a large number of editorial workers.

Qualifications for Editors. These editorial staffs seem to be chosen generally for experience or competence in two fields: subject-matter cores and grade-level area. Working under the direction of executive editors, there are usually several key text editors. They may be specialists in the language arts, social studies, sciences, mathematics, foreign languages, or the arts; or they may be concerned primarily with grade levels—elementary, high school, or college. Under their direction are other editors, copy editors, and assistants.

The qualifications for textbook editors, aside from that ill-defined but essential "editorial aptitude," are close to those for teaching. Many editors have come to the profession from brief experiences in the schoolroom. It would seem, however, that the key executive editors are developed within the profession itself, as often from the sales forces as from the editorial. The intricacies of rigorous competition and of the burdens of readability and regional, social, and grade-level controls create a very specialized technique in elementary and high-school publishing which makes it necessary for the industry to train its own craftsmen.

The educational or subject-matter expert from the outside becomes an important factor in the more advanced area. College publishers, even more than high-school publishers, use the advisory editor and the manuscript reviewing system extensively, especially in the more exacting subject disciplines.

Production Editors. Strong typographical, illustration, and production specialists have become essential to textbook publishers, particularly in the past half century. The individually designed and evocatively packaged textbook has become the rule at all levels, with color spreading like a forest fire from the elementary through the high-school and even into the college areas. Budgets for elementary-school books in color may show as much as 80 percent of the plate cost devoted to preparation of illustration and separation of colors on printing plates. The larger textbook houses must therefore carry a staff of expert typographers, illustration (art) editors, and production editors from a quarter to a half as large as the editorial force. The editorial and production staffs are sometimes combined in whole or in part, but they are more often separate departments.

Free-lance editors, typographers, and picture and text researchers play a minor but important role in textbook production. As with the advisory editor, their contributions are greatest in the college area.

Problems in Creating the Manuscript. In textbook even more than in trade book publishing the publisher and his editors are the dominant force in creating, revising, and editing the manuscript. Throughout the elementary and high-school areas, and more and more in the college, textbooks are written or rewritten to the publisher's order. They may even be written by a publisher's staff, working with carefully selected educational experts as collaborators or advisers.

This made-to-order character is not new in the textbook

field. Inasmuch as the basic concern is the presentation of accepted principles, original genius, unpredictable as to time and source, is not a prime factor. Recognizing a need, estimating its extent, developing an idea to fill the need, building a manuscript that will appeal to the majority of teachers who recognize the need, and producing a book that can be made and sold extensively in all markets at a reasonable profit—these call not so much for creative genius as for a combination of educational awareness, publishing skill, and business acumen, and for a strong financial reserve.

Once a textbook publisher has reached a decision to publish, where does the author come in and what does he do? From over a million and a half educators and teachers, the publisher must select the person most suitable for author-editorship. Perhaps from the ranks of article writers and convention speakers in the field, perhaps from those who have indicated, unsolicited or otherwise, an interest in educational writing, but more likely from the acquaintances of the publisher, of his editors, of his salesmen and consultants, the author or authors are selected.

Creation of manuscript independently by writers before submission does still exist, chiefly in the college field, but even there advance contracts are usually arranged. The creation of college manuscripts within the publisher's office is beginning to be more than an incident, and extensive editorial rewriting by the publishers of college manuscripts independently created is common.

Arrangements with Authors. The publisher-author arrangement must be confirmed by contract, usually at an early stage of publication. Under most textbook contracts, the publisher buys all rights, assuming the costs of editing and proofreading, illustration (usually), plate production, manufacture, copyright, promotion, and sale, in return for fixed royalty percentages. These contracts restrict the author to a limited amount of change in proof without charge and limit his freedom to write similar books for other publishers. They stipulate also that the author may be called upon by the publisher to make or to pay for the making of revisions. They give the publisher the sole right to the decision on acceptability, the need for new editions, and the discontinuation of publication.

Royalties, except for some instances in college areas, are based on the next selling price or on the net money received. Nearly all textbook publishers advertise list prices, but sales by the publisher at list prices are practically nonexistent. Royalty percentages range from about 3 to 8 percent on elementary-school books, 7 to 12 for high-school books, 10 to 20 for college texts. The author's typical "take" may, therefore, range from about 3¢ on an elementary workbook that may sell as much as half a million in five years to 10¢ on a textbook which may sell about as well. In the college area it may average 75¢ on a textbook which will sell 50,000 in a five-year period. "May"—that is the key to the author's fortune. An inquiry to most authors of textbooks will reveal that they are schoolteachers who do not dare to quit their school positions and live on their textbook royalties.

Techniques for modifying royalty to pay for the costs of authorship undertaken in the publisher's offices vary. In some cases, the author will pay outright the salaries and fees of all assistants and writers, recovering his expenditures, he hopes, from future royalties. More commonly, the publisher may lay out the money as an advance against royalties, to be deducted before the author receives any income. In still other cases, the publisher and author may agree on a modification in royalty arrangements, either on a flat rate or on a sliding scale. Costs for such expert assistance may be considerable and should not be undertaken lightly by publisher or author.

Planning and Writing. With the publishing arrangements generally agreed to, there begins a cooperative process of "bibliotecture" by publisher, author, and editor, centering usually about the most dominant and productive of the triumvirate. A thorough canvass of the school requirements, generally and regionally, a detailed analysis of the offerings of all competitors, a composite of the ideas of the collaborators—these must create the basic philosophy and detailed plan for the publication. The actual writing will follow, often drawing in writing specialists from within or outside the educational field. In a few publishing houses, particularly in the elementary and high-school fields, the function of the editor and the writer is combined.

The textbook editor will usually direct a group of author-editor collaborators through the stages of planning, creating, evaluating, revising, designing, illustrating, copy editing, and proofreading. He must be able to juggle successfully the demands of the publisher, the requirements of the salesman, the needs of the author, the impulses of the designers and art editors, the cautiousness of the copy editors and proofreaders, and the restrictions of the production experts.

One of the greatest concerns of the textbook editor will be to achieve a compromise between the controls necessary for national acceptance and the originality of the author's contribution to education. In the elhi fields particularly, he must balance skillfully the demands of contradictory curricular theories, of "progressive" educators and traditionalists, of exponents of the science-centered culture and the humanists, and above all of the majority and minority pressure groups. A Solomon the textbook editor is not, but delivering judgment is relentlessly forced upon him. That judgment must be sound without reducing each new textbook to a uniform product possibly acceptable by all and actually effective with none.

These editorial requirements have made writing and editing so involved that it is no longer possible for teachers to produce basal elementary and high-school textbooks independently. It has forced the publisher frequently to develop personnel especially trained in his own techniques for the creation, or at least re-creation, of books within the publishing house.

"PACKAGING"—DESIGN AND ILLUSTRATION

While the continued use of a textbook must be based upon its success in doing the educational task it was designed for, its initial adoption depends to a large extent on successful "packaging." To secure a favorable examination by a teacher or a rating committee, a textbook must be attractive physically as well as educationally.

Designers, art editors, editors, and production experts must cooperate to produce something that is pleasing enough to cause the potential customer to examine it with what a schoolman might call "buying readiness." As a result, a complete revolution in illustration and design has in recent years confronted the textbook publisher. Increased attention to book production techniques, typography, visual aids, and printing methods have been forced upon him. Full-color illustration throughout has become the rule in the basal elementary field and is rapidly spreading upward. Special attention to design has become necessary in every book. To put a brake on ever-increasing costs, the editorial-production editor has been forced to be alert to new and often revolutionary methods of simplification, standardization, short cuts, and unit economy through increased production, all to be processed in ever shorter and shorter periods of time.

The shift to full-color and direct separation from artist's

copy, following the success of the Alice and Jerry Readers (Row, Peterson) in the 1930s, introduced a staggering color separation cost into the competitive textbook picture. Within a twenty-year period production costs and selling prices have more than doubled largely because of the introduction of much color work to normally spiraling costs. With this change, it has become obvious that the earlier expectation of a publisher at least to break even on any publication is no longer realistic.

This steadily increasing cost of replacing popular titles has been further complicated by the fact that full color has come to be expected by the customer in all areas and all levels equally. What is possible at one price level in the great potential market of elementary reading is expected at the same price in the field of elementary science, which has perhaps one-fifth the sales potential. What is possible in the third grade with its high enrollment and severely restricted curriculum is wanted at the eighth grade, where smaller enrollments and more choice in subject areas cut down potential sales.

Until the 1930s the textbook industry favored flat-bed letterpress printing. With the extensive use of direct-separation of full-color copy, the cost of preparation of plates became excessive. Engraving methods for reproducing the popular open, irregular, fading-out water-color washes required costly handwork, and photoengravers were not interested in developing inexpensive methods to handle it, being already deeply involved in more profitable commercial and advertising work.

This opened the way for the offset method of color separation and printing to drive letterpress practically out of the schoolbook color field. Stimulated by the possibility of contracts for the repetitive presswork of textbooks, offset printers developed mass reproduction techniques with little handwork in color separation and platemaking that brought about an almost complete shift in the methods of production.

With offset printing able to lay on paper anything that can

be photographed, changes were many. Several publishers sold their captive plants and others converted them to both letterpress and offset. Editorial-production workers took over many of the steps in makeup formerly handled by more highly paid printing craftsmen. Illustration techniques and placement became more free. Photocomposition was developed to handle conventional printing types, and cold composition made use of the typewriter and hand-lettering devices.

To the many advantages of the new techniques were added disadvantages. Books became bulky, with stiff, springlike pages, particularly when they had to be side-wired or stitched to hold together in the hands of the book-wrecking schoolboy. The editorial staff found increased problems in checking and proofreading from scraps and pieces rather than sequential galleys. All were forced to accept the less attractive types and spacings of cold composition. Correction of single pages in printed books was no longer relatively easy. Greater variation in printing quality became noticeable. Yet over all, costs, particularly initial costs, were held to a more gradual increase.

Rotary presses, faster and larger, at first sheet-fed and then web-fed, were introduced to cut the cost of color presswork, and did so. As they operate, however, on only one of the smaller costs of book production—presswork—the results in the cost structure were not significant. With the highest cost of plate preparation in color separation and that in bookmaking in the binding, the unit costs of textbooks continued to increase. They may be expected to continue the upward trend until the printing industry can devise new and more fully mechanical methods, particularly for these two stages of book manufacture.

Where this pyramiding of cost will lead is a major problem for the textbook publisher. With each movement toward elaboration of format in textbooks, it has become increasingly important for the publisher to budget every step of his business. To keep in business, he must replace each title every four to eight years with an entirely new one which will cost him several times as much as the previous one.

COPYRIGHT AND THE TEXTBOOK PUBLISHER

Copyright protection is probably not as effective in textbook as in trade publishing. Since copyright basically protects originality of expression and not facts or ideas, it is easier to prove plagiarism of originality in a novel or play than in a textbook presenting principles so much repeated that they have become generally accepted. The textbook publisher, however, does copyright his publications and, if they are successful, renews the copyrights.

The life of textbooks has been greatly reduced in recent years. While it is still possible for a textbook to sell for a generation or more, such books must be given such frequent and thorough revisions that copyright renewal terms are more or less academic. In general, major revision must be made every five years or oftener, with minor revisions in between, to meet competition and to keep up with changing times. Some texts in social science and science must be revised yearly. School regulations have contributed to the need for frequent revisions by restricting adoption of books with old copyright dates, often asking at the same time for little change so that books on hand may be used up. Some textbook houses try to protect older copyrights by retaining older dates in copyright notices, but most drop the old dates entirely, hoping the unwary will mistake a new version for a new work.

The right to control copying for a limited time is not vigorously defended by textbook publishers, especially when the unfair use is made by customers. Photocopying devices are now widespread and have made copying so convenient and so deceptively inexpensive that teachers, schools, and libraries have become accomplished literary pirates. Educational television and radio now do extensive taping from copyrighted materials, usually claiming exemption from payment on the technical excuse that they are nonprofit educational adjuncts. Much copying is now obviously unfair use, but the textbook publisher has so far been reluctant to make an issue of it.

Copyright permissions represent a considerable problem to textbook publishers. Few textbook publishers, dealing as they do in restatements of accepted principles, have much to sell other publishers wishing to quote from them. Most requests received are from teachers wishing to copy selections for school use, with or without purchase of the book, from broadcasters and televisers wishing to convert printed material into their methods of communication, and from college teachers making up books by discussing the opinions of their colleagues. None of this brings in much revenue. On the other hand, textbook publishers must advance for their authors considerable fees for anthologized materials. A trade publisher has made the statement that subsidiary rights pay better than original rights. This refers primarily to reprint editions, movie rights, and so forth, but certainly he must also have had in mind the possibility of charging the textbook author for permission grants.

In general, plagiarism among textbook publishers is rare. Of course, a publisher seldom brings out a basic text without a thorough study of his competition and an attempt to include all the best features of all the successful books. He is obviously saved from plagiarism by his very thoroughness, being a scholarly eclecticist rather than a scoundrelly plagiarist.

DISTRIBUTION AND SALE

Textbook purchase and distribution is the area in which this branch of the publishing industry differs most widely from all others. Textbook selling is strongly competitive. Sales are for quantity orders, not single copies. Purchasing methods are varied and complex. Distribution methods are frequently dictated by school laws and regulations. Discounts are low in comparison to trade customs. Payment for sales comes largely in the third quarter of the calendar year.

Perhaps the most noticeable difference lies in the method of distribution. The trade area has discovered over the course of years that most of its initial market is concentrated in a handful of great urban centers which can be reached by advertising, direct mail, and relatively small agency forces. Only the paperbound reprint has reached a general distribution. The textbook publisher on the other hand is obliged to provide for school-to-school canvassing in the country as a whole and often over the whole textbook-using world. Sales forces of textbook publishers may, therefore, be as much as ten times as large as those of trade houses.

The textbook salesman and the consultant are in unique positions in the educational picture. They combine the function of book peddler, educational adviser, service man, and editorial scout. A large percentage of the two thousand or so men and women in this field have seen much service in school work. In the elementary- and high-school fields, the agent's territory is usually restricted to an area small enough to enable him to travel by car to his various schools several times a school year and still to be at home frequently for weekends or oftener. In the college area the territories are, of course, larger, and are sometimes so great that neither planes, trains, nor cars will permit the agent more than a yearly visit to some of his institutions, and will necessitate hotel or motel life for long periods.

Advertising, national and local, plays a considerably smaller role in textbook publishing than in trade work. There are few advertising media specializing in education of comparable circulation or pulling power with those in trade. The great communication media of popular periodicals, television, and radio are too diffuse in coverage to justify their cost for textbook selling. Instead of heavy budgeting for advertising, textbook publishers go in more extensively for the free samples, the direct mail circular, pamphlet, brochure, and chart, and for direct service to customers.

As in all other aspects of the industry, marked differences exist in the three grade-level areas. Most textbooks for elementary schools and to a lesser extent for high schools are furnished free to pupils through purchase from tax money. Two-thirds of the states provide all elementary textbooks free; of the other third, all but two states provide some free textbooks. In the high-school area, half the states furnish all books free; one-fourth provide some; the remaining fourth, none. In some cases rental of textbooks by pupils is required. In the college area, however, only a negligible amount of free textbooks is supplied.

Adoption Systems. The machinery for the provision of free textbooks is complicated, and the techniques diverse. Perhaps the most widely known of the systems for textbook purchase at the elementary-school and high-school levels is the adoption of one or more books in a city, county, or state for a fixed period of time. In this plan, the selection may be a basal listing (one title for all units concerned in the city, county, or state system) or a multiple listing (two, three, five, or so from which selection may be made). All purchases of textbooks are then made within the listing.

Adoptions call for a publisher to supply his books at a fixed price for a set period, usually five years, sometimes longer, regardless of the increasing costs of manufacture. School laws require also that all books must be sold at the lowest price at which they are offered to any other adopting unit in the United

States. In other words, Texas and Arkansas, regardless of potential markets, are entitled to the same price for the same edition of the same American history text adopted in the same year. The publisher may offer a revised edition at a higher price, however. With increasing preference for books with recent copyright, the publisher may, therefore, need to carry several copyrighted versions of the same text, multiplying considerably his inventory and accounting problems.

The single basal adoption, subject as it was in the past to the abuses that arose from unregulated competition, has been almost completely supplanted by the multiple-list adoption. This change for the better has been accomplished by the combined efforts of enlightened educators, public officials, and textbook publishers.

The state, county, and city adoption system may be varied considerably by the inclusion of exempt areas. For instance, a state may adopt for schools of certain size and for certain areas, but may exempt cities or counties, allowing them to make their own selections.

It must be noted that in multiple-list adoptions the publisher receives only what amounts to a license to sell his book. He will then need to compete with the other publishers listed for a share of the business, frequently with strict regulations about time allowed for selling, the number of salesmen permitted, and so on. Yet the results of this system are, in general, good. The school people have a choice of books. The adopting agency can take reasonable advantage of mass purchases. The sales are more evenly divided among publishers. And traditional political and financial abuses associated with the single basal adoption are avoided.

A further variation is the listing of all acceptable books offered. Such listings are often so extensive that they cannot be considered adoptions at all.

In two states, the state adoption system is approached not through purchase of individual books but through the rental of plates from publishers, with printing and distribution handled by the state. This system, like the single basal adoption, is questionable economically and educationally and is gradually being reduced in importance by the benefits of free competition.

In situations where adoptions are not made by states, counties, or cities, the choice is usually made in the name of local boards of education. In such cases, selection of books may be less subject to rules and regulations. Usually teachers, supervisors, and principals join in offering recommendations to superintendents, who make the actual purchases for the local school boards.

Private schools usually make selections by the class or the school. Parochial schools may follow the public-school systems but usually adopt on a diocesan basis rather than by state or other political subdivision.

In addition, adoption plus free distribution is usually confined to the textbook which is capable of being passed on from pupil to pupil for the full period of its adoption, if it can stand it physically. Supplementary books for school and classroom libraries, and particularly paperbacks, may or may not be included in adoptions. Workbooks, tests, and practice materials, which are consumed in one using, are usually not adopted but are chosen by the teacher or the school. They are more commonly purchased by the pupils than are basic texts.

A state adoption usually follows this procedure: the call for a new adoption by the state board of education; the appointment of a committtee, usually of educators, sometimes laymen, sometimes both, to study and evaluate available books; the rating of the books by the committee followed by its recommendation to the state board of education; and finally the action of that board in accepting, modifying, or rejecting the committee's recommendation. In general, practicing teachers make appraisals of the books available and school administrations select from their choices for actual purchase.

In open territories, each school or committee within the school or, in many cases, individual teachers are free to make selections, subject usually to the approval of school administrators and boards of education. Roughly the open territories are concentrated in the Eastern and North-Central states, while state adoption prevails in the Southern, Southwestern, and Far Western states.

In the college area, selection by the individual instructor or course committee is the general practice. Purchase by the student is the rule in most situations, with a quick turnover to the secondhand market. Rental systems, in which pupils pay a share of the cost for library or classroom use, are sometimes used.

Discounts in textbook publishing are considerably lower than in trade. In the elementary-school and high-school fields, discounts to schools regardless of the size of the order are usually 25 percent. In the college area, they are 20 percent. In addition, elhi publishers allow a 2 to 5 percent additional discount on exchange adoptions, that is, on adoptions where the seller takes in exchange textbooks replaced by the introduction of new titles.

DISTRIBUTION OF COSTS AND INCOME

What happens to the millions of dollars taken in annually by the textbook industry? The American Textbook Publishers Institute issues for its members an *Annual Survey of the Textbook Publishing Industry*, with statistics prepared by Stanley B. Hunt and Associates. The following table is condensed from the 1964 report.

These figures show an increase in net profit over the decade 1954–1964. More concentration on basal texts, and larger printings, made possible by increased school enrollment, combined with lower costs through the use of composition and platemaking improvements and faster presses—these may have reduced production costs somewhat; but plant and editorial costs have risen, nearly offsetting these economies. Authors' royalties show a slight increase. Selling and production costs combined have remained fairly constant. Improved and largely centralized warehousing has reduced warehousing and shipping costs, probably at the expense of longer times for delivery, a factor of less importance in the textbook than the trade field. Administration costs have increased, in part, at least, to provide greater fringe benefits for employees. Payroll and federal income taxes have, of course, gone up. In spite of increases in cost, the elhi publisher in 1964 was able to retain 7.7 cents net profit on the dollar, the college publisher, 9.8. From this relatively small margin of profit (compared with other industries) the textbook publisher must pay his stockholders for the use of their money and set aside an adequate reserve fund for financing new publications at ever-increasing initial and repetitive costs.

THE TEXTBOOK PUBLISHER AND THE FUTURE

Unlike the systems in many other countries, textbook publishing in the United States is almost entirely a private and independent enterprise. Only a bare minimum of textbooks is published and supplied free by federal and state governments. These are confined largely to technical areas needed for national defense, to adult education, to national efforts to improve library facilities, to the educational provisions for minority groups, and to fields not considered profitable for or not reached by commercial publishers. In the two areas where state

DISTRIBUTION OF INCOME FROM TEXTBOOK PUBLISHING

	ELEMENTARY AND HIGH SCHOOL		COLLEGE	
	1954	*1964*	*1954*	*1964*
Net Sales	100%	100%	100%	100%
Cost of Books Sold				
Production cost	35.6	31.9	25.9	22.7
Plant & Mfg. Dept. cost	4.5	5.3	8.8	6.4
Editorial cost	3.2	5.2	4.9	5.8
Authors' royalties	6.5	6.7	15.1	15.5
Total	49.8	49.1	54.7	50.4
Remaining Margin on Sales	50.2	50.9	45.3	49.6
Other Income from Textbooks	0.6	0.9	0.5	0.3
Total	50.8	51.8	45.8	49.9

Operating Expense				
Selling cost	15.5	13.9	8.9	9.0
Promotion cost (incl. samples)	6.3	7.3	6.9	6.4
Shipping & warehousing cost	4.6	3.9	3.7	3.3
Administration cost				
General	7.6	9.2	8.0	9.0
Housing	2.9	1.2	3.6	1.3
Payroll & other taxes (excl. Federal Income)	0.9	1.4	1.1	1.4
Total	37.8	36.9	32.2	30.4
Net Income from Textbook Operations	13.0	14.9	13.6	19.5
Other Non-publishing Income	0.1	0.3	0.1	- 0.2
Total	13.1	15.2	13.7	19.3
Federal Income Taxes	6.7	7.5	7.3	9.5
Net Profit	6.4	7.7	6.4	9.8

publication is a factor, textbook publishers have long resisted the trend. There are no direct federal subsidies to publishers. Federal funds allotted to the state (and to foreign countries) do play a strong part at present in the total of textbook purchases. Still, the textbook structure in America rests primarily on independent and private competition.

Many vexing problems face the textbook publisher. American education is in a transitional stage. Pressures for comprehension controls and child-centered motivation colored much of elementary-school publication of the past half century, tending to produce more highly illustrated books aimed at the slower groups of pupils. Now competition of the great powers for world leadership has greatly stimulated the emphasis on content, particularly in science and mathematics, reversing the trend toward easier textbooks. While this may serve as a brake on the rising use of color illustration, it is most certainly going to lead to the need for more books, books graded to varying levels of difficulty for the differing intelligences within the same subject and grade level. And the problems of our democracy have become more than a high-school subject to the textbook publisher. More attention to the current innovations in communication techniques may lead, as some now predict, to major changes from printed to electronic publishing. More immediately, the problems of majority and minority pressures in the field of religion, race, economic level, and social status will require continued and fundamental alteration in textbooks, and for a long time to come, alternate editions for groups unwilling to compromise on a common approach. The textbook publisher will no longer be able to take the cautious approach of ignoring controversial matters or of qualifying definite statements; he will have to face the facts that exist in order to stay effective in a changing world.

A solution will need to be found for the intrusion of the

private benevolent foundation and the federal government into the independent economic status of the textbook publisher. Educational groups sponsored with relatively unlimited foundation and government funds have entered the curriculum planning and development area in a number of subjects, attempting to force slow-moving educational practices to keep up with changing scientific and social concepts. This has tended to disrupt the responses of supply to demand in textbook publishing, and in some cases it threatens to reduce the publisher to the status of manufacture-distributor. It is probable, however, that when these emergency efforts have produced a reasonable consensus on what should be taught and when and where, commercial textbook publishing will again have a firm basis for operation in these areas.

Programing and teaching machines and devices will continue to be a factor and may supplement their present relatively minor position in the educational picture by changing the techniques in workbooks and in textbook teaching matter. Audio-visual and three-dimensional devices and educational games certainly will become more important, particularly in preschool, remedial, special, and adult education. The services, as yet vaguely understood, of the computer in typesetting and in the information storage and retrieval area are on the verge of entering the textbook arena.

All of the future is dependent, however, upon the passage by the Congress of a revised copyright act to provide an equitable compromise between the demands of educational associations for free and immediate access to all copyrighted materials for nonprofit educational use and the need of the author and publisher for compensation for original creations, for a reasonably limited time, subject only to the exceptions of fair use. Without such a solution, the financial structure of textbook writing and publishing as we know them may be so profoundly altered that federal subsidy of authors and publishers and educators must follow.

Textbook publishers have twice been flushed with merger fever. At the turn of the nineteenth and during the first decades of the twentieth century, textbook publishers merged and bought others to protect themselves from sure ruin through unprincipled competition. After half a century of relative stability, the fever returned. Publishers from various areas of publishing have combined to effect overhead economies and to balance income fluctuations. Newspaper, periodical, movie, and electronic concerns have set up combinations with textbook and trade publishers to broaden their scope within the overall field of communication. Industries outside the communications field with excess profits to invest have been looking long and hard at the relatively stable textbook publishing income. Financial writers are fond of projecting textbook publishing potentials mathematically upward in relation to the population explosion. Textbook publishers stocks are now listed and traded actively on the stock markets. Since about 1960, the textbook industry has become more glamorous to the outsiders than it often appears to the publishers themselves.

The textbook publisher in America is forced to be a vigorous, if not rugged, example of independent enterprise. Yet he is not free, for his every venture is conditioned by public needs. He is controlled by strong competition and by a multitude of specialists who evaluate and rate his books. He is regulated by states, cities, counties, and schools.

His is the task of knowing all the best that has been said and done in the world and helping to make it prevail. His product is firmly established as an essential part of the pupil-textbook-teacher situation in America. A strong and independent spirit, he must be no less astute than the trade publisher, certainly no less ethical, no less subject to economic and cultural compromise. Throughout our educational history, his position has been far more important than his share in the national economy would indicate. Often overcautious in matching strides with the educational process, sometimes venal in bargaining, sometimes impractical and ahead of his time, but always trying to give the public a little better product than it demands, he has been a powerful influence in education. And throughout the history of America, the leaven of the democratic process has worked. The textbook publisher has proved that he can meet every important publication need in the most extensive system of public education the world has ever seen.

FOR FURTHER READING

American Textbook Publishers Institute. Textbooks in Education. New York, The Institute, 1949.

—— Guidelines for Textbook Selection. Report of Joint Committee of National Education Association and American Textbook Publishers Institute. New York, The Institute.

—— Reprints of reports on annual meetings and seminars from *Publishers' Weekly*. New York, The Institute.

—— Textbooks Are Indispensable! New York, The Institute, 1956.

Carpenter, Charles. History of American Schoolbooks. Philadelphia, University of Pennsylvania Press, 1963.

Crofts, Frederick S. Textbooks Are Not Absolutely Dead Things. Third of the R. R. Bowker Memorial Lectures. New York, New York Public Library, 1938.

Cronbach, Lee J., ed. Text Materials in Modern Education. Urbana, University of Illinois Press, 1955.

Johnson, Clifton. Old-time Schools and School-books. New York, Macmillan, 1904; Dover (paperback ed.).

Lehmann-Haupt, Hellmut, and others. The Book in America. New York, Bowker, 1939, 1951.

Livengood, W. W. Our Textbooks, Yesterday & Today. New York, American Institute of Graphic Arts, 1953.

Nietz, John. Old Textbooks. Pittsburgh, University of Pittsburgh Press, 1961.

17

TECHNICAL, SCIENTIFIC AND MEDICAL PUBLISHING

By CURTIS G. BENJAMIN

CHAIRMAN, MCGRAW-HILL BOOK COMPANY

❋

EARLIER chapters of this book have dealt with the fundamentals of general publishing practice in the trade book field. Many of these fundamentals are applicable to technical book publishing as well, although any specialized field has its equally specialized problems. One of the first problems, in this case, is to define the technical book. Even Bigelow Buckram,* dean of technical book publishers in America, is hard put to make the definition. He likes to tell the story of a learned science librarian who was pressed to give the exact number of science titles published in 1963. The scholar consulted his records, studied a minute crack in the wall, and stated: "In 1963 there were exactly 2,569 science titles published in the United States. And nobody can prove otherwise."

THE SCOPE OF TECHNICAL BOOK PUBLISHING

Thus Mr. Buckram notes that, although everyone knows where technical subject matter begins, no one knows where it ends.

* Bigelow Buckram is a composite of at least a dozen technical publishers, embodying well over two centuries (in total) of experience. Apocryphal though he is, his comments express widely held attitudes and opinions.—C.G.B.

But regardless of extensions and borderline ramifications, everyone recognizes five broad yet fairly distinctive fields of technical subject matter:

1. Mechanical arts.
2. Mathematics and natural science.
3. Engineering and all other applied sciences, including agriculture, forestry, military science, medicine, hygiene and public health, psychology, psychiatry, nursing, pharmacy, dentistry.
4. The social sciences, which are becoming each year more quantitative and technical—anthropology, economics, sociology, government.
5. Industrial and business administration, which are based on both natural and social science.

When these broad fields are fractionated into all their natural subdivisions, one has a list of subject matter that would fill several pages. Clearly, then, the technical book publisher has almost unlimited scope for the development of his list. And the scope broadens rapidly year after year. New fields spring up overnight, and older fields become more fractionated and intensely developed. Indeed, a technical publisher has to scramble to keep up with his opportunities.

It may be useful, but certainly not very important, to list arbitrarily five major kinds of books that are found in almost every field of technical subject matter:

1. Practical how-to-do-it manuals. Elementary in content but demanding simplicity in organization and clearness in style.
2. Technical texts. Occasionally used as course textbooks and usually combining theory and application. Systematic general surveys of integrated subject matter, written at all levels.
3. Purely theoretical treatises. Usually written at advanced

levels by authorities in both general and specialized fields, for graduate study and professional reference.

4. Monographs. Short treatments of single subjects, theoretical or applied, written by specialists for fellow specialists.
5. Handbooks. Large, comprehensive compilations of working information and data, presented in the most usable and efficient manner and designed to answer the quantitative problems of the workaday mechanical, engineer, or practical scientist.

Anyone seeking large samplings of technical books of all types in all fields may refer to the standard bibliographies, *Scientific, Medical and Technical Books,* edited by R. R. Hawkins (Bowker). These volumes afford the most reliable guide to the scope and content of technical literature in America, but unfortunately they have not been updated in recent years.

There is a problem, too, in attempting to distinguish between the technical books and the textbook on a technical topic. The latter range all the way from an introductory chemistry textbook that may sell 100,000 copies or more a year to a senior-level college text on macroeconomics that may sell annually a mere thousand or two. Mr. Buckram is quick to admit that any technical publisher is happiest when given the opportunity to talk about technical textbooks, for on the horizon it would be difficult not to see and reflect happily on the ever-mounting student enrollments and an ever-increasing need for books, books, and more books. The discussion in this chapter, though, will by and large omit contemplation of this Elysian field, and limit consideration to those works published not as textbooks but primarily for professional readers.

So much for general definition and scope. Now, just how large is the technical book industry? Certainly it is considerably larger than is indicated by the comparatively limited markets for individual technical titles. According to the annual statistical report of *Publishers' Weekly*, from 1961 through 1964 technical books averaged about 30 percent of the total number of titles published. In 1965, of the total of 28,595 new titles and new editions published in all categories, 8,175 were numbered in the categories of Science, Medicine, Sociology and Economics, and Technical. But these impressive figures still fail to give a full picture of the comparative size of the technical book business. The physical size and price of the individual book must be taken into account. The average technical volume is at least 50 percent larger than the average nontechnical title, and its price is at least double that of the general book. In terms of either the amount of material published or the dollar volume of sales, technical books constitute a far larger portion of the total book industry than is suggested by the number of titles published annually.

THE FINANCIAL SIDE

In contrasting technical with trade book publishing, the important matter of finance comes first. A new trade book house may be launched on a relatively small investment, but a new technical publishing enterprise requires far more substantial financial resources that can be committed to long-term investments. For technical book publication from beginning to end is a costly process. Royalty and editorial expenses are high; composition of technical matter is very costly; illustrations of expensive nature must be plentifully used; only the best of paper, printing, and binding are acceptable. All this adds up to a large initial investment in each new book, and usually this investment goes into a small initial printing. (Even today, with burgeoning science and industry, first printings of most technical books only range from 2,000 to 5,000 copies.) On an initial unit cost basis—that is, the cost of each copy in the first printing—the cost of producing a new technical book is from two to ten times greater than the cost of producing a trade book of the same size. Of course, prices are higher too—but sales are much slower, and this is why an abundance of working capital is needed. The manufacturing cost of the average new book is regained in the first year's sales; and another year's sale usually is required to regain other initial out-of-pocket costs and overhead expense. (For large handbooks and other "monumental" works, twice this time may be required.) After that, if the book continues to sell steadily, the profit margin is large. But even with steady sales the turnover rate is slow. The publisher usually is happy if he can turn over his total inventory investment once a year.

Just how much capital investment is required for the production of a new technical book? It depends, of course, on the size and character of the book. A small, nonmathematical book may require an investment, at 1966 costs, of no more than $5,000. In contrast, a 3,000-page handbook, full of mathematical, symbolic, and tabular material, may require $50,000 to $200,000. In one such handbook, produced in 1964, the publisher had invested $150,000 in manufacturing costs alone before the first copy was sold.

On this subject of high investments, Bigelow Buckram likes to tell of an acquaintance in a fine old publishing house who was thinking of venturing into a small program of technical publishing and wanted to know how much it would cost to produce an engineering handbook like such-a-one. Mr. Buckram's answer was like J. P. Morgan's reply to the man who wanted to know the cost of owning a yacht—if you have to ask the cost, you cannot possibly afford it.

While the technical publisher must make larger and longer-term investments, he has the compensating advantage of a much smaller risk factor. Whereas the trade publisher is inclined to put his money on long shots, playing for the occasional best seller or major book club selection, the technical publisher wagers on less spectacular but almost sure-fire performance. He can measure the commercial worth of his authors, manuscripts, and markets with a rather high degree of accuracy, so he can be more confident of ultimate sales at satisfactory profits.

Further in this important matter of finance, the technical publisher must be prepared to make large commitments looking far ahead to indefinite dates in the future. And in recent years, the qualified author who announces merely his intention to write a potentially salable new technical work will find several publishers anxious to provide him with advances to spur him on with his task. Though advances are generally modest, especially in comparison with trade books, they sometimes can mount to $10,000 or more.

The preparation of a technical manuscript is a slow task, requiring usually from two to ten years. Certain "monumental" books have required as much as twenty years of intermittent work by a busy scientist or engineer. In addition, from four to twenty-four months are required for the editing and manufacture of a technical book. These lengthy gestation periods, together with an author's natural insistence on an early and binding publishing agreement with no manuscript delivery date specified, often force the publisher to pledge substantial investments far beyond the foreseeable future.

THE TECHNICAL BOOK AUTHOR

The busy scientist or engineer who requires twenty years to produce his *magnum opus* introduces the second major contrast between technical and trade publishing. Unlike most authors of trade books, the authors of technical books are not professional writers. Rarely is one even a skilled writer. Usually he is a scientist, an engineer, a teacher, or a technician. As a rule he has little interest in matters of style, but is vitally concerned about technical content, editorial accuracy, schedule, and production quality. Commonly he writes more for personal satisfaction or professional prestige than for the modest royalties his book may earn. Usually he only pursues an author's fame, knowing that such fame is likely to bring fortune in terms other than royalties. And so it often does—in terms of promotions, better jobs, higher consulting fees, and so on.

Unlike most professional writers, the technical author usually feels competent to deal directly with his publisher and his editor; hence he has no need of an author's agent. Writing is his sideline and his livelihood is not involved. Without financial or time commitments, he can afford to be more independent of his publisher than is the professional writer. So the technical publisher must have patience to wait hopefully, often for years, until his author produces a perfect—or almost perfect—manuscript.

Yet, for all of his slowness and independence, the technical author by his very nature affords his publisher distinct advantages over the trade publisher. In selecting his author, the technical publisher must look primarily for recognized technical competence. It is much easier, of course, to spot and measure outstanding competence in a chemist or engineer than in a novelist, poet, or biographer. If the technical publisher wants a book in a new field such as laser technology, for example, he will have little trouble in putting his finger on several outstanding technical authorities. Perhaps no more than fifty men in the whole country have at their command the latest, most authoritative information on this subject. A canvass of a few specialists usually will show general agreement on the very top ten or twelve men. The publisher then has only to persuade one of them to produce a manuscript, and thus he will be rather sure of procuring an authoritative and salable book. The trick, of course, is to persuade the man after the finger has been put on him, and then to help him produce a readable manuscript. This, obviously, is where the technical editor comes in.

THE TECHNICAL BOOK EDITOR

More often than not the technical book editor is not an editor at all in the true sense of the word. He rarely, if ever, does any substantive editing of manuscripts, and he usually does little or no copy editing. Actually, he is a generator, explorer, organizer, and developer of book ideas. He is a prodigious correspondent, writing thousands of letters to authors and would-be authors, to manuscript readers and general advisers, to educators and other readers of the books he has published. He is a recorder and reporter—a reporter of hundreds of interviews with authors, of consensuses of manuscript reviews, of technical and educational trends as they affect the book business. He negotiates agreements with authors and advisers, and he estimates markets for the books for which he contracts. In short, he is a complicated cross-breed, being partly managing editor, partly corresponding editor, and partly contracting agent and market estimator for the publisher.

Bigelow Buckram often says that the *best* technical book editor is like the Pecos River—a mile wide and an inch deep. However, he always qualifies this statement by adding that a *good* technical editor may be only a half-mile wide, but then he must be at least two inches deep in all areas. The deeper the better, of course, but breadth is the essential quality. For a technical editor can depend on outside specialists to compensate for his lack of depth in any area. And in contrast with the trade book editor (whose decisions are on his own head), the technical editor can feel secure in his decisions, for they are made on the advice of experts. Usually he can shrug off a mistake without great loss of confidence or reputation. On this point Bigelow Buckram constantly reminds his editors that it is ever safer to make a mistake on expert advice than on one's own judgment. So the technical book editor must be sure always to seek the best of expert advice on every manuscript. It is common for the editor to get two, three, or even more constructive manuscript reviews by outside specialists and consultants to provide the author with evaluations and helpful advice on the preparation of the final manuscript.

When the author has completed his creative task and his final manuscript is safely in the hands of his publisher, it is rare that the so-called editor undertakes any substantive editing. This does not mean, however, that technical manuscripts go unedited to the printer. On the contrary, most technical manuscripts are thoroughly worked over by highly skilled copy editors. This is a very important function in technical book production. When properly done it is a meticulous, time-consuming, and costly process, but it is indispensable for quality. Indeed, Bigelow Buckram often says that the prestige of a technical publisher's imprint usually can be measured by the size and quality of his copy-editing staff.

There is no need here to describe the rather staggering requirements of copy editors in such matters as outlines, headings, and sections; spelling, capitalization, hyphenation, and abbreviation; boldface and italics; tables, equations, symbols, formulas, and fractions; scripts, subscripts, and superscripts; overscoring and underscoring; inferior and superior numbers; primes, vectors, and radicals, *et cetera ad infinitum.* All these things and many others of equal importance in the editing and marking of a technical manuscript for the printer are described in detail in convenient booklets produced by the major technical publishing houses for their authors, of which several are available to the general public. (See list at the end of this chapter).

Since accuracy is a *sine qua non* of technical literature, as many as six readings of proof are usually required—three in the galley stage and three in the page stage, each stage being read and carefully corrected by the printer, the editor, and the author. (Yet errors still persist—but some editors explain that a few are intentionally left in just to keep the reviewers alert and happy).

Technical authors and editors alike give painstaking attention to bibliographies, glossaries, and indexes. Each of these is important to the professional reader, and a weakness in any is sure to impair the value of the book and handicap its sale.

THE PROBLEM OF ILLUSTRATIONS

As noted earlier, most technical books need many and varied and costly illustrations. Being functional, the illustrations must appear on almost every page, not conveniently grouped on separate pages that can be inserted almost anywhere. Since many of the illustrations invariably are half-tone engravings that require coated paper for proper reproduction, many technical books are still printed on heavy "slick-finished" paper.

More often than not, technical books require special types of illustrations as well as the conventional photographs and simple drawings. Maps, graphs, charts, sectional and exploded views, and three-dimensional pictorial drawings are frequently used. Occasionally, large, oversize illustrations must be reproduced on folded, "tipped-in" sheets, but these are avoided wherever possible as economic poison.

The larger technical publishers have facilities for helping

their authors with the production of finished illustrations of mechanical nature. This usually is not true of biological and medical drawings, which must be prepared by the author or under his close supervision. Further, biological and medical illustrations more often require the functional use of color, but this is kept to a minimum in the interest of cost. Absorbing the high cost of color plates in short-run printings greatly increases the unit cost of each copy produced. To authors who are blind to color costs, Bigelow Buckram always explains that if his technical books enjoyed press runs comparable to those of *Life* magazine, they, too, could be lavishly illustrated with color plates of the highest quality.

SPECIAL PROBLEMS OF MANUFACTURE

The special problems and processes of technical book manufacture also are described in the publishers' guides for authors. These processes are similar to those for trade books but much more complicated, time-consuming, and costly. Technical composition usually is done by Monotype, rather than Linotype, and much of it, including mathematical and symbolic matter, must be set by hand. Engraving, page make-up, plating, and "make-ready" of type forms or plates on the press also require many hours of handwork. Indeed, so much highly skilled handwork is involved in the backward art of fine composition and printing that it is not unusual for labor costs to constitute 80 percent of the total manufacturing cost of the first printing of a new technical book. The cost of type metal, paper, and binding materials (first quality though they must be) is only 20 percent of the total. In trade book manufacture, the relative cost of labor is far less, and of course the absolute costs of both labor and materials are considerably lower.

TECHNICAL PAPERBACKS

The paperback movement, which has made itself felt in almost all other areas of publishing, has had little effect on the technical book. True, a few low-priced technical paperbacks seem to appear each year, but these efforts are atypical and generally short-lived. The high first-printing costs and the small inelastic markets simply prohibit the sensible production of widely distributed and low-cost works of this type. Simple arithmetic will show that a technical book requiring an initial investment of $20,000 for composition, artwork, editing, and plate-making can hardly sell at a list price of $2.95 or $3.95, even though the publisher might save 20¢ on the basic $1.00 printing and binding costs by publishing in paper binding. Even on a substantial 5,000-copy printing, the unit direct cost to the publisher would be $4.80, or about $2.00 *more* than he would receive from the bookseller.

REACHING THE MARKET

As noted earlier, it is much less difficult to measure a technical book market than a trade book market. No one can tell how many general readers are likely to be interested in an absorbing new book on Lincoln's doctor's dog, but the publisher of a new book on physical optics can estimate with accuracy the number of his potential customers. He can easily learn the membership of the Optical Society of America and the readership of the Society's journal. Also, he can learn, but not so easily, the number and average enrollment of college courses in the subject. These collected figures give him a reliable measure of his market.

If a medical publisher intends to bring out a volume on

obstetrics, he can obtain a mailing list of 19,000 obstetrician-gynecologists in the country. He knows that he can obtain from a reliable source a mailing list of these specialists at a known rate per thousand names. In addition he can readily learn the number of medical libraries that will probably buy a book of this type. With such information, he is unlikely to overshoot his sales estimate through wishful thinking. This is why Bigelow Buckram admonishes his technical editors never to look at the ceiling or out the window when estimating markets—standard operating procedure for trade book editors. Solid facts and figures should always be at hand.

Since his product is addressed to specialized and limited markets, the technical publisher must have direct and full access to each market, using rifle rather than shotgun methods of promotion. This means that he must rely primarily on direct mail, and here lies the importance of a mailing list for each specialized field. Magazine subscription lists of membership in the various professional and trade organizations are valuable, but absolutely indispensable are the publisher's house lists of purchasers of earlier books. Without such lists, the publisher would be hard put to sell at a profit. Returns from house lists generally far exceed those from other lists. Accordingly, they are carefully maintained and guarded, and are used time and time again. Bigelow Buckram says emphatically that next to the prestige of his imprint and the good will of his authors, his house mailing lists are his firm's most valuable asset.

Space advertising in technical and professional journals is widely used to support direct mail promotion, though it is generally less effective in sales returns. Displays at conventions are often considered a must for house prestige, but they usually are the least effective form of sales promotion.

Bookstores generally do not carry representative stocks of the better-selling technical books. This is regrettable from all points of view, but no one has been able to break a long standing economic impasse between technical publishers and retail book dealers. The publisher cannot depend upon the local dealers to reach all the widely and thinly dispersed customers for a specialized book, so he must continue his costly rifle-shot promotion by mail. Yet having incurred this heavy direct mail expense, he cannot then afford to allow sufficient trade discounts to make technical book sales attractive to retailers.

A solution to this problem would be higher prices—prices that would provide ample margins to absorb *both* direct mail expense and longer trade discounts. But this oversimplified solution might defeat its purpose, for technical book prices already are comparatively high. In fact, technical books always have been held at the highest level in the book industry. In the postwar decade, the technical book publisher increased his prices in keeping with his rapid increases in production costs and with consumer commodity prices generally. This the trade book publisher failed to do, and he and the whole industry suffered accordingly.

In pricing his product, the technical book publisher has a great advantage over the trade publisher. He can and does get higher prices because his books are professional or vocational tools for which the buyer is willing to pay any reasonable amount. An engineer in 1966 does not hesitate to pay $20 for a handbook which in 1946 would have cost him $10. But the general book buyer would be shocked—or so the publisher thinks—if he were asked to pay $10 for a novel which, twenty years ago, he would have considered a bargain at $5. Here lies a basic reason for the marked difference in the economic health of the trade and technical branches of the book industry. On this critical subject of higher prices and sales resistance, Bigelow Buckram says that he may lose money on the books that he does not sell, but certainly he is not going to lose money on the books he does sell. Again Mr. Buckram is hard put when he tries to explain exactly what he means by this statement, but he firmly maintains that a general adhesion to this idea throughout the technical book business accounts for its robust health in a period when the book industry as a whole has not been highly profitable.

MEDICAL BOOKS—SPECIAL CONSIDERATIONS

Medical books certainly are technical in nature but not strictly *sui generis*. What has been said about the problems of selecting, editing, illustrating, and manufacturing technical books applies with even more force to medical books, for medical volumes generally are larger in size, higher in cost and price, and much more limited in distribution.

Unlike other fields of science and technology, the medical field is not a fast growing market for books. Our medical schools only produce about 8,000 new M.D.'s each year, and almost that many practitioners retire annually. Naturally, this condition has bred conservative publishing practices and has discouraged the building of new medical lists in recent years.

Medical publishers represent the only sizable segment of the technical book industry that widely utilizes book jobbers in the distribution of their product. A good number of these well-established, specialized jobbers operate regionally, serving retailers, medical schools, nursing schools, hospitals, libraries, and individual practitioners. Usually they sell books of all publishers through both field salesmen and direct mail.

Medical firms more than other technical book publishers have been constant importers of works from abroad, principally from Great Britain. The emergence of the United States as a leading country in medical education, research, and practice has diminished the number of titles imported in recent years, yet this practice remains an important aspect of medical publishing.

Overriding these technical differences is a deeper, philosophical distinction that sets medical publishing somewhat more apart. This is directly related to the physician's role—to cure illness, to preserve human life, to improve the general health of mankind. No other profession has a relationship that is so immediate, so personal, and so important to the individual, and this dramatic role is directly reflected in medical literature. Authors must be chosen for their unchallenged authority, for the use of a medical book can directly affect many human lives. Accuracy of the highest order is mandatory, lest wrong quantities, formulae, dosages, drugs, medications, and remedies be prescribed and administered tragically. Integrity in art reproduction is also mandatory, lest students, researchers, and practitioners be led into misinterpretation and wrong diagnoses. Frontier research must be proved and published in the professional journals and accepted conclusively at that stage before it can appear in medical books, for the physician and the public must not be given false information or false hopes.

Thus the medical publisher bears a greater weight of moral and social responsibility than does his colleague in any other technical field—except, perhaps, the publisher of books on A-bombs and H-bombs, whose product can have the same fatal relationship to the species as medical books have to the individual. What with the present dangerous drift in world affairs, his publishing conscience must bear the heaviest weight of all.

FOR FURTHER READING

Author's Guide. Englewood Cliffs, N. J., Prentice-Hall, 1962.

Benjamin, Curtis G. "Everything is Not Coming Up Roses," *Special Libraries*, November, 1965.

Benjamin, Curtis G. "The High Price of Technical Books," *ALA Bulletin*, January, 1965.

Burlingame, Roger. "Endless Frontiers—The Story of McGraw-Hill," New York, McGraw-Hill, 1959.

Century of Book Publishing, A, 1848–1948. Princeton, N. J., D. Van Nostrand, 1948.

First One Hundred and Fifty Years, The. New York, Wiley, 1957.

Guide for Authors, A. Cambridge, Mass., Addison-Wesley, 1965.

Hamilton, Edward P. "Author, Author," American Society for Engineering Education *Procedures,* 1944.

Hamilton, Edward P. "Engineering Literature," *Library Journal,* November 15, 1952.

Imprint on an Era. New York, McGraw-Hill, 1963.

Matheson, Martin. "Selling Books to Scientists," *Science,* April 17, 1953.

McGraw-Hill Author's Book, The. New York, McGraw-Hill, 1955.

Ransom, James. "How Medical Books Happen," *Journal of the American Medical Association,* April 20, 1964.

Richard D. Irwin Author's Manual, The. Chicago, Richard D. Irwin, 1960.

18

UNIVERSITY PRESSES

By LEON E. SELTZER

DIRECTOR, STANFORD UNIVERSITY PRESS

A UNIVERSITY PRESS is a nonprofit publishing house, owned by or an integral part of a university, engaged for the most part in publishing scholarly books (including reference works) and journals. The audience it serves is primarily a scholarly one, but the books it publishes will also necessarily serve the student and the informed layman. The advent of the "quality paperback," particularly, has very much enlarged the market for scholarly books, so that in recent years the marketing practices of university presses have come more nearly to parallel those of trade houses. But in addition to their nonprofit scholarly function, the university presses have one particular character that sets them off from the general book-publishing industry: they represent, as a species, a network of regional publishers, publishing books of regional interest.

ROLE IN THE INDUSTRY

If, from the 28,000-odd new titles and new editions published annually in the United States, are enumerated only those books of serious nonfiction that are either scholarly in nature or approach the scholarly, it has been estimated that the university press output of some 2,500 titles a year represents from 25 to

32 percent of the number of titles. A more conservative estimate—depending upon a broader view of the kinds of books to be considered—places the university press portion at about 15 percent of new titles published yearly. In either case it is clear that the forty-odd nonprofit American university presses, grossing nearly $20 million in sales, play an important role in American publishing.

WHY AND HOW THE PRESSES GROW

This role has been growing steadily larger for two main reasons. First is the growing strength as publishers of the university presses themselves. Second is the economic factor that has driven the "break-even point" of the commercial publisher higher and higher so that more and more books of serious nonfiction fall not so much out of their area of interest as out of the area of commercial feasibility. This is not to say that the commercial presses are in any way abdicating the important function of supporting the publication of serious scholarly work, but that they must necessarily forego the publication of certain works that in prior years would have found their way onto their lists. Here, the university presses have accepted the challenge and each year produce more of these worthwhile books.

In many ways, this has made for a more exciting kind of publishing on the part of the university presses, increasing the area in which their editorial initiative and judgment affect what is published and broadening the scope of their interests. This is demonstrated by the increasing frequency with which university presses are mentioned in connection with the annual Carey-Thomas Awards for creative publishing, and the increased sales their books are bringing in the academic world, through normal trade channels such as bookstores, and in foreign countries.

As a result of this, distribution methods have been improved and, corollarily, more university press books are classed as "trade books" to reach a wider market. Nevertheless, university press publishing continues to reach mainly a specialized market and to leave the commercial area of publishing (trade as well as text publishing) largely to the commercial publisher. Though most of a press's books come out of the work of the parent institution, each press publishes a good many books by authors from other universities and even from outside of academic life. The main criterion is the quality of the work and its contribution to serious knowledge.

In their day-to-day technical operations, the university presses are more and more like the commercial houses. This is especially true of the larger university presses, whose lists are great enough to support all the usual elements of editorial work, production, promotion, and distribution that characterize the trade houses. From the beginning of the process to the end, university presses will be found active in all such areas; they have, like commercial publishers, trade exhibits, bookstore representatives, seasonal catalogues, space advertising, direct mail, and general publicity.

If there is one great difference between the university presses and the commercial publishers in the technical aspects of publishing, it is the more tightly knit staff work. Because the university presses are usually smaller and because they must work within closely measured budgets, their staffs are smaller and less departmentalized. One person may do work that by its nature might be performed by several different persons in a larger publishing house. In some cases an editor has a good deal to do with production, or with promotion. This adds to the variety of his experience and to the interest of his job.

EDITORIAL CHARACTERISTICS

Since most of the books published by the university presses come out of the academic world, the area of editorial initiative is limited for most presses, though many of the presses are exerting themselves increasingly in this field. Because of this fact, however, most of the editors at university presses are highly skilled copy editors; fewer, in proportion, are "creative editors" in the sense commonly thought of in connection with a trade house. This is as it should be, for a book bearing the imprint of a university press must withstand the most careful scrutiny and must reflect the highest standards in its copy editing. Accordingly, more is spent, in proportion, for copy editing a university press book than is likely to be found for books of the trade houses. The amount of careful checking that is done probably varies little from press to press and is uniformly high. Nevertheless, some of the larger presses have scope enough to employ specialized editors for the various fields, such as science, humanities, or social science, but in most cases the burden of creative editing is carried by the chief editor or the director of the press himself.

PRODUCTION AND DESIGN

Most manufacturing of university press books is done by the same commercial printers that work for the commercial houses, though a few university presses own their own printing plants —for example, Illinois, Iowa State, Oklahoma, Princeton, Stanford, Syracuse, Yale. There are also printing plants at California, Chicago, Harvard, Kansas, Kentucky, Nebraska, New Mexico, and Texas, but these are operated by the universities rather than by the presses themselves.

University press books have long been noted for the excellence of their design and manufacture. An examination of the annual selections of the Fifty Books of the Year (judged by the American Institute of Graphic Arts) shows that since 1945 only one commercial publisher has had more books chosen than the leading university press (Princeton) in this category. Other leading presses in design were Yale, California, Columbia, Illinois, and Oklahoma; and almost every press can claim distinction for the craftsmanship of its formats and production.

The usual reason given for the dominance of university presses in design is that more expensive materials and printing processes are used. This may indeed be a factor, especially with respect to those books that have to stand up for long years of use and therefore have to be made of good materials. University presses have a great many books of this sort, more than most trade publishers do; their active backlists include titles ten, twenty, even forty or more years old. But good materials can be handled well or ill. The fact that they are typically handled with taste and craftsmanship by university presses is very probably because of an attitude, on the part of staff and management, that has come to demand consistent quality in design as in scholarship. Moreover, a university press designer may do everything from an art book to a complicated mathematics book—and will do a great many of them. This of course makes both for flexibility and for developed imagination and freshness of view.

THE TRUTH ABOUT SUBSIDIES

Since a university press is both nonprofit and subsidized, where does the money come from? In the first place, the university press works on a budget and is accountable to some agency—the university itself, the state legislature (in the case of state university presses), a board of trustees. Within the framework of its overall financial structure, it must operate efficiently and without waste. The kinds of subsidies vary from press to press, but all receive some kind of help. Universities themselves may provide direct help in the form of free space and rent, payment of salaries, furnishing of accounting services, use of university funds for working capital, or direct grants. The presses that come closest to being "self-supporting" are those that have their own printing plants (which produce income), large income-producing backlists built up over years of subsidized activity, or some kind of endowment.

In any case, these subsidies—direct or indirect—can account for only a small part of the losses incurred in publishing the small editions of specialized works that form the bulk of the presses' lists. While a commercial publisher can "break even" on from 5,000 to 10,000 copies of a book, a university press can often "break even," because of its subsidized nature, on 3,000 to 5,000 copies. Because of their limited market, however, the actual average sales of university press books are closer to 2,000 copies per title and often reach no more than 1,000 copies. Someone has to make up the difference between these low sales and the hypothetical "break-even" points. Funds for this purpose may come from the presses' own capital (either earned or given to it), but some of it must come, too, from individual authors, nonprofit foundations, or others interested in a specific book or series of books.

CONTRACTS AND ROYALTIES

For the scholarly book that might be expected to recover its cost, university press contracts are very much like those of commercial houses. The normal royalty is paid—10 percent or 12 percent—normal advances are made to the author, and the subsidiary rights and clauses are pretty much the same.

However, as just noted, most of the books published by university presses will not recover their costs, and accordingly the contracts reflect the subsidizing nature of many of the arrangements. These subsidies come from a variety of sources, mainly from the university itself, from the authors themselves, or from nonprofit organizations. Depending upon the expected sales performance of the work, the subsidizer may or may not receive returns from the sale of his book, but if he does receive returns, such returns will be very high (far exceeding the normal 10 or 12 percent), in accordance with the amount of money that has been furnished by the subsidizing agency.

ADVERTISING AND PROMOTION

University presses usually maintain their own advertising and direct mail staffs, but a number of them also use the regular advertising agencies that specialize in publishing, sometimes exclusively and sometimes to augment their own resources. Much of the space advertising, needless to say, is placed in scholarly journals or other specialized media in order to reach the specialized market for most of the university press books. There is, however, an increasing amount of regular trade advertising in the usual national media, keyed to the trade books of the university presses and to their other sales efforts in an attempt to reach the general public. Certainly a larger proportion of the university press promotion budget goes into advertising in the specialized media and into direct mail than is the case with most of the trade houses.

As an aid in direct mail promotion the university presses operate a cooperative mailing and addressing unit called the Educational Directory and run by American University Press Services, Inc. This maintains a large list of persons in academic life classified by various disciplines.

Exhibits now play an important part in university press promotion, and here, too, the presses have a cooperative exhibits program, also run by American University Press Services, Inc., through which the books of the presses are displayed at scores of annual meetings of various professional organizations across the country in the course of the year.

SALES EFFORTS

Most of the university presses employ the services of commission salesmen, many of whom also carry the lines of trade publishers. These sales efforts are augmented, as they are in commercial houses, by direct selling activities on the part of sales managers and other sales force personnel on the salaried staff of the press itself.

In one area of selling, however, the university presses have perhaps contributed something new in American practice. In recent years a number of the presses have joined in cooperative sales plans. These have been established in one of two ways. According to one method, a salaried salesman (not a commission man) may be hired to carry the lines of four or five presses in a particular area, with the expenses proportionately prorated among the presses concerned. By another method, an exchange arrangement is undertaken whereby the salaried salesman of a press in one area of the country (for example, the eastern seaboard) will carry the lines of one or more presses in another part of the country (for example, the west coast), and a reciprocal arrangement is made among the presses so that no money changes hands and no further accounting is necessary; this is an outright exchange of services. From the increasing frequency with which these two kinds of cooperative sales arrangements are being made, there is evidence that these sales methods are producing satisfactory results for the university presses. Another example of cooperative sales effort is the establishment of joint offices abroad—particularly in London—by groups of presses.

A particular area of difference between university presses and commercial houses exists in the proportion of foreign sales. Because American books are high in price, most foreign purchasers will be exceedingly discriminating in the American books they buy. However, when a book is vital to a man's area of interest, he will buy it no matter what it costs. Because university press books are largely of a specialized nature and usually represent the foremost thought in a particular academic discipline, these books are much in demand. As a result, the foreign sale of university press books is almost always over 10 percent of the annual gross (for all presses it was 13 percent in 1964), for the larger presses perhaps averages close to 20 percent, and in some presses goes as high as 30 percent of total sales. This is a far higher proportion than the commercial houses have, for their foreign sales are likely to hover around 8 percent of total gross.

Since the Second World War, foreign sales have been stimulated particularly by two main factors—the scholarly paperback and the great educational efforts being made in all countries.

INVESTMENT IN SCHOLARSHIP AND BACKLIST

With all their similarities to ordinary publishing, the university presses nevertheless, by the nature of the books they publish, have certain special problems. These problems revolve around a number of disadvantages that commercial publishers do not bear, but these disadvantages involve the whole special responsibilities of the university press and can never be thrown off. One of the most important of these is the necessity to invest money in worth-while, scholarly books that will have a small market—books that will either lose money or make it back very slowly. This is a responsibility to the new scholar and the new work of the mature scholar. A second responsibility of the university press is to keep in stock a backlist of books far greater in both number of titles and copies of manufactured books than any commercial house could tolerate—whether in books or in anything else. Both these handicaps are well recognized and happily borne: they are the reason for the existence of the university press. (Another special quality of the university press is the "regional-publishing" aspect of some of their work. In many cases the university press is the only publishing house in a large area of the country, and has accordingly accepted and promoted its role as the publisher of books about the area).

ASSOCIATION OF AMERICAN UNIVERSITY PRESSES

To help face some of these problems, the university presses of the country in 1937 set up an organization called the Association of American University Presses (AAUP), formalizing an informal group that had been operating for a number of years (and calling itself, at one especially informal stage, "The Pure Tobacco Growers Association").

The Association consists (1966) of some 70 members located in the United States (36 states and the District of Columbia), Canada, and Mexico. (There are a number of other smaller university presses that, because of the irregular nature of their output and their special organization, are not members of the Association.) The members of the Association meet annually, in different parts of the country, to discuss common problems, to examine their relations with scholarly authors, markets and other publishers, and to hold workshop sessions.

In 1964 it reorganized into the Association of American

University Presses, Inc., and a wholly-owned subsidiary, American University Press Services, Inc. (above). The most ambitious of the latter projects is *Scholarly Books In America*, a descriptive quarterly bibliography, arranged by subject matter, of all books published by all members of the Association.

This program, instituted in 1953, provides more than 200,000 scholars throughout the world regularly issued information on the titles, authors, and general scope of the principal books in the broad scholarly areas, published by the member and affiliate presses.

In 1949 the Association, with help from the Rockefeller Foundation and the American Council of Learned Societies, published *A Report on American University Presses*, written by Chester Kerr of Yale. A reexamination of the material in that book was undertaken in 1955 by Mr. Kerr for the Association.

It is perhaps fitting, therefore, that we should close this chapter with some remarks made by Mr. Kerr in discussing university presses. He said, half in jest, that university presses make up "the most foolhardy branch of book publishing: we publish the smallest editions at the greatest cost and on these we place the highest prices and then we try to market them to the people who can least afford them. This is madness." Madness it is, but, as Mr. Kerr agreed, there is more than a little reason in it and certainly a great deal of excitement, creativeness, and satisfaction.

FOR FURTHER READING

An Advertisers' Guide to Scholarly Periodicals, 1966–67. 6th ed. New York, American University Press Services, 1966.

Cargill, Oscar, and others. Publication of Academic Writing. New York, Modern Language Association, undated.

Harman, Eleanor T., ed. *Press Notes.* Periodical. Also in annual volumes. Toronto, University of Toronto Press.

—— The University as Publisher. Toronto, University of Toronto Press, 1961.

Hawes, Gene R. To Advance Knowledge: A Handbook on American University Press Publishing. New York, American University Press Services, 1967.

Hogan, John C. and Saul Cohen. An Authors' Guide to Scholarly Publishing and the Law. Englewood Cliffs, N. J., Prentice-Hall, 1965.

Kerr, Chester. A Digest of A Report on American University Presses. (Norman, University of Oklahoma Press, 1949.) New York, Association of American University Presses.

Scholarly Books in America. Quarterly. Descriptive bibliography, with articles on author-publisher relationships and other university press matters. New York, Association of American University Presses, 20 W. 43d St., New York 10036.

Underwood, Richard G. Production and Manufacturing Problems of University Presses. New York, Association of American University Presses, 1960.

University of Chicago Press, The, 1891–1965. Pamphlet. Chicago, University of Chicago Press, 1966.

Trans-Pacific Scholarly Publishing. Paper. Honolulu. East-West Center Press, 1963.

Putting Knowledge to Work: A Tribute to Datus C. Smith, Jr. Princeton, N. J., Princeton University Press, 1952.

Welter, Rush. Problems of Scholarly Publication in the Humanities and Social Sciences. New York, American Council of Learned Societies, 1959.

19

MASS MARKET PAPERBACKS

By FREEMAN LEWIS

VICE-PRESIDENT FOR PUBLISHING, SIMON & SCHUSTER, INC.

❋

THE PAPERBACK REVOLUTION of the twentieth century began in the 1930s, became effective with the arrival of Pocket Books, Inc., in 1939, and really mushroomed as a dynamic force in American book publishing after the end of World War II.

It was essentially a revival rather than a wholly new development. And as with so much of our book publishing history, it followed after developments in Western Europe, particularly in England, France and Germany. It was also largely a revival of the flourishing era of paperback publishing in the 1870s and 1880s. That era ended in general bankruptcy. The paperback, curiously enough, then helped furnish the raw material for an era of hardback reprints (paperbacks were rebound and became "bargain" books), which reached its height in the late 1920s and 1930s.

New machinery, low-cost materials, and a revival of distribution through techniques used by magazine and newspaper publishers sparked the paperback revolution, which ended, as a "revolution," in the middle 1950s. (For history, see the best single book yet written on the subject: *The Paperbound Book in America*, by Frank L. Schick; (New York, Bowker, 1958.)

THE BUSINESS PHILOSOPHY

Paperbacks owed much to the depression in the sense that they represented a drive to attain a larger market for books through very low retail prices (25¢) in a very large number of retail outlets, with titles which had a demonstrated or at least a highly likely mass appeal and by a paring of costs, discounts, royalties, and the gambles which normally characterize all trade book publishing. For instance, in the late 1930s, good book paper cost 4¢ to 5¢ a pound. Magazine wholesalers received a 36 percent discount and gave retailers a maximum of 20 percent. Royalties were 4 percent of retail, and guarantees were negligible. Paperback reprinting took its place as an extension of the marketing tools of trade publishing through two major accomplishments: very low retail prices and wide availability.

THE EARLY DAYS

Title Acquisition. In the early days, there were only a small number of paperbacks published. The emphasis was heavily on popular fiction; the book clubs and hardback lines of Grosset & Dunlap, Blue Ribbon Books, and the Garden City Publishing Company offered an easily read record of low-priced book popularity. There was some original publishing, chiefly nonfiction and anthologies, but essentially paperbacks were reprints. In relation to needs there was a seemingly large reservoir of titles which was being adequately replenished each year by the trade book publishers.

The contract was an adaptation of that used for hardback reprints. The seller, almost always the trade publisher, granted the right to publish in English in paperback for a limited period of time and to sell the product in certain specified territories. Royalty was paid on net sales and there was usually a modest guaranty against royalties whether earned or not and usually payable six months after the publication date. These earnings were customarily split 50 percent to the author and 50 percent to the original publisher.

Distribution. Magazines are distributed by wholesalers who receive copies in bulk, deliver predetermined quantities by truck to the dealers they serve, pick up unsold copies when the issue is out of date, and handle the credit and collection functions. It was these wholesalers who became the chief mechanism for the distribution of paperbacks. Originally, every effort was made to treat books as nearly like magazines as possible. Each dealer received a prepackaged bundle at stated intervals. There was little knowledge of individual titles and little effort made to serve book readers' needs. The entire process was on consignment and operated to a large extent on the premise that the customer is always wrong. But this belt-line system did deliver paperbacks into over 100,000 retail outlets and did bring about the exposure of books to more people than ever before had had a chance to see and buy them so cheaply and so conveniently.

One immediate effect of this system was on packaging. The competition for visibility was tremendous, not only within the confines of the book racks but also with the magazine displays. Paperback publishers therefore treated book covers more flamboyantly as posters than trade book publishers needed to do. Novelty and shock effect were sought. Copy sometimes was deliberately misleading. Change became the order of the day and there was much anguish at some of the results.

But the public was pleased and the business of paperback publishing flourished. By the early 1950s there were about twenty mass market paperback publishers issuing nearly 1,000 titles a year and selling close to 250 million copies. The goals sought had essentially been reached. The revolution was over, by accomplishment of its initial objectives, and the great changes which have happened since, and which will continue, had begun.

Mass paperback publishing is today almost a misnomer except for the very small companies. Since the space I have been allotted is very short, I refer the reader necessarily to the earlier chapters dealing with trade book publishing, for paperback publishing today is increasingly trade book publishing—plus the many and diverse peculiarities which it is inventing for itself.

In large part, mass market paperbacks began as an attempt to overcome the limited capacity of retail bookstores and book jobbers to bring books to more than a very small audience. And the mass market paperback publishers largely disregarded this area because it was too small and too demanding. (In the early days, the regular book trade accounted for less than 4 percent of Pocket Books' sales.) It is noteworthy that in *Publishers' Weekly*, December 27, 1965, President Louis Epstein of the American Booksellers Association announced that the American Booksellers Association's annual convention in 1966 "will emphasize paperback publishing and the major contribution paperbacks have made to booksellers' prosperity."

These figures will help explain the change:

PERCENT OF MASS MARKET BUSINESS IN COPIES

Outlet	*1955*	*1964*	*Ten Year Change*
U. S. magazine wholesalers	77.3	60.4	−16.9
U. S. other	8.6	27.0	+18.4
Canada	7.3	6.0	− 1.3
Other foreign	6.8	6.6	− .2

These are industry averages. The larger companies have all experienced greater declines in the proportion of their business done through magazine wholesalers.

THE SITUATION TODAY

The situation today is fluid. Here are some of the major factors.

Title Acquisition. The supposedly adequate reservoir was in fact inadequate. As lists increased in size and as trade paperback lines multiplied and took back titles from the mass market reprinters, three kinds of attempts at solutions became increasingly evident: 1) a growth in the number of original versus reprint titles; 2) republishing—this is the reappearance in paperback from another company of a title previously published in paperback; 3) an extension in editorial range far beyond any reasonable likelihood of an appeal to a mass audience.

Acquisition Costs. As competition increased, the amount of minimum guarantees required rose sharply, the terms changed sharply, and the payment requirements in point of time more and more made mass market paperback publishers bankers without even interest. The standard royalty rates of 4 percent on the first 150,000 and 6 percent thereafter are still used, but the exceptions grow in number and wildness—up to 17½ or 20 percent. Competition is so great for much-wanted titles that the winner of the auction today (in the mid-1960s) is likely to be the company which estimates its loss most optimistically.

But the huge sums paid for single titles have really had a less serious effect on mass market paperback publishing than the rising costs of acquiring bread-and-butter books. Titles which formerly had values of $2,000 to $5,000 and could be acquired at that cost have not changed in value but their prices now run $10,000 to $25,000. And there are a hundred such titles for every blockbuster. Probably no other single factor has been more important in pushing retail prices upward.

Such pressures have forced the publication of more originals and have stimulated efforts to publish in areas of less competition and smaller sales potentials. When, as is now the case, it is not uncommon to be able to buy all book publishing rights to a manuscript (assuming, of course, the full trade publisher's risks and potential rewards) for less than the later cost of acquiring limited paperback reprint rights, the urge to publish "originals" rather than "reprints" becomes almost irresistible.

Because such changes have occurred, mass market paperback houses now need editors with the full range of regular trade publishing skills, plus the original rather simple mass market reprint skills, plus specialized skills in seeking out manuscripts for more limited markets including, at least potentially, the textbook market.

Distribution. To reach the outlets covered by magazine wholesalers, mass market paperback publishers use their own sales forces if they are also magazine publishers (such as Avon, Dell and Fawcett), or they use the services of national distributors. (A national distributor supplies a publisher's paperback books to local or regional wholesalers, who in turn supply the retail outlets.) Bantam, for instance, uses Select Magazines (S-M) for this purpose. New American Library uses Independent News Company. Pocket Books and Ballantine Books use the Curtis Circulation Company. Popular Library uses Hearst's International Circulation Division (ICD).

In earlier days, there was competition in the wholesaling of magazines and paperback books. The American News Company, through its branches, served many publishers and the local independent wholesalers served the rest. This gave publishers a choice, an alternative. But the American News Company gradually began losing out and finally when its losses from magazine and paperback distribution grew too great (reputedly about $5 million a year), it simply gave up. The result is a monopoly for magazine distribution through retailers and the loss of an alternative for paperback publishers within this particular area of sales.

The independent wholesalers appear to like their monopoly position though it has placed many new demands and burdens on them. The outpouring of paperback books floods their warehouses. When they try to stuff this oversupply into the racks of the retailers they serve, there just isn't room to take the load or to leave most titles on sale long enough to have a chance to be bought. Consequently, net sales of mass market paperbacks through magazine wholesalers currently are running less than 50 percent of distributions to them from publishers, an immensely wasteful and expensive result.

But magazine distributing techniques cover only one sales area. Direct sales to book and college and department stores, to chain and syndicate stores, to discount outlets, to schools and libraries and the jobbers that serve them, to export markets, even mail-order sales are becoming increasingly important. So the mass market paperback publisher today needs a sales staff skilled in all these other areas, particularly in the trade book areas described elsewhere in this book.

And accompanying the need for such diversified sales skills are the promotion and advertising skills required to exploit these many markets. Paperback publishers today are using the full panoply of advertising, publicity, and public relations techniques which go with aggressive trade book publishing.

The Educational Market. The most visible example of change from the former simplicities of mass market paperback publishing lies in the issuing, promotion, and distribution of books intended for use by students in secondary schools and in colleges. Over the past ten years this has grown from a trickle to a tide. Increasing support is coming from the educators themselves. The top five mass market paperback publishers are probably in the mid-1960s, getting about 20 percent of their net sales from this area, and they are devoting more than that percentage of their efforts to the acquisition and publishing of suitable titles and to improving their capacities to promote and distribute them.

This is also the primary area for sales of trade paperbacks

and the area which has caused the greatest growth in sheer numbers of titles, both reprints and originals, in paperbacks of all shapes, sizes, and prices. And since education is becoming or perhaps already has become the biggest business in the United States, it is easily predictable that this trend will grow for publishers of all kinds.

That means that new and different kinds of editors are needed. It means that new and different kinds of promotion and advertising are needed. It requires different kinds of services to the eventual customer, whether that be the school or library or the retail outlet to which the student goes to make his purchases.

The chapter on textbook publishing in this volume can tell only part of this story, since the mass paperback publishers are not as yet really publishing books which have no other customers than schools. But some of them, particularly Bantam, Dell, New American Library, and Washington Square Press (a subsidiary of Pocket Books) are coming very close to pure textbook publishing and will undoubtedly go all the way in the near future. So if you wish to understand mass market paperbacks, read the parts of this volume that deal with textbooks.

This part of the new revolution has also markedly changed magazine wholesalers. At their conventions during the 1960s, it has often seemed that "How to Sell More Books to Schools" had become the topic of Number 1 importance and interest to them. It may well be that a wholly new structure of jobbing will come about because of these new needs and opportunities. For instance, it seems clear that not all the approximately 600 magazine jobbers can successfully be "school and college" book wholesalers if they stay within the geographic limitations of their magazine deliveries. Within their industry is the capital, interest, intelligence, and manpower and warehousing resources which could produce a major change in the structures through which schools and libraries get the books they need, but this is unlikely to happen unless they depart even farther from their traditional magazine distribution practices.

Packaging. Mass market paperbacks over the past twenty-five years have customarily been in two sizes, both made on the same highly efficient presses and both fitting into the standard racks in which so many millions of dollars have been invested. But the surplus of production and the limited or specialized sales appeal of so much of this product is currently forcing a change in sizes, in pricing, in marketing methods. At the moment this is a probing rather than a solution. But one factor is relatively clear: the mass market publishers of the 1960s have many more alternatives than were available to the same sort of publishers who went bankrupt under remarkably similar conditions in the 1890s. It would seem reasonable to guess that the past paperback revolution will evolve into structures and products which can have even more dynamic effects on American book publishing than the mass market revolution has already had. If so, it would probably be as a result of a further cultivation of standard trade and textbook publishing techniques.

THE OUTLOOK FOR PAPERBACKS

"You pays your money and you takes your choice." Today paperback publishers are issuing titles at all levels of potential sale from truly mass (say over a million copies) to highly selective (say down to 10,000 to 15,000 copies). They are publishing for adults and for teen-agers and for children. They are publishing at a great variety of prices—increasingly over $1.00 but also going back once more to 25¢. They are publishing in a wide range of shapes and sizes and bindings, including hardbacks (Washington Square Press published a 3-volume boxed new translation of Dante's *Divine Comedy* at $19.95 in 1966). They are marketing through almost every known device, including book clubs. The simple structures by which they were formerly defined still exist but are less and less definitive.

It would seem probable that the biggest area of expansion will be in the educational market but almost certainly not with the product as before. They will probably seek markets beyond the United States with more vigor than in the past. Three major mass market publishers already have domesticated companies in London to serve the British Empire. Despite the flood of rumors, the electronics industries had not at this writing tapped them for merger, but that is certainly a possibility.

It is clear that mass market paperback publishing as formerly defined has vanished. The shape of the future will be governed by economic pressures, by opportunities, and by chance. This part of book publishing remains the most dynamic force in the industry without knowing precisely where it is going or how it will get there, but intent on growth and capable of almost any achievement.

FOR FURTHER READING

Anderson, Vivienne, ed. Paperbacks in Education. New York, Teachers College, Columbia University, 1966.

Gross, Sidney, and Phyllis Steckler. How to Run a Paperback Bookstore. Paper. New York, Bowker, 1963.

Guinzburg, Harold, and others. Books and the Mass Market. Urbana, University of Illinois Press, 1953.

Schick, Frank L. The Paperbound Book in America: The History of Paperbacks and the European Background. New York, Bowker, 1958.

20

THE TRADE PAPERBACK

By PYKE JOHNSON JR.

EDITOR-IN-CHIEF, DOUBLEDAY ANCHOR BOOKS

❋

THE TRADE PAPERBACK derives its name from the means by which it is distributed. Unlike the mass market paperback, which reaches the consumer through a chain of national and local distributors, or the paperback textbook, which is distributed through the regular educational channels, the trade paperback is sold through the book trade, by which is meant the country's bookstores, and most especially the college bookstores. It also differs, therefore, from the school book services, such as Scholastic, whose product is sold directly through the elementary and high schools and is not, normally, available in bookstores. It should be emphasized, however, that no definition of paperbacks by distribution is rigid, and that it is possible for one type of paperback to find its way into the distribution system of another.

During the current phase of paperback publishing, which may be said to have begun with the appearance of the first Pocket Book in 1939, the first trade paperback was probably the Barnes & Noble "College Outline Series," which also began in 1939 and which was directed at a special, though broad, market. In 1951 Dover Publications introduced a series of paperbacks, chiefly scientific in nature and with a price of $2 or less, which represented the first time that serious material was presented in paperback format at a relatively low price.

But the real beginning of the trade paperback as it is known today took place with the appearance of the first Doubleday Anchor Books in April, 1953. The original concept of Anchor Books was to offer "paperback books for the permanent library of the serious reader." These books were in the format of the mass market paperbacks (Doubleday, which is one of the few trade publishers to do its own printing, owned a press which had been purchased to print a mass market line known as Permabooks), with slightly higher cover prices, slightly better paper and binding, lower initial first printings, and a standard trade discount to bookstores. An astute bookseller, Bob Marshall of Ann Arbor, who participated in the early planning for Anchor Books, has pointed out that the most important aspect of this new series was that it was issued by a trade publisher who did not have a textbook department. Mr. Marshall opines that, had Anchor Books been issued under textbook discounts, as were the Rinehart paperback "College Editions" in 1948, the widely heralded paperback revolution might have been delayed for many years.

The first Anchor Books were selected for their appeal to the "academic community," towns such as Berkeley, Ann Arbor, Chapel Hill, Cambridge, and Washington, D.C. They were not chosen primarily with the needs of the student in mind. However, the initial sale of Anchor Books in these academic communities quickly brought them to the attention of professors, who just as quickly saw in them new educational possibilities and began to use them in their classes. This classroom use was accelerated with the appearance of a number of new trade paperback lines: in 1954 came Knopf's Vintage Books, the Grove Press Evergreen Books, and Doubleday's Image Books (a series for Catholic readers); and one year later, Meridian Books, Viking Paperback Portables (to which were added Compass Books in 1956), Harcourt Brace's Harvest Books,

Beacon Press Paperbacks, and Van Nostrand's Anvil Books. One interesting side result of the appearance of these quality series was that it made the college stores realize, for the first time, the possibilities of selling books other than textbooks, a realization that grew steadily and is still growing.

EDITING

The initial success of the trade paperback in the college market determined the direction to be taken in the future by this entire area of publishing. All trade paperback lines, in contrast with the mass market lines, appeal to a specific, not a general, audience. The major areas of specialization, all of which overlap, are educational, religious, and scientific. When he evaluates a book for publication, the first question a trade paperback editor usually asks is: "What college course use does it have?" If the answer is, "None," the likelihood of the book's being accepted is very slight. Moreover, unless an editor is working for a house that has a large textbook department, he is not interested in the educational market below the college level, and even here the chances are that the selection and handling of a paperback book for the elementary or high schools will be done in the educational, not the trade, division of the publishing house.

At the beginning, all trade paperbacks were reprints. But as the number of titles in print and the number of publishers doing their own paperbacks proliferated, it became increasingly difficult to obtain suitable reprint titles. The result has been a vast increase in the number of paperback originals, in some series running well over 50 percent. These originals may be of three kinds: the book published only in paperback, the book published simultaneously in hardcover and paperback, and the book contracted for originally as a paperback, but published first in hardcover, with the paperback edition appearing at some time later, usually a year or more.

Trade paperback editors have a number of sources for new titles. They scan carefully the advance reviews in such professional journals as *Library Journal* and *Choice*. They read the reviews in the literary quarterlies and various professional magazines, such as *The American Historical Review* and *The American Sociological Review*. They pay particular attention to the *London Times Literary Supplement* (a publication with a large influence on the American campus) and various Continental literary magazines. Most trade paperback houses have paid consultants or scouts, most of them teachers, and many new titles are uncovered by college travelers, working either directly for the paperback department or for the college department of the parent house. And, as in all branches of publishing, a certain number of books are created in the house or come in, unsolicited, through the mail.

The one area of publishing in which the trade paperback has been signally unsuccessful has been in the publication of contemporary fiction, either as originals or reprints. Here again the academic orientation is evident. Without class adoption, the trade paperback novel cannot compete successfully, because of its higher price and narrower market, with its mass market counterpart.

After the selection of the title has been made, editorial work, in the case of reprints, is limited. A scholar or critic may be chosen to edit, revise, or write an introduction for a book. Footnotes may be moved from the bottom of the page to the back of a book, bibliographies updated, and, sometimes, a new index prepared; but beyond this, little is done, or indeed needed. Editorial work on original books is the same as with the normal serious hardcover book. However, in the case of both reprints and originals, copy for the back cover is usually written by the editor.

CONTRACTUAL ARRANGEMENTS

The standard royalty payment for the trade paperback is 7½ percent of the retail price. This may be for all copies sold, or may advance to 8½ percent or higher after a certain number, usually 50,000 copies, has been sold. A lower royalty is sometimes paid on collections, depending on the contribution of the editor. When an original manuscript is signed up with an agreement to publish it in both hardcover and paper edition, the author is given an option of the standard contract specifying he is to receive full hardcover royalties and 50 percent of the paperback royalties, or he may elect to take the full paperback royalty, with a hardcover royalty starting at 7½ percent, rising by stages to 15 percent after 15,000 copies have been sold. Some houses offer full royalties on the hardcover and 10 percent of the net on the paperback; there are almost as many variations on the basic scale as there are publishers.

The average advance on the trade paperback is between $1,000 and $2,000. When there is competition for a title, the advance may go considerably higher. It is rare, however, that a trade paperback publisher can compete successfully with a mass market bid. In such a competitive situation, when a trade paperback bid wins out, it is usually because the author is influenced by the prestige of being in a certain series. A book with a broad educational appeal can be sold as well by a trade paperback publisher as by a mass market publisher, as the history of *The Lord of the Flies,* published in Putnam's Capricorn series at $1.25, demonstrates.

There has been an interesting development in publishing as a result of the large number of originals of high scholarly quality published by trade paperback houses. This is the sale of hardcover reprint rights, which is made usually to university presses or to smaller general publishers. Advances are small and the royalty is usually 15 percent of the retail price, divided equally between the author and the paperback publisher. The hardcover publisher is able to save the cost of composition by photographing the paperback book. The author gets the satisfaction of having a hardcover edition, which is usually enlarged in size from the paperback version, and also reviews and library sales which are not always accorded paperback books. The hardcover affiliate of the paperback line is usually willing to relinquish the rights to books whose markets it considers small and specialized.

MANUFACTURING

Those trade paperbacks which are the same size as the mass market books are normally printed on the same type of press and are usually completely reset for this purpose. Books in larger formats (the Harper & Row Torchbooks are an example) are either photographed from existing books or use the same plates. The smaller size use "perfect" (adhesive) binding; some of the larger books are sewn. Slightly higher grade papers are used and the tops are rarely stained. Initial printings are seldom over 15,000 copies and are usually considerably lower. Certain publishers will make an initial printing and bind some copies in cloth and some in paper, saving the remaining sheets to be bound as sales of the two editions indicate.

SALES AND DISTRIBUTION

Sales of the trade paperbacks are largely dependent upon the activities of the trade sales force of the publisher. This is usually the same group of men who handle the hardcover books; separate selling forces have been tried at one time or another, but have usually been abandoned. Prices range from 85¢ to as high as $9.00, although the average price in the mid-1960s was somewhere around $1.50. Discounts offered to booksellers are usually the standard trade discount, starting at 40 percent and rising as the number of copies bought rises. Full return privileges apply, although it is seldom that paperbacks returned can be resold. As of 1966 there had been very little remaindering of trade paperbacks, although there were indications that this might become more prevalent in the future.

The most serious problem confronting the trade paperback publisher has been the lack of satisfactory wholesale outlets. The giant in the field has been the A&A Distributing Company of Holbrook, Massachusetts, whose distribution has been heavy in the East, but has also extended west of the Mississippi. In the New York area, Dimondstein in New Rochelle, which, unlike A&A, does not carry mass market books, is an example of a good regional wholesaler. So, on a slightly larger basis, is Ray Surguine of Boulder, Colorado, a mass market wholesaler, who services the area from California to Iowa and Minnesota. These wholesalers usually receive a discount of 50 percent, sometimes on all books purchased, sometimes after a certain number of copies, usually 10,000 assorted titles, have been bought.

A small number of mass market wholesalers carry selected trade paperback titles. The Mahoning Valley Distributing Agency in Youngstown, Ohio, a wholesaler so devoted to the educational market that its warehouse is arranged by subject rather than publisher, is typical.

A significant factor in the distribution of trade paperbacks has been the specialized wholesaler, best exemplified by the National Association of College Stores. From its home base in Oberlin, Ohio, NACS has had for some time an arrangement to carry all of the paperback books issued by university presses. More recently, it has set up a separate corporation, NACSCORP, to sell trade paperbacks to its member stores.

NACSCORP, which has a fairly complicated arrangement with the publishers whose books it handles, is intended to serve the *trade* needs of college stores and discourages orders from its members for textbook adoptions. Only a relatively small number of publishers have been using the services of NACSCORP. Another important specialized wholesaler is the National Catholic Reading Distributors, operated by the Paulist Press, which distributes paperback books to Catholic outlets.

One effect of the vast differences in the distribution systems of the mass market and trade paperbacks has been to enable two paper editions of the same book, usually separated in price by about one dollar, to coexist successfully.

A major opportunity for sales growth in the paperback field, both trade and mass market, lies in the schools and public libraries of the country. Awareness of the possibilities of the paperback and also of its special nature was slow in coming to the country's libraries and its professional organizations. Too often confronted by the paperback, the librarian's initial reaction has been to convert it as quickly as possible, through rebinding, into a hardcover book. Increasingly, however, libraries, particularly in schools and colleges, are setting up special paperback collections and using paperback editions to lighten the demands on reserve collections. The increasing number of original paperbacks of scholarly appeal has helped force a change in attitude. This change has also been reflected in the growing activity of professional library groups and publications in listing and evaluating paperback books.

ADVERTISING, PROMOTION AND PUBLICITY

The low profit margin of all paperbacks does not permit of extensive advertising for any individual title. In publications designed for the general public, list advertisements for trade paperbacks are occasionally run, particularly in the special paperback supplements issued by some of the larger newspapers. More important advertising outlets are to be found in those publications read by educators: the weekly opinion magazines, professional journels, and even college newspapers. Probably the single most important medium for reaching the college market is the Bowker *Paperbound Book Guide for Colleges*, which is distributed free of charge to professors and for which publishers pay a fee for each title listed.

All trade paperback promotion in the educational field is devoted to the single end of getting a book in the hands of the professor who may be in a position to adopt it. To achieve this end many techniques are used: direct mail offering free examination copies, exhibits at educational meetings, college travelers who call on professors, book fairs run in college bookstores for the benefit of the faculty, permanent exhibits in departmental libraries in larger colleges, and arrangements by certain publishers with leading college bookstores, permitting teachers to take from the store's stock examination copies which are then replaced by the publisher.

It should be emphasized that, as opposed to similar activity with hardcover books, the aim of trade paperback advertising and promotion is to generate multiple sales. Advertising and promotion resulting in the purchase of individual copies rarely pays its way.

Compared to the hardcover field, trade paperback publicity plays a small role. The large book review media have been singularly obdurate in refusing to review paperback books. Cynics comment that the resistance is not unconnected with the small amount of advertising done; book review editors reply, and not without justice, that the content of the trade paperback is too scholarly for their readers. However, it has not been untypical to find that a paperback book published at

$1.95 was not reviewed, whereas the hardcover reprint edition, published some months later at $6.50 by a university press, received a full-dress review in a leading book section. Of course, there have been occasional important reviews of trade paperbacks and these reviews have contributed significantly to sales. But the actual case history of an original trade paperback which sold over 50,000 copies before it was reviewed anywhere indicates clearly the relative unimportance of book reviews in this area.

Personal publicity, such as radio and television appearances or autographing parties, is rarely done for the author of the trade paperback book. Again this is a reflection of the specialized appeal of the books. Most publicity effort must, perforce, be concentrated on trying to obtain reviews in those publications which are read by teachers.

EXPORT

Sale of the trade paperback usually is confined to the fifty states. Prices of American editions do not permit competition with other English-language editions of the same book, and, even with noncompetitive titles, prices are too high. The one major exception is Canada, where increases in college enrollment have brought about increases in sales of trade paperbacks from this country; and there have been occasional sales of some size in other English-speaking countries elsewhere in the world.

FOR FURTHER READING

Titles listed at the end of the preceding chapter.

21

PUBLISHING BOOKS TO SELL BY MAIL

By JOHN TEBBEL

BOOK INDUSTRY HISTORIAN;
PROFESSOR, NEW YORK UNIVERSITY SCHOOL OF JOURNALISM

❋

SELLING BOOKS BY MAIL is a field whose boundaries are difficult to define. It includes book clubs, which may be independently operated (Book-of-the-Month Club), an adjunct of a magazine (Reader's Digest Condensed Book Club), or part of a general publishing house (Doubleday's Dollar Book Club). It encompasses such relatively recent marriages of book and magazine techniques as Time-Life Books and the American Heritage Publishing Company, whose products are sold by highly developed mass marketing techniques. Many leading general publishers have mail-order departments or divisions which not only sell books on the regular trade list by mail, but also develop their own items. There are also variations on subscription selling, including that part of the encyclopedia business which sells by mail, and in supermarkets by weekly purchases. And there are the special arrangements between publishers and manufacturers of other products, as in the case of packaged food producers who promote cookbooks by mail.

All these and more are forms or variants of mail-order publishing. In all, this category of publishing may comprise as much as 25 percent of the $2 billion book industry, and it is growing. Certain built-in limitations affect its growth. The cost of producing and selling books by mail places them, with some exceptions, in the upper price brackets, although books can be sold to mass markets in series or other kinds of subscription. Then, too, a saturation point will be reached eventually where serious consumer resistance to coupons and mailing pieces can be expected. Nevertheless, as the market for books continues to expand, mail-order publishing will expand with it, and the end is nowhere in sight.

THE PROCESS OF SELLING BY MAIL

The basic assumptions upon which all mail-order bookselling is based are, first, the idea that a market for books exists among people who either cannot or will not buy from regular retail outlets; and second, that specialized audiences among book readers generally can be reached more directly and effectively by mail. There are also some books, especially those on sex, which buyers would be embarrassed to ask for in a store but have no hesitation in buying under the anonymity provided by the post office. The size of this particular market can be estimated by the fact that a single such volume grossed $800,000 in its first year of publication, and shows every sign of selling for years.

A definitive description of mail-order publishing would require a book far larger than this one, but there are enough common denominators to make a general description possible. Probably the most important of these commonalities is the list. List-making and selling is an industry in itself. The companies which compile and sell them can provide almost any listing of human segments in the population a publisher desires—people divided by age groups, by occupation, by income, by geographical distribution, by buying habits, and dozens of other divisions. The publisher usually begins with these, but he soon supplements or combines them with his own, compiled from previous successful mail-order campaigns, from magazine subscription lists, or as time goes on, from the people who have bought at least one of his products.

Mailings go out to these lists in widely varying quantities, ranging from a few hundred thousand to as many as eight million or more. A book may be sold entirely through these mailings, in which the customer returns either a coupon or a card ordering the book, or entirely through coupon advertising placed in magazines or newspapers, or both. Mailings and advertising are also used in combination. What happens after the order arrives until final payment is received, including shipping, billing, and collecting, is known as fulfillment.

Direct mail solicitation may go to a general list, or to specialized groups—accountants, for instance, who may be prospects for a tax book. Coupon advertising has the same flexibility. It can be placed in general magazines and newspapers, or it can be concentrated in periodicals directed to a specific audience. In such advertising, coupons are almost always placed at the bottom so that it will be easier to tear them out. For small publishers who want to sell a single book on their list by mail and lack both the machines and manpower to do it, there are mail-order fulfillment houses ready to do the entire job for them, under arrangements in which there is considerable variation.

Described so simply, it would seem that the venerable truism, "anyone can go into the mail-order business," has more than an element of truth in it. To sell by mail successfully, however, is another matter, requiring an entirely different set of techniques, and even a different philosophy, than traditional trade selling.

To begin with, the mailing piece or the advertisement represents an art in itself. The layman looks at a full-page coupon advertisement in his newspaper or magazine and wonders disdainfully who reads all that type packed into its borders; he is accustomed to the clean, spare impact of most national advertising. Or he may open his mail and find as much or more type in a brochure or a broadside, accompanied by a selling letter and perhaps some other single sheets containing special offers, and quite possibly he will throw all of it in the wastebasket and remark irritably about the quantity of junk mail he gets.

The layman cannot know of the endless hours which have gone into those presentations he dismisses so casually. Their conception has been argued and reargued, they have been designed with the utmost care, the writing has been done by specialists, some of whose salaries would astonish the recipient. Artwork, if it is used, is carefully selected and executed. All this expert preparation is based on the certain knowledge that, if it is done well, a profitable percentage of recipients will read all the type and look at the pictures and fill out the coupon. For the secret of direct-mail selling is simply that there are always people to whom the idea of advertisement or mailing piece appeals directly, and these people are not only willing but eager to read about what is being offered them. They are in a receptive mood to be sold. The Civil War buff is a case in point, and there are as many other cases as there are kinds of books.

Once the coupon has been mailed and the fulfillment process begins, the whole world of mail-order selling opens up in all its variation. Probably it can be best understood by examining its principal types in more detail.

THE BOOK CLUBS AND HOW THEY WORK

Among the book clubs, the Book-of-the-Month Club is the prototype of this contemporary phenomenon which has become a formidable business within the book industry. It was originally devised by Harry Scherman, who remains the Club's chairman of the board. Scherman invented the book club in its twentieth-century form, although the idea dates back to the early nineteenth century, or possibly even earlier. In the forty years of BOM's existence (it began in April, 1926), the Club has distributed more than 200 million books to its members, or 618 selections chosen from more than 87,000 titles—an average of 2,500 books submitted by publishers every year. Another 20,000 titles have been recommended (and sold) to members.

BOM is the only book club with an autonomous editorial board making the selections, from galley proofs (usually) or bound books submitted to them. Everyone in the executive hierarchy, however, is invited to submit possible titles to the board. Besides Scherman, there are only two chief executives, a president and an executive vice-president. Since the BOM publishes its own editions of the books chosen, the remainder of its organization resembles that of a trade publisher, at least in some respects. It has advertising and promotion people, an art department which employs artists and layout experts, and copywriters particularly trained for mail-order selling. Such copywriters have often begun their careers working for other book and record clubs; they need only to adapt their style to the Club's, which is somewhat more restrained, like the sales effort of American Heritage.

Unlike the regular trade publisher, however, BOM has a group of statisticians employing market research techniques in an effort to predetermine how much a particular title may sell. Computerization has come to be a help in this respect, as it has in other kinds of merchandising. Nevertheless, the book business being the uncertain affair it is, the Club turns out what it calls a "pessimistic" first printing, but is able to return quickly for more books as the members' response warrants. Selections are shipped from whatever plant they are printed in, but all the billing is done at the Club's headquarters in New

York City. Its lower price structure is based on volume, and also on the fact that it leases plates from the original publisher rather than buying from him at the usual discounts.

Mailing lists are developed in the Club by the means described earlier. Some lists are rented, and of course the organization has built up its own list from its customers. About 40 percent of these are replaced every year, but many resubscribe later. Mailings run anywhere from one to eight million, after pretesting of the market. One list, for instance, may respond quite differently from another to a particular mailing.

As in other businesses, computerization has pretty well taken over the order and shipping departments at BOM, but the Club still employs about 500 people. From a vocational standpoint, however, BOM offers a limited job market. It has few executives and they have been drawn largely from advertising agencies and related enterprises. The editorial board is composed of distinguished writers and critics. Copywriters come from other mail-order operations, while employees in the advertising and art departments are likely to have had previous backgrounds on magazines or in book publishing houses.

What computers have meant to book clubs can be seen from a study of automatic and nonautomatic operations in fulfillment. The automatic club ships in cycles—a week, a month, or even longer—and it may or may not offer a return privilege. The Reader's Digest Condensed Book Club is an example, issuing its volumes quarterly without previous announcement. Nominally the subscriber is intended to keep the shipment, but there are some returns nonetheless. The BOM is a nonautomatic club, operating on a rejection privilege basis, but it has a subsidiary automatic club, the Young Readers of America. Nonautomatic clubs have special problems rising from their frequent, repetitive transactions. For example, there is the problem of stopping shipment when a reader refuses a book in a particular month. Another is the matter of substitution, which is the customer's privilege. Then there are the procedures common to all—processing returns, changing addresses, applying payments, effecting cancelations, and so on. Computerization has helped materially to speed up all these standard operations.

When a book club is part of an extremely large publishing house, difficulties are multiplied, particularly so in the case of Doubleday, which has about thirty clubs and "programs" of various kinds enmeshed in its corporate structure. The number is not constant because a program which is not doing well may be dropped, perhaps to be resumed later. Meanwhile, it may be replaced by one or more unrelated programs.

The range of Doubleday's mail-order selling is impressive. For years the Literary Guild, chief rival of BOM, was the company's chief activity in the field. Closely following it came the Doubleday Dollar Book Club, which has now surpassed its older brother. The other clubs and programs are centered around specialized audiences, for the most part, and the publications include both books and pamphlets, supplemented by such educational materials as microscopes, arrowheads, slides, and similar articles, offered as premiums. The Nelson Doubleday Personal Success Program, to cite an example, is a series of booklets. Doubleday's mail-order business, in brief, is the selling of printed materials.

Besides those already mentioned, these programs include, at this writing, the American Garden Guild garden books; the Around-the-World Program; Best In Books, a competitor of the Reader's Digest Condensed Book Club, and operated in much the same way; a companion piece, Best In Children's Books; and another, Best Loved Girls' Books; Book Club Associates; Book League of America; Catholic Family Book Club; Catholic Youth Book Club; the Cookbook Guild; the Dollar

Mystery Guild; the Family Reading Club; the Fireside Theatre; the International Collectors' Club, distributing better quality editions of classics; the Junior Deluxe Editions Club; the Know Your America Program; the Know Your Bible Program; the Junior Literary Guild; the Literary Guild Retail Division, selling the Guild through the book departments of department stores; Macy's Literary Guild of America; the Paint-It-Yourself Art Program; Real Books; the Reading For Men Club; Amy Vanderbilt's Personal Success Program; the Science Fiction Book Club; the Science Program; and the Sports Book League.

In addition, Doubleday operates a small mail-order department, composed of only two men and three girls, who follow the usual procedure of selecting books from the Doubleday list with mail-order potential—they are mostly of the self-help variety—and promoting them by mail. This relatively modest enterprise sometimes grosses more than $500,000 annually. One of its recent outstanding successes was the selling by subscription of the Anchor Bible, in forty volumes, for which 15,000 subscribers had been obtained by early in 1966, only a few months after initial publication.

General Dwight D. Eisenhower's volume of reminiscences, *Waging Peace*, was also sold by this department, employing among other devices a political list compiled largely from campaign contributors. This ploy was used earlier in selling Richard M. Nixon's book about political crises. The department began to develop a new series in 1965 called Zenith Books, designed for young readers in various ethnic groups.

Doubleday possesses, in addition, an educational mail-order department, dealing mostly in paperbacks, and sending its mailings primarily to teachers for the use of both themselves and the students. This department will (and does) sell whole shelves of books by mail for school libraries.

Completing the company's mail organization is a Subscription Book Department, involved in such activities as selling a deluxe volume, *The World of Birds*, employing the lists of the Audubon Society and working with the Society to merchandise the volume.

In spite of this complicated network of diversified merchandising, mail-order selling at Doubleday has a streamlined organization. One fulfillment department serves all of the clubs, programs, and departments, including the sending out of mailing pieces. This mechanism is centered in Garden City at the old Country Life Press, where the company began its career. Shipping is done from wherever the books are produced, either at Berryville, Virginia, or at another Doubleday printing establishment, in Philadelphia. Billing is done from the Garden City center.

There is an editorial vice-president in the Doubleday corporate organization who is in charge of the clubs, and each club has its own editorial staff, varying in size according to the scope of its activity. Copywriting and layout for the firm are centralized, and mail order also uses the company's art and production departments. Mailing materials and advertising are separate departments especially for the clubs and programs, and the recruiting of new members is handled separately. Doubleday does not do as much market research as, for instance, BOM, but it too is rapidly becoming computerized.

MAIL ORDER IN A TRADE PUBLISHING HOUSE

The Doubleday colossus is not typical of what regular trade publishers do about mail-order selling. Much more customary is the mail-order department of a firm like Harper & Row, a small organization which publishes its own books as well as combing the house's trade list for mail-order possibilities. This department's list is heavily loaded with reference and self-help books—encyclopedias, dictionaries, health, self-improvement, and specialized volumes in such activities as bridge, golf, and business management. The aim of such a department is not to establish large initial sales, although that sometimes happens, but to create books which will sell in satisfying quantities over long periods of time. It is not unusual for a book to keep on selling, albeit in decreasing quantities, for ten or fifteen years. The mail-order department also publishes a few "prestige" books—art books, or so-called coffee table items.

Trade departments in publishing houses operate by means of a shotgun technique, scattering their shots over a broad area. Mail-order departments cannot afford this method. They must try to get long-selling volumes into print, and develop series which will continue over a period of years. Harper, like many of the others, does occasional pretesting, but relies mostly on test mailings. The department is not in competition with the house's other divisions; it tries to originate books outside the areas in which the trade department may be working. Its art and production work is channeled through the regular Harper departments.

When a book is developed by the department, particular attention is paid to advance organization of the content, so that the end result is a detailed table of contents which can be used in the advertising and mailing pieces. This is common to most such departments. The theory is that a table of contents constitutes an excellent selling tool, since it gives the potential customer a comprehensive idea of what is in the book, whets his interest, and impels him to buy out of curiosity, if nothing else.

Harper & Row mail-order books are often in the $6 to $10 price range. Their titles, following uniform practice in the field, are specific and short. They avoid cuteness; the mail-order customer is a no-nonsense fellow. Every book carries an index.

In writing advertising copy, the Harper staff also follows standard practice in trying to make the presentation as complete as possible on the theory that, unlike the usual advertisement, the mail-order ad must do the entire selling job for the book. Consequently the layman's complaint of "too many words," as pointed out earlier, is not a realistic basis for judging this special kind of salesmanship.

The Harper & Row department could be described as a basic kind of mail-order operation within the structure of a large publishing house. Other houses vary principally in the variety of their activities, as in Doubleday's proliferation of clubs and programs. Similarly, Prentice-Hall has an extensive list of book clubs and reader services. McGraw-Hill and Simon and Schuster are other leaders in the field with multiple mail-order offerings. Grolier, whose principal stock-in-trade is encyclopedias, which are sold in part by mail, has a variety of mail-order activities, including a recently acquired correspondence school.

CREATING BOOKS TO SELL BY MAIL

Mail-order selling by regular trade publishing houses is old enough to be traditional. Its chief rival is the kind of mass market merchandising represented by Time-Life Books and by the American Heritage Publishing Company. The rise of these enterprises has been phenomenal. Scarcely more than a dozen years old in 1966, American Heritage is one of the most successful publishing operations in the industry, while Time-Life Books, only five years old in that year, accounted for 8 percent of Time, Inc.'s corporate business in 1965.

The two enterprises have in common an adroit blending of magazine and book techniques, and both are sold and distributed by the general mail-order methods common to all. Otherwise they differ, in that Time-Life sells primarily through coupon advertising, while American Heritage does about three-quarters of its business by direct mail. There are differences in organization, too. Time-Life is a mixture of news magazine and regular trade procedures; American Heritage is much closer to the standard pattern of the trade house. Again, Time-Life sells most of its books in series, thus enabling it to function within a lower price structure, while American Heritage—aside from its hardcover periodicals—produces more luxurious, one-shot books at higher prices, and concentrates more or less in the field of American history, whereas the Time-Life range is wide.

The Luce organization was actually first in the field, experimenting as early as 1950 with a half-dozen or so expensive one-shot books. These were spinoffs from *Life* magazine, using both art and text from that periodical. The experiments were successful enough to convince Time, Inc.'s executives that mail-order bookselling was a profitable business to be in, and in 1959 they hired Doubleday's advertising manager, Jerome Hardy (later publisher of *Life*), to develop a book division. As a separate entity, this division stopped using material from the parent organization's magazines, except for an occasional plate, and began creating its own products, beginning with the World Library in 1960. In the following year four more one-shots were introduced, including an atlas in a joint venture with Rand-McNally, and a nature series was added. Expansion was rapid after that, until the Book Division became one of the largest such organizations in the world, with total sales in its first five years of more than 40 million copies of more than 200 books in the United States and Canada, and at least 5 million more abroad, translated into thirteen languages.

Time-Life Books in 1966 had seven different "libraries" or series in operation: the Life Nature Library; the Life World

Library; the Life Science Library; a series on the Great Ages of Man; a twelve-part Life History of the United States; the Time Reading Program, a series of soft-cover editions of contemporary literary classics; and the International Book Society, a book club distributing special editions of foreign books, printed abroad and sold to members at prices in the upper brackets. An example of the latter would be Rose Macauley's *Pleasure of Ruins*, a large book 10¼ by 14 inches, with 160 full-page photographs and many hand-mounted color plates. This volume, designed to retail for about $30 in the regular market, was offered to members for $17.50. Thus Time-Life encroaches on American Heritage territory; its other products have been selling from $2.95 to $4.95.

As is evident, Time-Life Books are divided rather neatly between science and the humanities. They are written by noted scholars and authors, under the direction of an editorial staff numbering nearly 250, and the photography is by equally eminent practitioners of the art, including some of the noted free-lancers who work for *Life*.

A planning department has the overall direction of these complex activities, working under a manager of sales development, a manager of special projects, and a circulation manager, but ideas for books are welcomed from anyone in the organization. All ideas are subjected first to market research, after which the publisher decides on the basis of the figures whether the project is commercially viable. The editors must then decide whether the book is editorially feasible. Seven people comprise the Planning Department, as a general rule. The market research is done by standard mail-order testing techniques, usually sample mailings, sometimes supplemented by telephone surveys. Every idea is thoroughly pretested; mistakes are prohibitively expensive in this business. Even after a series is decided upon, the editors create the first volume and try it out on the public before they commit themselves to a long-range program.

There is a general editorial staff in charge of the books, but each series also has its own staff, and each has its own design. Thus Time-Life Books has an editor, an executive editor, a text director, an art director, a chief of research, an assistant art director and an assistant chief of research, working under an overall executive staff which includes a publisher, a general manager, a business manager, and a circulation manager. A series like the Great Ages of Man, for example, will have a series editor and an editorial staff which includes an assistant editor, designer, copy editor, two staff writers, chief researcher, picture researcher, and five text researchers. There is also an editorial production staff numbering a color director, a three-girl copy staff, five art assistants, and a two-girl picture bureau. Production itself goes first through the Traffic Department, then comes under the control of Corporation Production, which handles production for all of Time, Inc.

A series may, and often does, draw on the resources of the parent organization. Great Ages of Man gives credit to the chief of *Life's* picture library, to the chief of Time, Inc.'s Bureau of Editorial Reference, to the chief of the Time-Life News Service; and to Time correspondents in Rome, London, and Paris.

The promotion department at Time-Life Books functions on behalf of all the series, employing five people to handle institutional advertising, news about the projects, reviewers, and displays at conventions and elsewhere. There is a permanent display of the division's projects which travels around the country.

In its merchandising, Time-Life employs the usual method of renting lists, which are supplemented by the corporation's lists from its magazines, and the constantly growing lists of its own customers. Fulfillment is carried out in Chicago, where Time, Inc., has several operations, including printing. Lists of customers are carried there on tape, for use by the computerized order and shipping departments. Printing is done in seven or eight printing establishments, and the binding in four other shops. The shipping label comes from Chicago to wherever the book is waiting for it. Three warehouses, one in Indianapolis and the others in Crawfordsville and Hammond, Indiana, house the books.

Time-Life Books is essentially more of a magazine than a book publishing enterprise, evidenced not only in its *Life*-like layouts but in its schedules, where sometimes as many as four books may close in a single month, creating the rush and tension more characteristic of periodicals than of trade houses.

Although they are in the same business, broadly speaking, American Heritage offers a contrast to Time-Life Books in many respects. It too sprang from a magazine, but not from an already highly successful commercial enterprise with the resources of a large and high-powered corporation. James Parton and Joseph Thorndike, its chief entrepreneurs, started from scratch, or a little below. The idea took root as early as the mid-1940s in the minds of two men, Courtland Canby, son of the noted *Saturday Review of Literature* editor, Henry Seidel Canby, and the historian Allan Nevins. Canby had come to work for Nevins on the scholarly publications of the American Association for State and Local History and The Society of American Historians. They conceived the idea of a history magazine for these times, perhaps recalling the nineteenth-century success of the *Magazine of American History* and similar periodicals of that era. This idea was developed skillfully by Parton after he acquired the historical societies' property. It emerged concretely in 1954, under the sponsorship of the two societies, as a hard-cover bimonthly in a picture-and-text format, declaring as its purpose to depict "the history of the American experience, in all its varied aspects." Parton was joined in his venture by Joseph Thorndike, who brought to it the rich experience he had gained as editor of *Life* for many years. The result was a gold mine.

As a magazine in hard covers, *American Heritage* is, at this writing, a handsome book of 8¾ by 11¼ inches, with 112 pages on which are reproduced a great variety of historical illustrations, about a fourth of them in color, on good quality paper, and selling at $3.95 a copy, or $15 a year for six issues. The senior editor in 1966 was Bruce Catton; the editor, Oliver Jensen.

American Heritage appeared at an opportune moment. In the mid-1950s Americans were engaged in a search for their national identity, a search reflected in numerous magazine articles, books, and editorials on the subject. Instinctively they turned to their own past for the answer, and American history became a more important part of publishing than it had ever been. Through mail-order selling, Parton was able to capture a large part of that considerable audience which liked to read but had not learned or been persuaded to buy in bookstores.

By 1957 the magazine was so well established that Parton and Thorndike were encouraged to bring out their first book —*The American Heritage Book of Great Historic Places.* It sold 150,000 copies at $12.50 by mail, entirely aside from its sale through regular trade channels. Convinced that they were on the right track, and a highly profitable one, the partners began the line of books which quickly placed them among the leaders in the mail-order book business. The series included volumes on the American Revolution, the pioneer spirit, the Civil War, Indians, flight, natural wonders, World War I and World War II in separate books, the West, and an illustrated history of American eating and drinking packaged as *The American Heritage Cookbook.*

Of them all, the outstanding success by 1966 had been *The Civil War*, with a text by Bruce Catton. Selling for $19.95, with a deluxe edition for $25, it grossed a remarkable $8 million against a production cost of $2 million.

Branching out in another direction, the company introduced a similar magazine of the fine arts, *Horizon*, with a comparable book division, although, as at Time-Life, the books were original creations, not taken bodily from the magazine. They, too, were splendid and expensive productions, using text and pictures in the same way as American Heritage books, and including such titles as *Ancient Greece*, *Christianity*, *The Age of Napoleon*, *Lost World*, and *The Renaissance*.

Invading the field of children's books, the company produced a line called the American Heritage Junior Library, began in 1959, and in 1962 expanded it to include another series known as Horizon Caravel Books. These volumes, like the magazines, are published at two-month intervals, six to the year, under the general title of Adventures in History. The Junior Library concentrates on American history, the Caravel line on world history and art. These publications are sold by subscription on a yearly basis at $2.95 each, or at retail for $3.95.

American Heritage is also in the mail-order map business, offering early maps of America, 1½ by 2 feet, printed in full-color gravure on heavy paper with a matte finish; the story of the map is printed on the back.

Unlike the Time-Life products, American Heritage books are distributed by means of contracts with individual trade publishers, using their sales and distribution machinery, as well as through the mail-order mechanism at Heritage. Parton boasts that his company publishes only best sellers, and it is sheer economic necessity that they be so, because of their exceptionally high production costs. A book must sell at least 75,000 copies before it begins to make money for its publisher, and in some cases this figure rises to 100,000. Scientifically planned mail-order campaigns are organized for every book. These result in initial mailings as high as 7 million.

Departing momentarily from its successful formula, American Heritage produced one of the most spectacular mail-order sales in history after the assassination of President John F. Kennedy, with a book about the event and the funeral called *Four Days*. Distributed through United Press International and its clients by means of coupon ads in the newspapers, the book sold 2.5 million copies; in a single day one paper alone recorded 25,000 orders.

At the top of the company's organization chart, Parton heads the business side and Thorndike is chief editorial executive. There is an editorial director for the books, and there is for the individual magazines, and seven or eight editorial staffs work on the various projects. The magazines, of course, have their own permanent staffs, and the book divisions also have permanent overall editorial direction. Senior editors conceive the ideas for books in conjunction with those responsible for sales. Planning is projected several years ahead; a major book will take a year or even two years to produce. There is a picture research staff to work with the editorial people, while art, design, and production are concentrated in another department. Promotion and sales are handled within the organization, but advertising goes through an agency. As at Time-Life, lists are developed through rentals and cumulatively from past customers. Fulfillment (i.e., subscription and order processing and billing) is carried out by the Fulfillment Corporation of America, in Marion, Ohio, using the now virtually standard computer tape. Much of the organization's printing is done in New York, but a good deal also is assigned to presses in Switzerland, Italy, and other European centers noted for superior color work. Shipping is usually from the bindery. The company uses two of these for the most part, H. Wolff in New York and

Riverside in Cambridge, Mass. These firms also take care of the warehousing.

A unique characteristic of this kind of mail-order organization is the absence of remaindering unsold books, a perennial problem in trade publishing. Printings are geared to anticipated sales, both retail and mail, and the long life of these volumes virtually guarantees that they will all be sold eventually.

It is obvious from the foregoing description of the Time-Life and American Heritage organizations that people seeking a career in this part of the mail-order field must bring to it an armament of skills from other occupations. Those with experience on picture-text magazines, art and production people from both book and magazine operations, specialists in mail-order copywriting—such are the backgrounds of the personnel producing the books turned out by these companies.

The roster of mail-order bookselling organizations is not exhausted by those already discussed. There seems to be a virtually endless number of approaches to disposing of books by mail, and not all of them are the organizations whose names are so well known to the public through advertising. The housewife who buys encyclopedias in parts of her supermarket probably does not notice the publisher's imprint on backstrap or title page, but in the trade, Golden Press, Dell, and Meredith are among those recognized as leaders in this kind of selling. These and other houses produce a wide range of books sold in a variety of ways.

Mail-order selling well illustrates what is perhaps the most significant thing that has happened to American publishing in this century—the multiplication of outlets for the distribution of books. Where once the retail bookshop and the department stores were almost the only links between books and the buyers, save for a relatively minor amount of subscription selling, publishing today has a broad choice of distribution points to supplement the traditional outlets, including the mails, supermarkets, drug stores, the college bookstores, even gas stations which handle travel guides.

While the commercial advantages of this proliferation are readily recognized and understood by the book industry, and most publishers are now busily engaged in exploiting its possibilities in one way or another, there remains a traditional distaste for some aspects of it on the part of old-line publishers. It is directed particularly against the kind of product produced by Time-Life Books and American Heritage. The term "made books" is sometimes used in a disparaging way, although the "idea book" is firmly entrenched in every house when it means a book conceived inside the firm, which then finds an author to write it and, if necessary, picture researchers to illustrate it. But the big, handsome book, using the picture-and-text techniques developed by *Look* and *Life*, is often called a "coffee table" book by its critics, as noted earlier, meaning that it is bought as a status symbol and displayed to guests on the coffee table, where it testifies to the owner's affluence and culture but remains unread.

Reader surveys, however, do not bear out this contention. While status is certainly involved in an indeterminate number of cases impossible to measure, there is good reason to believe that if the list of American Heritage, for example, were measured against the list of a regular trade publisher, there would be substantially more overall reader attention paid to the Heritage books, for reasons which perhaps are obvious. A large number of books on the regular publisher's list will inevitably have small audiences, reaching the vanishing point in the case of some novels. Conversely, a high sales figure does not guarantee readership. Many a best seller remains relatively unread after it gets into the home. But the studies available show that Heritage's books on American history, to continue the example, are closely and devotedly read by the growing number of history buffs in our country. Similarly, the Time-Life books on science, to cite another instance, are meat and drink to a growing generation enchanted with the astounding technological society they are inheriting. Indeed, many educators believe that the mail-order books of these two companies alone are a powerful educational force, particularly in making subjects which were once regarded with distaste by young students far more palatable through the use of graphic illustration, and text freed of the academic ineptitudes characteristic of so many textbooks.

While there is little likelihood that mail-order books will take over publishing, as some enthusiasts earnestly believe, they will unquestionably continue to play an increasingly important role, particularly with the further expansion of education, which is on the verge of becoming the nation's largest industry. Consequently mail-order publishing has an exceedingly bright future. In an era when specialized publishing has come to dominate all of the print media, it is clear from the experience of the mail-order organizations already in the book business that there is an enormous market of Americans hungry for information and culture if it is attractively packaged. That market, in spite of the impressive sales figures cited in this chapter, remains relatively untapped. In the mid-1960s, the tapping process had only begun.

FOR FURTHER READING

Lee, Charles. The Hidden Public: The Story of the Book-of-the-Month Club. New York, Doubleday, 1958.

Titles listed at the end of Chapter 7, especially those containing information on advertising by mail.

SECTION VI

THE FUTURE

22

THE CHANGING FACE OF PUBLISHING

By DAN LACY

SENIOR VICE-PRESIDENT, MCGRAW-HILL BOOK COMPANY
FORMERLY MANAGING DIRECTOR, AMERICAN
BOOK PUBLISHERS COUNCIL

IN THE postwar decade, the future of books and of book publishing was thought a bleak and limited one. Exciting new forms of entertainment, of communications, and of the storage and retrieval of information had seized the imagination. It was to broadcasting, it was thought, that people would turn for news and entertainment, and television and other audio-visual aids would replace textbooks in the classroom. The book stacks of libraries would be succeeded by compact stores of microforms, from which information would be drawn by computer and projected to the waiting inquirer. It seemed to many that the reading of books, like the riding of horses, would remain only as the elegant and somewhat archaic pastime of a small elite. So informed a body as the University of Chicago's Graduate Library School convened a conference in 1954 to consider "The Future of the Book"—and generally found it wanting.

THE BOOK REVOLUTION

But the prophets would have done better to have kept their eyes on the maternity wards, for it was in the delivery rooms rather than in the electronics laboratories that the immediate future of the book was being determined. The annual number of births, which had fallen as low as 2.25 million in the 1930s, rose abruptly in 1946 and 1947, and for almost twenty years stayed above 4 million a year. By 1952 this postwar generation had begun to enter school, and within a decade there were about 12 million more schoolchildren than in the preceding decade, demanding children's books and textbooks in enormous numbers.

Moreover, education assumed a new role in American life. The G. I. Bill of Rights established a pattern that made a college education the normal expectation of most young men and women rather than the privilege of a few, and college enrollment had tripled as compared with the prewar years even before the first postwar baby was out of high school. That enrollment was to double again when the postwar generation came of college age in the latter 1960s. But it was not only that many millions more youngsters stayed in school for far more years that we had ever known before. The change in American education was qualitative as well as quantitative. It was filled with a new seriousness. Students worked harder, and they read more. School, college, and public libraries were packed, and the budgets to support them were increased by hundreds of millions of dollars. Paperbound books by the tens of millions of copies were consumed by high-school and college students.

Their parents read more, too. They bought more paintings, visited more museums, attended more concerts, owned more classical recordings, viewed more ballet, and bought more books. Whatever one may think of the development of the content of American cultures, the last decade has seen a revolution in its instruments and institutions.

The consequence of all these trends is that there has been not a decline, but rather a correspondingly revolutionary increase in the number of books published and sold in the United States. In 1955, 12,589 titles were published, of which approximately 750 million copies were sold for about $800 million. In 1965, only a decade later, 28,595 titles were published, and over 1.25 billion copies were sold for about $2 billion. This growth was so large and so swift as to become a change in kind as well as in degree and to have profound consequences for the whole structure of publishing.

NEW MONEY, NEW STRUCTURES

In the first place, it required an unprecedented increase in the working capital applied to publishing. Between 1955 and 1965 it is probable that between $750 million and $1 billion of new capital had to be invested in publishing to meet society's new demands. It was, of course, totally impossible to generate a sum within the industry. The reinvestment of every nickel of post-tax profits over the decade would not have approached the required amount. Some reinforcement was achieved by mergers within the industry that enabled better financed companies to increase resources for those less well financed. But most of the money had to come from outside the industry.

It came in two ways. One was by public stock flotations which enabled the general public to invest new capital, while a majority control remained in the hands of the owners. The other was through the entry of outside companies into book publishing, either through the acquisition and expansion of existing companies or through the initiation of new book-publishing ventures. In the latter cases, new management has often accompanied new money.

The mergers have probably been of less consequence than has been supposed. Rarely have they reduced the number of competing firms in any area of publishing. Rather they have been intended to round out companies. They have been typified by such mergers as that of Harper and Brothers, publishers in almost every field except elementary and high-school textbooks, with Row, Peterson and Company, publishing such textbooks almost exclusively; or that of Harcourt, Brace and Company, publishers of trade books and college and high-school textbooks, with the World Book Company, publishers of elementary textbooks and tests.

Potentially somewhat more significant has been the process of "going public." Though it may not have changed the management or control of a company, it has charged the management with a responsibility to outside stockholders who may have invested only for income and profit. That responsibility has to be publicly expressed in published reports, stockholders meetings, and conferences with securities analysts. A concern for profitability, which has of course always been actually present in publishing as in other businesses, has been, if not accentuated, at least formalized and patterned. Eccentricities peculiar to publishing have tended to disappear as publishing firms have conformed more nearly to the management practices of American corporations generally.

Most significant of all may be the entry of new firms into the book publishing field. Major magazine publishers have expanded into books, usually employing the editorial approaches successful in their magazines and seeking to serve a very similar market. Time-Life, Inc. and Meredith have initiated major book enterprises, following the lead of the *Reader's Digest.* More recent has been the acquisition of book publishing companies by firms in other areas of communications or information transfer. The Times-Mirror Company, a Los Angeles newspaper publisher, became by 1966 the owner of five book publishing houses, in the fields of trade, Bible, dictionary, juvenile, mass market, paperbound, law, medical, and art publishing. Such diverse firms in the electronic and related worlds as RCA, IBM, Xerox, Raytheon, and General Electric became in the 1960s the owners of or associates in book publishing enterprises.

This latter group have been motivated by a conviction that the educational materials of the future are likely to take the form of systems rather than isolated units, and to be made up of a synthesis of printed and audio-visual materials, probably controlled and presented by electronic devices. They have believed, hence, that success in the vast educational market would go to those companies that embodied in themselves such a synthesis of printed, audio-visual, and electronic approaches. Here the intention of the new investors has been active and creative, rather than passive, and their interests and special competences will no doubt be impressed upon their publishing subsidiaries.

One result of the growth of the industry, mergers, and the new investment is an increase in the size of companies. In 1950, a book publishing house doing a business of $5 million a year would have been thought a large one; and one doing $10 million, very large indeed. Fifteen years later there were several firms whose total business probably exceeded $100 million annually, and quite a number whose turnover was $25 million or more. The difference is not merely one of degree; the larger houses require, and can afford, specialized management staffs, computerized accounting and management controls, systematically organized marketing services, research facilities, personnel office, and in general a more professional and impersonal management.

Such companies, with ample financing, are more able to shape both their products and their markets than were publishing houses of a generation ago. Books conceived and created by publishing houses or by writers commissioned by them have always played an important part in publishing, but their proportion of the total output of books has sharply increased. These include not only encyclopedias and textbooks, but art books, children's books designed for supplemental school use, books and series intended for mail-order sale, international publishing projects produced simultaneously in several countries, reprint series, cook books, and many other varieties; and will include such products of the marriage of print and electronics as may appear in the future. Publishing of this kind begins with a market and a method of selling and seeks to create a book salable by that method to that market, where traditional publishing began with a book and sought to find a market for it. To the degree that a publishing firm can indeed control the entire process from creation of a work to its final sale it is freed from the expensive uncertainties that have always menaced publishing enterprises that must gamble on the unpredictability of authors, the vagaries of public taste, and the operations of a spotty and inadequate distribution system.

The ability to control both the source of manuscripts and the marketing of books has been sought within traditional patterns of publishing as well. Trade publishers, for example, have established their own inexpensive reprint lines, rather than relying solely on the sale of reprint rights to other houses. Conversely, reprint houses have entered original publishing in order to have a dependable source of titles. Direct mail sales to the public have markedly increased, as have direct sales to schools and libraries. In both cases marketing remains under the publisher's control, independent of jobbers and retailers.

Another principal influence on publishing has been the increased importance of the school and library market for juvenile and adult trade books. The institutional market now absorbs perhaps 80 percent of the output of children's books (other than inexpensive mass market editions), and probably a majority of the more serious adult nonfiction. This startling increase in the number of titles published annually is almost entirely responsive to this demand. The doubling, in a decade, of the number of new children's titles published annually, from about 1,500 to more than 3,000, was made necessary primarily to provide supplemental books for school libraries, specifically planned to support the curriculum. The principal increase in new adult titles published annually has been in scholarly and informative works for the university and public library market. Similarly the ten-year rise in paperbound titles produced annually from about 1,500 to 7,500 has been occasioned primarily by the school and college demand for copies for supplemental reading.

These changes have disturbed many. Where once they feared that books and publishing might disappear altogether, they are now concerned that the very flood of print may submerge the traditional forms of publishing and the traditional values of books. Will a publicly held company, responsible to its stockholders for achieving a maximum return on their investment, be free to undertake the risky publication of the works of untried authors? Will excellence be entirely replaced by profitability as a criterion? When hundreds of millions of dollars are invested in books written to order to fill a particular need or suit a particular market, will there be opportunity for books written to express the author's encounter with meaning? Amid giant corporations, will there be room for the small personal publisher? Will there be a role for the bookstore in an era of direct selling?

So far, the answers can be reassuring. Large, publicly held firms have not in fact eliminated the high quality trade title from their lists. The number of novels and of volumes of new poetry and drama published annually has increased, not decreased. A rapidly growing market has made possible the publication of many more scholarly books and the issuance of paperbound books of high intellectual caliber. The largest publishing houses, concerned to maintain a high reputation in the educational world, have been jealous of the range and quality of their trade publishing programs in literary and scholarly fields. Very small, one-man, publishing houses are probably even more difficult to launch successfully today than a generation ago; but there are dozens of relatively small to medium-size independent publishing houses that play a vigorous and distinguished role. A rapid growth in university press publishing—both in the number and in the size of university presses—has greatly extended the range of scholarly publishing and has increased the number of outlets for poetry. Bookstores, which languished for many years after the war, seem to have experienced a renaissance, with the number of members of the American Booksellers Association increasing from 1,125 in 1955 to 2,400 in 1966. This growth has probably been occasioned primarily by the availability of higher-priced paperbounds and by the almost explosively growing college market, but it has extended across the entire range of bookselling.

In general, it can be said that the influx of new money and of new management into publishing, and the rise to a dominant position of what might be called market-oriented publishing, has by no means smothered traditional forms of what might in distinction be called author-oriented publishing, but rather has given it new vigor and resources.

What of the future? Two powerful new factors, or rather two factors newly and powerfully reinforced, will affect publishing. One is the massive entry of the federal government into the financing of education and especially of the purchase of books for school and library use; the other is the further development of the technology of information storage, retrieval, transmission, and copying.

GOVERNMENT PROGRAMS

Through a series of acts—the Library Services and Construction Act, the Elementary and Secondary Education Act, the Higher Education Act, the Medical Libraries Act, and others—the federal government has moved swiftly and massively to support library programs at all levels of education and in public libraries as well, with special emphasis on books for hitherto deprived areas and social groups.

The total flow of federal funds into the purchase of books for educational and library use is difficult to determine, since much of it will appear only as a component in comprehensive projects for improving the education of the culturally deprived or for vocational training under anti-poverty programs or the like. But it seems clear that it will probably grow rapidly from the 1966 level of $200 million to $300 million. For the industry as a whole this is a very big increase; largely concentrated on children's books as it is, it will probably double or even triple demand in that section. There can be no doubt that the educational market, broadly defined, will continue to expand in breadth, volume, and complexity and will come to occupy an even more dominant position in the publishing world. But even less than in 1965–1966 will it be a market only for textbooks. On the contrary, education will draw on every medium and every kind of book for its purpose.

As a result of both the increase and the broadening of the educational market, the distinctions between textbook and trade book publishing are likely to diminish. Editorial judgments of trade book as well as textbook publishers will be increasingly influenced by educational needs. Library and school binding standards will govern the production of an increasing proportion of adult as well as juvenile books. The sales and promotional efforts of trade publishers, including paperbound publishers, will be increasingly oriented toward the educational and library market.

There may be structural changes as well. Very large further increases of working capital are necessary to meet this enlarged demand, probably on the order of $150 million to $350 million before 1970. Again, most of this is coming and must come from outside the industry, and its source will affect the character and organization of the industry.

TECHNOLOGICAL CHANGES

As to the other major factors, for the last half-century major changes in, or even destruction of, the book industry have been foreseen as the consequence of technological advance. First it was the movies, around the period of World War I, then radio in the 1920s and 1930s, television in the 1940s, the marriage of computers and microfilms in the 1950s, and teaching machines in the early 1960s. Movies, radio, and television were expected in their turn to replace reading as recreation; and each of the developments was expected to revolutionize education, replacing books as its primary instrument. For that matter, Henry Holt once foresaw that bicycle riding would bring the doom of reading. Movies, radio, and television did indeed become enormously popular instruments of entertainment, far exceeding books in the size of their audience; but they complemented and stimulated reading rather than replaced it. And so far as the revolutionizing of education is concerned, none of these waves of the future quite reached shore, in spite of the special stimulus given the so-called newer (but by then quite venerable) media by the National Defense Education Act of 1958.

This is not to say that these media have not achieved an important role in education. They have. They can do many things a book cannot. A book cannot present action visually as a film can. It cannot reproduce music or the sound of poetry as a disc or tape can. It cannot reproduce art with the fidelity a slide can. It cannot let a student compare his pronunciation of French with that of a native speaker as a language laboratory can. It cannot allow a whole school to hear a lecture simultaneously or witness a Senate hearing as television can. The point is that these media do *not* do better what a book does, and hence tend to replace it; they do what a book *cannot* do, and hence tend to supplement and reinforce it.

It is well established that a film based on a novel increases rather than inhibits purchase of the book, that television stimulates rather than interferes with reading, and that the schools that make a liberal and effective use of the newer media are also the ones that make a liberal and effective use of books. It is also evident that the prophecies of a "library of tomorrow" that were common in the mid-1950s—prophecies that foresaw libraries whose contents would be embodied in microforms or the memory of computers and which would render service by projection of desired pages or information on a screen in a carrel or in the user's home—have not been fulfilled. The more experience we have in such matters, the more apparent become the astronomical costs and the formidable, perhaps insuperable, intellectual and conceptual obstacles to such an achievement. We have become more familiar with the limitations as well as the amazing powers of the computer; and the reduction of the Library of Congress to a giant instrument seems an even remoter fantasy than it did at the dawn of the computer age.

Nevertheless, it is true that what might be called the second generation of electronic and related devices in documentation has extremely important implications for publishing. Especially significant are the advances in electrostatic and other copying equipment. These have simplified copying from books and have reduced the per-page cost—when overhead factors are removed from cost computation—to a level already approximating that of short-run scientific and technical books. When the typical unit of use of a work is a defined segment of some kind, the reproduction of desired segments as an alternative to buying the entire work will increase. Notably is this true now of articles from scientific, technical, and scholarly journals, where reproduction from a single copy may supply the needs for individual articles of dozens of users. Some fundamental reexaminations of the methods and economics of journal publishing may become necessary as this practice increases.

The availability of more efficient and sophisticated copying equipment has also opened new possibilities to publishing. It is now practical to publish a book by traditional methods only if there is an estimated market of several thousand, or at the very least, many hundreds of copies. If no such demand could be anticipated, book-length materials, however important intrinsically, have usually been reproduced by mimeographing or similar impermanent methods and have not usually been listed or cataloged as books and hence have not been placed under adequate bibliographical control. The newer devices create the possibility of giving a work full bibliographical treatment, but of reproducing copies only as demanded.

This is not a novel idea. Doctoral theses have been published in this form for years by University Microfilms, and no American university now requires the printing of dissertations. Probably few titles now conventionally published will be relegated to this form, but thousands of works not now formally "published" may be disseminated in this way in the future. The tailor-making of anthologies and collections of readings for individual classes will become economically feasible, though presenting obvious copyright and policy problems.

To turn more specifically to the computer, it is unlikely to substitute in any way for books published to be read in their entirety—novels, biographies, children's books, etc.—or those used to look up single items of information approached in a uniform way—e.g., telephone directories and dictionaries. Those reference works consulted for individual facts, but in varied and unpredictable ways that cannot be foreseen and provided for in an alphabetical or numerical arrangement or index, may indeed in special instances be replaced by a computer, but this is likely to affect only a tiny percentage of all books. Books are efficient now only when several thousand people want the same text, or access to the same information by the same approach (as in searching for a telephone number by the name of the subscriber) and for that kind of use the book is inherently more efficient than the computer, whose advantage lies rather in its ability to manipulate or rearrange data.

The principal role of the computer in relation to books will no doubt be to provide organizations of and access to the oceans of data that underlie books. It is more likely to mediate between the raw data and the book than between information organized in book form and the user. That is to say, when a computer has organized masses of raw data into a form and arrangement in which it will be useful to hundreds or thousands of users, the most efficient way of fixing and disseminating the data in that form will be to publish it as a book, rather than to leave it in the computer to be repetitively and expensively recalled for one such user at a time.

A further and extremely important use of the computer will be in the organization and editing of tape to operate typesetting equipment for metal or film. This use promises, for the first time, major reductions in plant cost, thus bringing to the short-edition book technological economies that have been hitherto found only in very long-run printings.

One major result of all these developments has been to demand new abilities in the publishing executive. Where once a sense of style and literary taste, a flair for sales and promotions, a knowledge of conventional printing, and routine business acumen equipped a publisher completely, he—or his firm—now requires far more complex attainments. A sense of the range and potentiality of technology and an ability to master and apply its fruits, an awareness and sensitivity with respect to educational innovation, the sorts of professional management skills to control integrated enterprises of wide scope and large staffs—all are essential to a future publisher. But at the heart of all the technological and management apparatus that will provide the *means* of publishing, there will remain the question of its *substance*. Publishing will no doubt always be judged by *what* it disseminates even more than by how widely or efficiently it achieves that dissemination. And the central concern of the successful publishing executive must remain the fostering of those acts of creation to which publishing can give only a means of expression.

Meanwhile, whatever the changes in the character of publishing, or whatever marginal effects may result from the replacement of certain specialized uses of particular kinds of books by other media, it seems certain that the increase in the demand for books in more or less conventional form will continue to increase very rapidly throughout the foreseeable future as a result of population increases, the massive extension of education, the greater support of libraries, and the enlarging foreign market. For as far as one can see in the future, publishing will remain a "growth industry."

FOR FURTHER READING

Annual meeting and special conference reports reprinted from *Publishers' Weekly* by American Book Publishers' Council, One

Park Avenue, New York 10016; American Textbook Publishers Institute, 432 Park Avenue South, New York 10016; Association of American University Presses, 20 West 43d Street, New York 10036; Book Manufacturers' Institute, 20 West 43d Street, New York 10036.

Annual summary numbers of *Publishers' Weekly*, latter part of January each year.

Various titles listed at end of first chapter, especially: Lacy, Freedom and Communication; Bowker Annual; Economic-Media Study of Book Publishing; Jovanovich, Now Barabbas.

APPENDIXES

A: REFERENCE BOOK PUBLISHING

FINANCIALLY, one of the largest segments of the book industry (see the introductory chapter of this book) is the reference book business. This includes the subscription-reference book business; the publishing of reference books designed for supermarket sale, a volume at a time (mentioned also in the chapter on mail-order publishing); and the publishing of reference books as single projects by general publishers.

Although this broad area of publishing is organized, for the most part, quite separately from the other areas of publishing covered in this book, and is not given a full chapter, a word should be said about it here.

This field embraces such famous projects as the *Encyclopaedia Britannica*, *Encyclopedia Americana*, *Collier's Encyclopedia*, *Compton's Encyclopedia*, *World Book*, the *Book of Knowledge*, and many other distinguished or less-notable reference works, the production of which is predicated upon the taking of orders in advance of publication, by mail or by personal solicitation.

A twelve- or twenty-volume reference work of established reputation requires tremendous investments, not only to launch it originally, but also to keep it frequently revised and updated; and it must be shrewdly sold. For the best reference works a corps of full-time editors is employed, each an expert in a specific discipline, and the services of still larger numbers of specialists and scholars are engaged to write specific articles in the work.

Here, too, sales techniques are carefully tested and geared to the market sought—from school systems and libraries to families approached by canvass or through selected lists of citizens. Many expert salesmen devote their whole careers to subscription reference book sales. Many firms in this field maintain full-time regional sales offices. Selling methods have at times earned federal scrutiny, but today the subscription reference industry is, with certain overly aggressive exceptions, as straightforward as it is prosperous.

Other Reference Books. Trade publishers, specialized and general, who regularly issue reference books, may have large or small reference editorial departments, depending on the nature and frequency of their publications. The editorial department of the Columbia University Press, for example, employs for *The Columbia Encyclopedia* a small permanent full-time staff (some of whom may at times have other duties), augmented to about 150 as a new edition approaches. In several cases the technical and medical publishers fall within the reference publishing category. As for the great dictionaries, what has been said here about the major encyclopedias applies with full force: full-time specialists must be employed, massive clipping files of current usage must be fed daily, elaborate systems and the whole complex mechanics of modern lexicography must be maintained, quite aside from the necessarily specialized procedure of manufacture and sale. Similarly, all the directories, who's-who's, and professional and business indexes an industrial society devours, require set-ups in which clerical exactitude, editorial organization, and mechanical ingenuity must combine. A parallel set of techniques, complicated by the need for skilled cartographic departments, is found among successful publishers of maps and atlases.

B: "VANITY PUBLISHING"

A WORD should be said about the books known in the trade as "vanity books," of which several hundred a year are issued by a small group of firms. Most of these titles are of low interest and slight literary quality and get their nickname from the fact that the producers *solicit* would-be authors to pay for the production and for the selling, if any—in fact, for virtually all the costs of publishing. The "vanity publisher" does not assume the risks; it is the author who does so.

The regular book publisher, on the other hand, either assumes the total risk or, for a needed book of limited appeal or great expense to produce, obtains a subsidy for specified purposes and, still paying his own overhead costs, engages in a truly cooperative venture with the author or sponsoring agency. Such an agency may be a scholarly foundation or an historical society or a business firm interested in having its story printed—to take typical examples.

In recent years the Federal Trade Commission has issued orders against a number of vanity houses, as a result of inquiries and complaints. These firms, under such orders, are supposed to mute their more blatantly flattering come-ons, deliver all that they promise in their contracts, make no actual or implied promises, in their solicitations for manuscripts, that are not carried out in practice, cease to offer "40 percent royalties" when what they really mean is a return of a small part of the author's investment provided any sales are made, and so on.

It should be emphasized that in the "vanity" operation the author typically does not own the books he has paid for, and would be better off dealing with a competent printer in his own neighborhood, handling sales through friends or local stationers, newspapers, and institutions. But for those authors who do wish to pay, with their eyes open, for the services spelled out in a "vanity" contract, the vanity operation has sometimes been successful. Properly observing FTC rules, the vanity house may justify its typical claim to the title of "subsidy" or "cooperative" publisher. But "vanity" operations remain under the scrutiny of Better Business Bureaus and the FTC, because in the past they have relieved unsuspecting would-be authors of many thousands of dollars.

C: SOME STATISTICS FREQUENTLY QUOTED

ESTIMATES OF TOTAL BOOK SALES, 1963, 1964, AND 1965

Receipts of Publishers
(In thousands of dollars; add three zeros)

CATEGORIES OF BOOKS	*1963* (Census Year)	*1964*	*1965*
Adult trade			
Hardbound	$ 108,515	$ 117,000	$ 127,000
Paperbound	17,029	20,000	21,500
Subtotal	125,544	137,000	148,500
Juvenile books			
Under $1 retail	31,257	33,000	39,000
$1 and over retail	72,678	79,000	88,000
Subtotal	103,935	112,000	127,000
Bibles, Testaments, Hymnals, Prayer Books	34,622	34,000	35,000
Other religious	46,498	49,000	56,000
Subtotal	81,120	83,000	91,000
Professional books			
Law	57,384	65,000	69,000
Medicine	24,148	28,000	30,000
Business books	14,800	17,000	19,500
Technical, scientific, and vocational	69,218	76,000	79,500
Subtotal	165,550	186,000	198,000
Book Clubs	143,418	159,000	181,000
Wholesaled (mass-market) paperbound	87,380	99,000	106,000
University Press	18,274	20,000	23,500
Other books	102,056	104,000	113,000
Total	$ 827,277	$ 900,000	$ 988,000

Textbooks and Reference Books
The following are sales tabulations reported by the American Textbook Publishers Institute for textbooks and reference books:

Subscription reference books	379,750	410,950	439,700
Subtotal	$ 814,750	$ 919,800	$1,024,700
Textbooks	$ 462,000	$ 508,850	$ 585,000
	$1,669,000	$1,819,800	$2,012,700

Note: The 1963 figures are from the U.S. Census of Manufactures, *except* for the following four categories in which the census figures appear not to accord completely with the categories used in the industry surveys and for which estimates have been made: adult trade paperbound books, business books, wholesaled paperbound books, and university press books. The 1964 and 1965 estimates are primarily projections of the 1963 figures based on the percentage increases shown in the trend reports compiled for book industry associations.

Sources: American Book Publishers Council and American Textbook Publishers Institute, as printed in *Publishers' Weekly*, August 15, 1966.

TRENDS IN NET SALES OF BOOKS, 1957–1965

Based on Reports of 145 Publishers Reporting Data for this Survey

BOOK CLASSIFICATION	NET SALES—ANNUAL INDEXES[a]						
	1957	*1958*	*1959*	*1960*	*1961*	*1962*	*1963*
Adult trade books:							
Hardbound	94.1	100.0	109.8	128.6	138.1	153.7	151.3
Paperbound[d]	81.6	100.0	112.7	179.1	231.0	300.7	288.7
Total adult trade books	93.0	100.0	110.0	132.9	146.0	166.0	162.9
Juvenile books:							
Under $1 retail	93.0	100.0	170.3	246.1	273.3	291.2	181.3
$1 and over retail	83.5	100.0	127.6	154.7	149.0	169.1	167.8
Total juvenile books	85.1	100.0	134.9	170.3	170.2	189.9	170.1
Religious books:							
Bibles, testaments, hymnals and prayer books	98.5	100.0	104.2	105.2	109.2	113.1	107.4
Other religious	94.6	100.0	108.8	121.1	123.3	127.7	138.8
Total religious books	97.2	100.0	105.7	110.7	114.1	118.1	118.1
Professional books:							
Law books	Insufficiently Reported						
Medical books	96.7	100.0	112.6	119.7	129.8	145.1	153.9
Business books	93.2	100.0	100.8	117.0	131.0	150.3	157.6
Technical and scientific books	94.4	100.0	113.8	125.4	148.8	166.0	187.1
Total professional books	95.1	100.0	110.2	121.1	136.9	153.9	166.7
Other books:							
Book club books[e]	93.7	100.0	110.3	124.5	137.8	151.1	163.9
Wholesaled paperbound	87.2	100.0	120.2	128.7	148.3	166.2	170.9
University press hardbound							
University press paperbound							
Total sales of this survey books	88.7	100.0	110.4	129.9	145.5	156.1	176.9
Other books	100.4	100.0	108.1	139.7	155.9	180.5	196.2
Total other books	91.3	100.0	113.8	127.1	143.1	158.4	169.0
Total sales of this survey	91.6	100.0	115.3	133.2	144.7	160.8	162.8
Foreign sales[f] as a % of total sales in each classification:							
Book club books	5.9%	5.8%	5.9%	5.9%	5.7%	5.5%	5.3%
Wholesale paperbound books	14.7	14.7	13.9	13.6	13.8	12.8	12.0
University press books	14.7	13.5	13.1	12.4	12.2	12.2	12.2
All other books	6.6	6.8	7.3	7.5	7.4	7.2	8.3
Total sales of this survey	7.9	8.0	8.3	8.2	8.3	7.9	8.4

[a] 1958 Net Sales = 100.0

[b] 1958 Copies = 100.0. 1958 base period for copies derived by applying Average Price per Copy reported in earlier survey against 1958 Dollar Net Sales reported in this survey.

[c] Per Cent Change from 1964 to 1965.

Source: American Book Publishers Council, 1966.

1964	1965	% CHANGE[c] DOLLAR VOLUME	COPIES ANNUAL INDEXES[b] 1964	1965	% CHANGE[c] COPIES	% OF TOTAL NET SALES 1964	1965	% OF TOTAL SALES 1964	1965	AVERAGE $ PER BOOK[g] 1964	1965
160.9	173.9	+ 8.1%	146.5	152.7	+ 4.3%	18.1%	17.7%	7.0%	6.9%	2.42	2.50
341.4	370.9	+ 8.7	342.3	329.5	− 3.7	3.5	3.5	4.7	4.3	0.70	0.79
176.1	190.5	+ 8.2	190.4	192.3	+ 1.0	21.6	21.2	11.7	11.2	1.72	1.85
189.0	224.6	+18.8	128.0	140.5	+ 9.8	3.0	3.2	13.9	14.3	0.20	0.22
167.5	186.4	+11.2	154.2	164.5	+ 6.7	12.7	12.9	9.0	9.1	1.33	1.38
171.2	192.9	+12.7	137.1	148.9	+ 8.6	15.7	16.1	22.9	23.4	0.64	0.67
102.0	106.4	+ 4.3	104.3	104.1	− 0.2	3.7	3.4	1.3	1.3	2.50	2.61
146.0	165.6	+13.4	134.8	144.4	+ 7.1	2.7	2.8	2.7	2.7	0.95	1.01
117.1	126.7	+ 8.2	122.7	128.4	+ 4.6	6.4	6.2	4.0	4.0	1.47	1.53
177.2	188.5	+ 6.4	161.7	181.9	+12.5	3.8	3.7	0.6	0.6	5.71	5.40
179.8	208.0	+15.7	145.1	173.6	+19.6	2.3	2.4	0.4	0.4	6.58	6.37
203.9	212.9	+ 4.4	134.7	168.9	+25.4	3.9	3.7	0.5	0.6	6.94	5.78
187.4	201.9	+ 7.8	147.4	174.9	+18.6	10.0	9.8	1.5	1.6	6.34	5.76
182.0	207.5	+14.0	153.9	180.9	+17.6	23.0	23.8	11.6	12.8	2.29	2.09
192.8	205.1	+ 6.4	117.3	120.8	+ 3.0	17.2	16.6	45.7	44.3	0.353	0.363
192.4	223.6	+16.2	151.4	173.3	+14.5	3.3	3.5	0.8	0.8	3.93	3.99
210.7	256.8	+21.9	184.2	206.8	+12.3	0.5	0.5	0.5	0.6	0.85	0.92
194.6	227.5	+16.9	163.2	185.4	+13.6	3.8	4.0	1.3	1.4	2.68	2.76
199.6	217.4	+ 8.9	227.4	251.6	+10.7	2.3	2.3	1.3	1.3	1.71	1.68
187.8	208.6	+11.1	125.1	132.9	+ 6.2	46.3	46.7	59.9	59.8	0.75	0.78
175.8	193.7	+10.2	133.4	141.7	+ 6.2	100.0	100.0	100.0	100.0	0.96	0.99

5.5%	5.5%	+14.6
11.9	11.8	+ 5.2
13.0	13.1	+17.3
8.2	8.1	+ 7.4
8.4	8.3	+ 8.5

[d] Adult Paperbound does not include University Press Paperbound books.

[e] Book Clubs Net Sales are at "Retail" prices. Book Club Number of Copies includes both those sold and distributed. Book Club Average $ per Book covers Books Sold only.

[f] Foreign Sales include U.S. Territories.

[g] Publishers' receipts, not resale prices.

MAJOR CATEGORIES OF PUBLISHERS' INCOME AND EXPENSE, 1965

		ADULT TRADE				
	Overall Total	*Total*	*Hard-bound*	*Paper-bound*	*Small*	*Large*
Total net sales	100.0%	100.0%	100.0%	100.0%	100.0%	100.0%
Total production cost and authors' royalties	50.4	56.0	58.3	49.2	57.4	55.8
Gross margin on sales	49.6	44.0	41.7	50.8	42.6	44.2
Other publishing income	3.3	8.1	9.8	0.1	4.3	8.6
Total selling expense	8.1	6.3	6.2	7.4	6.1	6.3
Total advertising, promotion and publicity expense	8.5	11.9	11.4	6.8	13.2	11.7
Total shipping and warehousing expense	4.3	5.1	5.1	6.7	4.2	5.2
Total administrative expense	14.6	14.4	14.5	15.2	14.1	14.5
Net income *before* State and Federal income taxes	10.6	7.1	6.9	9.8	0.1	8.0

JUVENILE			TEXT-BOOKS	RELIGIOUS			PROFESSIONAL		
Total	*Small*	*Large*	*Total*	*Total*	*Bibles**	*Other Hard-bound*	*Total*	*Medical*	*Tech. and Science*
100.0%	100.0%	100.0%	100.0%	100.0%	100.0%	100.0%	100.0%	100.0%	100.0%
54.1	53.8	54.1	46.0	61.3	68.4	53.0	45.4	45.2	40.2
45.9	46.2	45.9	54.0	38.7	31.6	47.0	54.6	54.8	59.8
3.4	2.8	3.4	0.6	1.4	1.4	1.4	0.5	0.3	0.7
7.5	5.2	7.7	9.9	4.9	5.2	4.8	8.3	11.7	6.3
6.2	10.5	5.9	7.2	7.8	5.3	10.8	9.7	8.9	9.7
5.7	5.4	5.7	3.4	5.4	5.2	5.5	3.6	2.8	4.3
12.6	16.4	12.2	14.0	12.2	10.2	14.6	15.5	14.6	16.8
11.9	2.7	12.9	11.3	5.2	3.9	6.5	9.9	9.0	14.8

* Bibles, testaments, hymnals, and prayer books.
Note: Miscellaneous additional expenses are not given in this table.
Source: American Book Publishers Council, "Financial and Operating Ratio Report" for 1965.

AMERICAN BOOK TITLE OUTPUT, 1961–1965

CLASSIFICATION WITH DEWEY DECIMAL NUMBERS	*1961* New Books	*1961* New Editions	*1961* Totals	*1962* New Books	*1962* New Editions	*1962* Totals
Agriculture [630–639; 712–719]	194	37	231	215	68	283
Art [700–711; 720–779]	539	81	620	590	136	726
Biography [920–929]	622	168	790	667	256	923
Business [650–659]	286	64	350	308	90	398
Education [370–379]	461	73	534	559	123	682
Fiction	1,645	985	2,630	1,787	1,155	2,942
General Works [000–099]	231	44	275	279	70	349
History [900–909; 930–999]	796	253	1,049	812	400	1,212
Home Economics [640–649]	143	48	191	156	69	225
Juvenile	1,513	113	1,626	2,328	256	2,584
Language [400–499]	248	59	307	226	106	332
Law [340–349]	203	53	256	219	97	316
Literature [800–810; 813–820; 823–899]	617	271	888	771	326	1,097
Medicine [610–619]	595	181	776	688	264	952
Music [780–789]	114	41	155	137	51	188
Philosophy, Psychology [100–199]	433	132	565	436	217	653
Poetry, Drama [811; 812; 821; 822]	517	98	615	505	131	636
Religion [200–299]	1,098	192	1,290	1,174	281	1,455
Science [500–599]	1,193	301	1,494	1,309	434	1,743
Sociology, Economics [300–339; 350–369; 380–399]	1,289	324	1,613	1,603	456	2,059
Sports, Recreation [790–799]	381	63	444	367	109	476
Technical Books [600–609; 620–629; 660–699]	665	116	781	780	151	931
Travel [910–919]	455	125	580	532	210	742
Totals	14,238	3,822	18,060	16,448	5,456	21,904

Sources: Annual Summary Numbers of *Publishers' Weekly*.

1963			1964			1965		
New Books	*New Editions*	*Totals*	*New Books*	*New Editions*	*Totals*	*New Books*	*New Editions*	*Totals*
219	67	286	209	76	285	214	56	270
664	158	822	776	130	906	763	208	971
680	292	972	697	251	948	455	230	* 685
396	127	523	411	164	575	437	100	537
777	164	941	934	298	1,232	789	165	954
1,859	1,265	3,124	1,703	1,568	3,271	1,615	1,626	3,241
346	231	577	361	171	532	384	250	634
847	477	1,324	834	524	1,358	209	773	1,682
205	60	265	188	49	237	241	59	300
2,605	371	2,976	2,533	275	2,808	2,473	422	2,895
334	154	488	414	387	801	385	142	527
269	114	383	256	90	346	291	145	436
861	452	1,313	1,038	416	1,454	1,166	520	1,686
752	302	1,054	876	335	1,211	871	347	1,218
139	40	179	156	58	214	183	117	300
505	214	719	528	238	766	582	397	979
578	209	787	681	255	936	775	219	994
1,459	324	1,783	1,441	389	1,830	1,428	427	1,855
1,648	563	2,211	1,923	815	2,738	1,850	712	2,562
1,932	555	2,487	2,445	827	3,272	2,372	870	3,242
427	141	568	452	130	582	474	117	591
960	197	1,157	939	186	1,125	942	211	1,153
595	250	845	747	277	1,024	635	248	883
19,057	6,727	25,784	20,542	7,909	28,451	20,234	8,361	28,595

* Figures for 1965 in nearly all categories are somewhat distorted by a shift in the Library of Congress classification of biographies; some titles formerly designated as biographies are here counted in other groups.

TRENDS IN AVERAGE RETAIL TRADE BOOK PRICES 1952–1965, HARDCOVER BOOKS ONLY

NOVELS, AVERAGE RETAIL PRICES

1965—115	vols.	from	34	publishers	$5.18
1964—145	vols.	from	32	publishers	$4.86
1963—146	vols.	from	38	publishers	$4.82
1962—145	vols.	from	35	publishers	$4.52
1952—204	vols.	from	46	publishers	$3.26

BIOGRAPHY, AVERAGE RETAIL PRICES

1965—108	vols.	from	47	publishers	$6.92
1964— 86	vols.	from	52	publishers	$6.24
1963—114	vols.	from	55	publishers	$6.88
1962— 89	vols.	from	46	publishers	$6.43
1952—138	vols.	from	53	publishers	$4.66

HISTORY, AVERAGE RETAIL PRICES

1965—161	vols.	from	60	publishers	$7.81
1964— 95	vols.	from	51	publishers	$7.85
1963—165	vols.	from	64	publishers	$6.98
1962—133	vols.	from	51	publishers	$7.08
1952—118	vols.	from	47	publishers	$5.45

Compiled by *Publishers' Weekly* from trade books in the indicated categories, advertised in the Fall Announcement Numbers of *Publishers' Weekly* in the years noted.

INDEX